CRETE

Contents

Written by Donna Dailey and Mike Gerrard

Copy edited by Rebecca Snelling
Page layout by Nautilus Design (UK) Limited
Verified by Christopher Somerville
Indexed by Marie Lorimer

Published in the United States by AAA Publishing,
1000 AAA Drive,
Heathrow, Florida 32746
Published in the United Kingdom by AA Publishing

ISBN 1-56251-831-3

Color separation by Leo Reprographics
Printed and bound in China by Leo Paper Products

10 9 8 7 6 5 4 3 2 1

A01027

the magazine

The Ties that Bind

First a Cretan, then a Greek. This proud statement of "who I am" is shared by Cretans across several generations, from humble villagers to the renowned writer Nikos Kazantzakis. To understand the Cretan character you must look to the bedrock of island life – the family and the land.

Although Cretans spent decades striving for *énosis*, or union, with Greece, which was finally achieved in 1913, it was motivated by practical concerns for security, rather than a sense of "roots". Physically separated from the rest of the country by the Sea of Crete, Greece's largest island has its own unique history. There is often distrust of the government in Athens, and resentment of imposed rules.

Centuries of resistance to foreign occupation (▶ 14) and the long struggle for freedom have left a deep imprint on the Cretan soul. Cretans are survivors, and value independence and self-reliance with a fierce pride, particularly in rural areas. The national costume worn by men at parades and festivals, with a dagger or firearm tucked into a waist sash, symbolises the importance of freedom and *philotimo* (honour) in Cretan tradition.

Elefthérios Venizélos

Streets and squares throughout the island bear the name of Crete's great statesman Elefthérios Venizélos (1864–1936). Born in the village of Mourniés near Chaniá, he fought against Turkish rule and in 1897 led a protest that saw the first raising of the Greek flag on Crete. He became prime minister of Greece in 1910 and under his rule Crete's union with Greece was achieved.

Background: 17th-century engraving showing Europa being abducted by Zeus

Page 5: Madonna and Child, an eternal icon

All in the Family

When a taxi driver takes you to his cousin's shop or his brother's hotel, it's not just nepotism at work, it's the Cretan way of life. Family means extended family – it is common for three generations to live together under one roof, and close family members help each other in times of need.

Socially, the generations mix happily in Crete. You'll often see hip youth in trendy clothes sitting side by side at the local bar with grandfathers in baggy breeches and high boots. Though many young people are leaving rural villages for softer jobs in tourism and the cities, most return for local festivals or to help with the olive harvest. And few would miss the grand celebrations of a family wedding or christening.

Wearing Black

Why do older women in the villages so often dress in black? Traditionally, Cretans wore black for three years out of respect for a dead relative. Foreign oppression brought such a cycle of loss and mourning that it gradually became the national colour.

Left: Traditional costumes are still worn by Cretan villagers

> " It is common for three generations to live together under one roof "

Are all Cretans Liars?

The philosopher Epimenides, a Cretan himself, said so 2,000 years ago. St Paul quoted him and the claim stuck. Most likely it stems from an ancient Cretan belief in a fertility god who died and was reborn annually. The Cretans claimed their "Zeus" was buried beneath Mount Gioúchtas, near Knosós, but the northern Greeks, for whom Zeus was immortal, were outraged by this heresy and branded them liars.

In general, Cretans are an honest lot – at least with strangers. What is true, however, is that they enjoy a good story. They love to talk,

The First Europeans?

According to Greek mythology, the god Zeus was besotted with a Phoenician princess. One day, while she was gathering flowers near the shore, he disguised himself as a pure-white bull to trick her. Playfully he let her ride on his back, then suddenly jumped into the sea and swam off with her to Crete. There he ravished her under a plane tree at Górtys, and they were later married in the Diktaean Cave. King Minos of Knosós and his brothers were their offspring. The princess's name? Europa.

An Amári Valley shepherd tends his flock

and often exaggerate or make promises that are forgotten the next day. It's all part of their mercurial nature – alternately warm and indifferent, relaxed, passionate and glum, sometimes unreliable but always genuine in the moment.

A Stranger and a Guest

The Greek word "*xenoi*" has a dual meaning: "stranger" and "guest". It is the custom that a stranger is automatically a guest in one's country and in one's home. Although the

sheer number of visitors to Crete today threatens this tradition, you will often be surprised by sudden gestures of hospitality – fresh figs from someone's tree, a complimentary *raki*, an invitation to share a meal. Such generosity can't be repaid, for Cretans take pleasure in the giving. Show your appreciation with a smile, or a simple word of thanks (in Greek if you can manage it).

Cretan Institutions

The *kafeníon* (café), part coffee-house, part bar, is to Crete what the pub is to Britain. There's at least one in every town or village and you'll recognise it by the men sitting outside drinking strong Greek coffee or brandy, playing cards or backgammon, exchanging news or arguing politics. The *kafeníon* is a male domain, as much an unofficial men's club as a public café, and although few Cretan women would buck tradition by coming here, exceptions are made for visitors.

The *voltá*, or evening stroll, introduced by the Venetians, is the time for socialising in mixed company. Whether it be around the village square or along a seafront promenade, families and couples stroll arm in arm, stopping to chat with friends, and groups of young men and women gossip and flirt. It's a chance to dress in one's best, to see and be seen.

These Cretan children may belong to the 21st century, but traditions will prevail

Dancing with Bulls

Greece may be the birthplace of the Olympic games, but long before the first torch was carried through a stadium in classical times Cretan athletes awed the crowds by turning somersaults over the horns of charging bulls.

Crete was the home of Europe's first civilisation, which flourished here from around 3000 BC until 1100 BC. Amazingly, it lay hidden until the 20th century, when the Englishman Arthur Evans began excavating Knosós (▶ 76).

He called this ancient race the Minoans after the mythical Greek King Minos. It seems, however, that Minos was a title, not a personal name, rather like the Egyptian Pharaoh, and at least 22 rulers bore this name.

These priest-kings built impressive palaces – Knosós, Faistós, Mália and Zákros are the largest discovered to date – where they presided over a rich, artistic culture that was

The bull's head *rhyton*, or drinking cup, from Knosós

The Snake Goddess

Another potent Minoan religious figure was that of the Snake Goddess, a woman holding a snake in each hand. Her bare breasts symbolised fertility while the snake, which sheds its skin, symbolised healing and rebirth.

highly ritualistic. The Minoans loved games and athletic contests. Bull-leaping satisfied both their appetite for sport and their religious obligation. The athletes would grab a charging bull by the horns, somersault over its back, and land on their feet with arms raised in victory. Both men and women took part in these dramatic feats, which required great courage, agility and skill.

Impossible? Spanish bullfighters claim it is, and some scholars believe that the bull-leaping scenes featured in Minoan frescoes may be only symbolic. Indeed, bulls had a strong religious significance in Minoan society. They represented virility and were depicted on vases and in figurines, and enormous sculpted "horns of consecration" adorned the palace walls.

Ceremonial drinking vessels called *rhytons* were carved in the shape of a bull's head. In sacrificial rites thought to be connected to agricultural cycles, a bull was captured and bound, its throat cut and its blood drained into these sacred cups. This ritual honoured the bull and connected the Minoans to its divine life force. Bull-leaping, whether or not it actually occurred, may have symbolised the triumph of man over the unpredictable forces of nature.

"

... grab a charging bull by the horns, somersault over its back, and land on their feet with arms raised in victory.

"

Carved ivory figure of an athlete, found at Knosós

The famous bull-leaping fresco, on display in the Archaeological Museum in Irakleío

Life as Art

Much of what we know about the Minoans has been gleaned from their beautiful artworks. Impressive frescoes once decorated the walls of the palaces showing people, animals and scenes of Minoan life. The paintings, incorporating movement and sensuality, were skilfully executed in vibrant colours made from plants, minerals and shellfish. The artists painted women's skin white and men's red: thus we know from the frescoes that women played

an important role in society.

Exquisite sculptures, pottery, mosaics and decorative arts suggest that the Minoans lived an ancient version of the "good life". Their palace homes had roof terraces, light wells, baths and sophisticated plumbing systems. They were well fed, with huge granaries and giant vessels, called *pithoi*, to store wine and olive oil. The Minoans were also great

The hall once displayed the bull-leaping fresco

" ...the Minoans lived an ancient version of the "good life" "

Giant storage jars

seafarers, trading their agricultural produce far and wide to acquire copper and tin to make bronze, and gold, silver and precious stones to make jewellery and works of art.

One of the most curious facts about their palaces is that they were built without fortifications, suggesting the Minoans lived peacefully and did not fear enemies. At their height, the Minoans are thought to have numbered over 2 million, a figure four times greater than the population of Crete today.

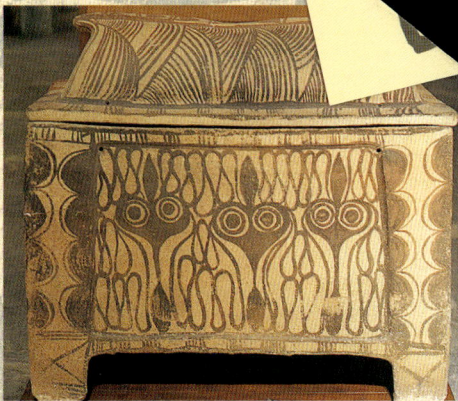

The Legend of the Minotaur

Poseidon, god of the sea, sent King Minos a white bull, but when he later requested that it be sacrificed Minos could not bring himself to kill the beautiful animal. In revenge the angry god caused the king's wife, Pasiphae, to fall in love with the bull and their mating produced the Minotaur, a hideous creature with a bull's head and man's body. Minos kept the monster in a labyrinth beneath the palace and every nine years fourteen youths were shipped from Athens and fed to the Minotaur.

When Theseus, son of the king of Athens, heard of this he vowed to stop the slaughter. Volunteering to be one of the victims, he entered the palace and then seduced Minos's daughter, Ariadne, who gave him a sword and a ball of thread with which to kill the bull then find his way out of the labyrinth.

Catastrophic Ending

This great civilisation came to a sudden end around 1450 BC, when some unknown catastrophe occurred that destroyed all the palaces at the same time. Many believe the volcanic eruption on the nearby island of Santorini (Thira) created a deluge of tidal waves, earthquakes and fires on Crete, which could explain the charred remains found at some of the palaces. Others favour theories of outside invaders such as the Mycenaeans, or an internal rebellion against the palace rulers. Whatever the cause, within 200 years the Minoans had all but disappeared, though the reason may always remain a mystery.

The Double Axe

The double axe was also a dual symbol, representing both the waxing and waning of the moon and the religious and political power of the priest-king.

Top: A Minoan sarcophagus in Chaniá's Archaeological Museum

Background and centre: Theseus slays the Minotaur

FOREIGN POWERS

Crete was ruled by a series of foreign invaders from the demise of the Minoans until the early 20th century. Later, it was occupied by Germany during World War II. Centuries of foreign domination and the long struggle for freedom shaped not only the landscape and the cities, but also the character of the people.

The Greeks

Mainland Greeks were the first to invade the island. Mycenaean warriors from the Peloponnese rebuilt Knosós and other Minoan settlements. As their power waned, the Dorians from northern Greece moved in and established city-states at Górtys, Lató and elsewhere. The original Cretans, known as Eteocretans, withdrew to settlements in the mountains.

This mosaic of Dionysius and Ariadne dates from the Roman period

"
the fairest and noblest race of men that ever lived
"

What's in a Name?

Crete's capital has been known by many names. Though its origins are much older, the town served as a port under the Romans, who called it Herakleium, from which its present name is derived. After the Arabs conquered the city in the 9th century they built fortifications, dug a moat around it and called it Rabdh-el-Khandak (Castle of the Moat), or Chandax. In medieval times the Venetians called both the city and the island Candia. Under Turkish rule the Cretans referred to the city as Megalo Kastro, or "great fortress". The official name of Irakleío (Iráklion, Heráklion) was adopted in 1922.

Byzantine churches have survived throughout Crete

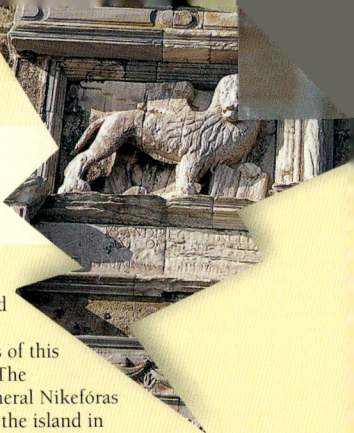

The Romans

The Romans conquered Crete in 67 BC and established their capital at Górtys (▶ 81). It was a time of peace and prosperity, with the building of roads, aqueducts and irrigation systems. St Paul brought Christianity to the island in AD 59.

became a pirate den and slave market. Little remains of this dark period. The Byzantine general Nikefóras Fokás retook the island in 961 after a grisly siege in which captured Saracens were decapitated and their heads catapulted over the fortress walls.

The lion of St Mark, symbol of Venetian rule

The Venetians

Following the break-up of the Byzantine empire, Crete was sold to Venice for 1,000 pieces of silver. Venetian rule, which lasted 465 years, brought prosperity, culture and the building of great fortresses and harbours. Handsome mansions, buildings and fountains from this era still remain in Réthymno, Chaniá and Irakleío. But Cretans periodically rebelled against the harsh feudal system their rulers imposed.

Below: Turkish fort at Áptera, near Soúda

The Byzantines

With the fall of Rome, Crete became part of the Byzantine empire, ruled from Constantinople. During both the first and second Byzantine periods, Christianity and art flourished. Many churches were built across the island, some of which survive today.

The Arabs

The Saracens, a band of Arabs who had been expelled first from Spain, then from Alexandria, captured Crete in the 9th century. Górtys and other cities were destroyed, and Chandax (Irakleío)

Timeline

1450–1100 BC
Mycenaean period
1100–67 BC Dorian period
67 BC–AD 337 Roman rule
337–824 First Byzantine period
824–961 Arab occupation
961–1204 Second Byzantine period
1204–1669 Venetian period
1669–1898 Turkish occupation
1898 Crete gains autonomy
1913 *Énosis* (union) with Greece
1941–45 German occupation during World War II

The Turks

The Turks attacked Chaniá in 1645, but it was another 24 years before they subdued the rest of the island. Under Ottoman rule the island fell into economic and artistic decline, Christians were persecuted and Cretans suffered great cruelties. Heroic freedom fighters continuously rebelled, particularly the Sfakiots of western Crete, who launched attacks from their mountain strongholds.

Priests and Patriots

Monasteries have played a pivotal role in defending Crete from invaders, with priests and abbots figuring among some of the island's bravest heroes.

The very name of Moní Tóplou (▶ 116–117) – it means "cannon" in Turkish – signifies resistance. During the 1821 uprising the Turks captured it and hanged 12 monks at the gate for harbouring rebels. Later, during World War II, Tóplou was a shelter for Cretan and British fighters; when the Germans discovered a radio transmitter there, Abbot Silignákis and several monks were shot.

Melhisedek, abbot of Moní Préveli (▶ 144), raised the first revolutionary flag against the Turks at Rodákino in 1821. He was fatally wounded in battle two years later. During World War II

Préveli monks risked their lives to help dozens of Allied servicemen escape by submarine from nearby beaches after the fall of Crete.

The most famous figure of all is Gabriel Marinákis, the abbot of Moní Arkadíou (▶ 130–131) who, during the 1866 rebellion, gave the order for the gunpowder stores to be blown up rather than surrender to the Turks. The sacrifice of hundreds of lives and the heroic deaths of so many clergymen shocked politicians and intellectuals in Europe and the United States, moving them to support the cause of Cretan liberty.

This monk (top) lives at the beautiful monastery at Arkadíou (above)

Left: The monastery at Préveli, peaceful today

The Battle of Crete began with the biggest airborne invasion in military history. So determined was Germany to capture the island that it launched an offensive on 20 May, 1941 that turned the skies black with planes and paratroops. Tens of thousands of German soldiers invaded the island in an event that lives on in the mind of every Cretan, whether alive at the time or not.

The Battle of Crete

The value of Crete lay in its size and location. At the time of the invasion some 32,000 Allied troops were recuperating on Crete, having been evacuated from Greece and the other Balkan countries. The Italian army had invaded the Greek mainland in October 1940, and with German help had pushed their way through the country, forcing the evacuation of troops to Crete. Crete's location in the southern Mediterranean, conveniently placed for access to Greece, the Middle East and North Africa, meant it was tactically of great importance.

The British war leader Winston Churchill had described Crete as his island fortress, believing it to be impregnable, and for some time the Allied naval forces succeeded in keeping German forces at bay. It was then that Hitler took to the skies.

Below: German grave at Máleme

Losing the Battle, Winning the War

Hitler had planned to start his invasion of Russia in April 1941, but when it came to it he chose to throw more troops into the task of capturing Crete, thus delaying the attack on Russia until June. It may have been a decision that cost him the war, because as a result of this delay his armies had not succeeded in capturing Moscow or Leningrad (St Petersburg) by the time the Russian winter struck. Instead, Hitler ordered his southern troops to attack Stalingrad (now Volgograd). A million German soldiers were killed in this exercise, a defeat from which Hitler's army never fully recovered. Though losing the Battle of Crete, the Allies went on to win the war.

The Battle Begins

At 6 am on 20 May an initial bombardment began. At 8 am, after a short lull, another wave of planes flew over, and at 8:15 am the paratroopers began to arrive. Many thousands of them filled the skies, concentrating at first on Chaniá and the important airfield near by at Máleme. German losses at first were heavy, as ordinary Cretans rushed to help the troops defend their island. Men, women and children, armed with pitchforks, rifles and makeshift weapons, killed many of the invaders as they floated to earth.

Eventually, though, the sheer scale of the attack proved too much for the islanders. After several hours

Cretan villagers surrender to the German forces

The Battle of Crete through a child's eyes – from the Naval Museum in Chaniá

Casualties

Official casualty figures necessarily include estimates, and probably underestimate the numbers involved. Greek figures are not known, but the German air corps recorded taking 5,255 Greek prisoners. The Allied forces reported 1,751 killed, with 1,738 wounded and 12,254 prisoners of war. In addition, the Allied naval forces estimated that well over 2,000 of their men were killed. The Germans estimated about 4,000 men killed or not accounted for, and another 2,600 wounded. It seems likely that at least 10,000 people died during the battle, and many more during the 1941–45 German occupation of Crete.

of heroic defence the Germans seized Hill 107, a strategic position that enabled them to take control of the airfield. After this, German planes were able to land and bring in more troops and weaponry.

By the afternoon, German troops were also landing at Irakleío and Réthymno, although it took them until 31 May to capture Réthymno. By this time the Allies were in retreat; crossing the White Mountains, heading down the Ímpros Gorge and evacuating to Egypt from the little port of Chóra Sfakia.

Many Cretans joined the resistance movement

" **Men, women and children, armed with pitchforks...** "

Patrick Leigh Fermor

British travel writer Patrick Leigh Fermor was an intelligence officer in the British Army, serving on Crete. After the German invasion he lived in the Cretan mountains for two years, disguised as a shepherd and helping coordinate the Cretan resistance. In 1944 he was responsible for the audacious kidnap of the German Commander on Crete, General Kreipe (► 88, Anógia). The story is told in *Ill Met by Moonlight*, written by Fermor's fellow conspirator W Stanley Moss. The resistance fighters succeeded in kidnapping Kreipe from the very heart of the German headquarters, spiriting him away to the mountains and eventually taking him off the island to Egypt for interrogation.

The Cretan Diet is the healthiest in the world, as several studies have shown (see box). Fortunately the diet is not only healthy but also very tasty, blending pulses, olive oil, fresh fruit and vegetables, lots of fresh fish…and the island's robust red wine. In addition, it incorporates most of the other requirements for healthy eating, including nuts, spices, garlic, bread, cheese and meat.

EAT, DRINK &

Vegetables

Part of the diet's strength is its emphasis on fresh vegetables, which are rich in vitamins and fatty acids and thus help fight off heart disease. Cretans consume three times as many vegetables as other Europeans, with artichokes, tomatoes, cucumbers, spinach, aubergines, beans, carrots, potatoes and leeks all organically grown on the island.

Fruit

Cretans are also said to eat four times as much fruit as the average southern

Top: A healthy lunch

Centre: Oranges grow in abundance on Crete

Left: The market at Chaniá overflows with fruit and vegetables

In a study of heart patients in Lyon, French doctors divided their patients into two groups. One group was given a conventional low-fat/low-cholesterol diet, as recommended by the US Society of Cardiology for sufferers from heart disease, while the second was put on the Cretan Diet. The results were astonishing. After two years, mortality rates in the second group were 75 per cent lower than the first group.

European, and six times as much as their northern European counterparts. Most notable among the fruits is the vitamin-rich orange, which grows in such profusion on the island, even in winter, that often landowners cannot even give away their crop. Grapes too are widely eaten, and their skins have antioxidant elements that are believed to offer protection against cancer.

Bottom: Olive oil for sale: healthy contents in a decorative bottle

BE HEALTHY

Extra Virgin
Olive Oil
from Crete

Fish

Although Crete is a large island, its long, thin shape means that nowhere is so far from the sea that fresh fish cannot be obtained. Commonly available are swordfish, tuna, bream, sea bass, mullet, squid, whitebait and sardines. There are also trout farms in the interior. As well as being full of vitamins, fish oils are known to help protect against heart disease.

Wine

Moderate amounts of red wine are believed to be generally good for health. Red wine has antioxidants that help fight several diseases, and studies have shown that people who drink a glass or two a day live longer than either teetotallers or heavy drinkers.

Fish is an essential part of the Cretan Diet

Olive Oil

Crete produces especially good olive oil. Olive oil reduces the unhealthy LDL (low density lipoprotein) cholesterol in the blood stream, which can lead to clogged arteries, but increases the amount of HDL (high density lipoprotein) cholesterol, which helps break down these fatty deposits. Next time you have a Greek salad, there is no need to refuse the olive oil in the belief that it is bad for you. Far better to cut down on dairy products, for example eating your bread without butter and having a modest amount of cheese in the diet.

The Cretan Diet

Research begun in 1956 by American nutritionist Dr Ancel Keys compared diets, diseases and death rates in seven countries, including Japan, Italy and the USA. Greek studies were undertaken in Corfu and Crete, with Crete showing by far the lowest mortality rates for heart diseases and cancer. In Finland, for example, there were 972 such deaths per 100,000 people in 1986, whereas the figure for Crete was just 38, the lowest in the world. Similarly, Crete had the lowest rate of deaths from other causes, and the lowest incidence of disease. So impressed was Dr Keys by this that he began to follow the Cretan Diet himself...and is now well into his 90s!

The Beat
of Crete

Music is the heartbeat of Crete

> "
> **Tell me with a laugh,
> tell me with a cry,
> Tell me you do not love
> me: What care I?**
> "

played on the knee like an upright violin. Backed by the *laouto* (lute) and *tambouras* (bouzouki), it is the true sound of Crete.

Music is the heartbeat of Crete

Even the great novelist Nikos Kazantzakis (▶ 33) wrote song lyrics, so deeply embedded is music in the Cretan soul. This extract is from the most common type of Cretan song, the *mantinada*. Dating back to the 5th century BC, the form is made up of rhyming couplets containing 15 syllables, often expressing extremes of joy and sadness.

Other types of music include *rizitika*, or rebel music, most often played at weddings, baptisms and other feasts, and *erotokriti*, which are folk songs derived from the 10,000-line epic of the same name written by Vitsentzos Kornáros (▶ 111).

The main instrument is the *lyra*, a three-stringed instrument traditionally made of mulberry wood and

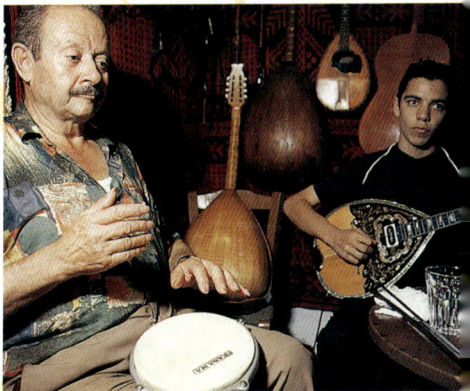

Musical Masters

The music shops of Irakleío (▶ 69) are a good source of authentic Cretan music. Look out for Nikos Xilouris (one of the greatest players), and his brother Antonis, known as Psarantonis. Thanassis Skordalos is another contender for the title of "the greatest". One of the best places to see contemporary artists is at the O Gounas taverna, Réthymno (▶ 152).

Festivals

Crete is big on festivals. In addition to the public and religious holidays, and the Saints' Days and Name Days (the equivalent of birthdays) celebrated nationwide, the island rejoices in its fertility with festivals devoted to wine, sultanas, chestnuts and other produce, and the major towns also hold annual arts and cultural festivals.

April

23 The Feast of Ágios Giórgios, St George, the patron saint of shepherds. Much feasting in many rural communities.

Easter The dates vary and are usually different from the Christian Easter. It is the biggest festival in the Greek Orthodox Year. Religious processions build up to Mass on Saturday night, and feasting follows on Easter Sunday.

May

1 May Day, when many people traditionally go on picnics into the countryside.

20 The Battle of Crete. Commemorated with events in and around Chania for up to a week.

21 The Feast of Saints Constantine and Helena, celebrated in many churches and monasteries named after them, most notably Moní Arkadíou.

June

24 The Feast of St John the Baptist.

Late June Naval Week, principally celebrated in Soúda Bay.

January

6 Feast of the Epiphany and the Blessing of the Waters, celebrated in ports around the island.

March

25 Public holiday celebrating the commencement of the 1821 Revolution against the Turks.

Carnival Celebrated 40 days before Easter (see below) in many places, notably Siteía.

in Kritsá, to which all visitors to the island are invited.

Late August On the night of the last full moon in August, there's a cultural event in the fortress at Siteía.

September

14 Feast of Ágios Stavrós, a religious holiday celebrated in villages around Chaniá.

Ochi Day parade in Réthymno

Summer

The Summer Arts Festival at Irakleío continues throughout the summer months. From **early July** to **mid-August** the cultural festival called Kornaria takes place in Siteía.

In **August** and **September** there is a Renaissance Festival, including international drama and music performances, in Réthymno.

July

Late July Réthymno Wine Festival. Two weeks of tastings with music and dancing.

August

6 The Metamorphosis consists of religious services and feasting, notably in Voukoliés (southwest of Chaniá), Máles (near Ierápetra) and Zákros.
15 Feast of the Assumption, a public holiday.
25 Feast of Ágios Títos, Crete's patron saint. Celebrated across the island and with large processions in Irakleío.
Mid-August The Siteía Sultana Festival lasts for a week and celebrates not only the local sultanas but the original grapes...and the wine made from them. Much feasting.
Late August A traditional Cretan wedding is performed

October

Mid-October The Chestnut Festival takes place in western Crete in and around the village of Élos (► 167).
28 Ochi Day, celebrated throughout Greece to commemorate the occasion when the Greek General Metaxas gave a one-word response, Ochi (No), to Mussolini's request to allow Italian troops into Greece in 1940.

Good Friday procession through the streets

November

7–9 The great explosion at Moní Arkadíou (► 130–131) is commemorated there.
21 A local holiday dedicated to the Mother of God with a service in the cathedral in Chaniá.

December

6 Feast of Ágios Nikólaos, the patron saint of seafarers, celebrated most notably in Ágios Nikólaos itself (► 106) but also in other smaller places around Crete that have the same name.

Cretan Creatures

Hippos in Chaniá? Elephants at Elafonísi? Though these creatures roamed the island in times past, Crete's landscape – and its flora and fauna – has been changed considerably by human habitation.

Crete's defining natural features are its mountains, which cover two-thirds of its surface. Four great ranges slice through the island from east to west. The highest and most dramatic are the Levká Óri, or White Mountains, in the west. The central Psiloreítis range contains Crete's highest peak. In the east are the Díkti and Siteía ranges. Made primarily of limestone, the mountains are riddled with caves that vary from great caverns with impressive formations to unexplored pot-holes.

Habitat

Looking at Crete's dry landscape today, often covered in stubby kermes oak and *phrygana* (a low scrub), it's hard to imagine it was once densely forested with cedar and cypress. The seafaring Minoans were the first to fell the ancient trees – using the timber for ships and buildings – but the Venetians and Turks continued the deforestation and today only small pockets of native woodland exist, mainly in remote areas.

With the loss of this habitat, Crete's deer and many other larger woodland species of mammal largely died out. Of the small mammals that remain today, the endemic Cretan spiny mouse with its characteristic back spines is notable.

Growing wild on many

> **" Four great ranges slice through the island from north to south "**

hillsides are aromatic herbs such as oregano, thyme, sage and marjoram. Cretan dittany, or *diktamo*, is a medicinal herb that grows in remote gorges, used in ancient times to heal arrow wounds and ease childbirth pains.

The *kri-kri*, sometimes called *agrimi*, is a large, wild goat with sweeping horns much like those of an ibex. Its summer coat is reddish-brown, and males have a rather large beard. Plentiful in ancient times, it was often depicted in Minoan art but was subsequently hunted to near extinction. The only natural population left is in remote areas of the White Mountains (where happily numbers have increased since the establishment of the national park there in 1962). Some animals were also moved to Dia and other offshore islands for protection. The *kri-kri* is very shy, but if you are lucky you can sometimes spot young animals in the Samariá Gorge (➤ 140–141).

On the Wing

Crete's geographical position and diverse habitats of high coastal cliffs, rocky islets, wetlands and meadows make it a mecca for birdlife. Out of Greece's 420 species, 350 have been spotted on Crete, and the island is also a stop-over for winter migrants.

Crete is the last breeding ground in Greece for the rare and endangered lammergeier, or bearded vulture. This magnificent bird has a wingspan up to 3m. Fewer than ten breeding pairs remain but the vulture is occasionally spotted above the Omalós or Lasíthiou plateaus. You are more likely, however, to see a griffon

Hunting – the magnificent lammergeier in flight

The beautifully vivid yellow-horned poppy

The Ímpros Gorge in Western Crete

vulture, with its distinctive white head. These, though also rare, occur in larger numbers. You could also be lucky enough to spot an Eleonora's falcon or a golden eagle.

Floral Crossroads

In spring the countryside is ablaze with colour as wild flowers bloom in every field and crevice. One third of Greece's 6,000 plant species are found on Crete, of which nine per cent are endemic. One of the more unusual is *Phoenix theophrasti*, a native date palm (▶ 117). Several dozen African and Asiatic species, as well as plants from the Balkans and Western Europe, are also present.

Above all, however, Crete is renowned for its wild orchids – there are some 67 varieties growing on the island – and bulbs, including wild tulips, Cretan iris and Cretan ebony.

Europe's Oldest Forest?

Along the tree line (1,650m) of the southern White Mountains are cypresses over 1,000 years old. Not only are they among the oldest trees in Europe, but early signs of coppicing suggest they may also be the world's oldest managed forest. At this height the trees seldom grow above 2m tall, but are often larger in diameter than usual. The annual rings on the trunk record climatic changes since Roman times.

In spring the hills are alive with beautiful flowers

Loggerhead turtles are protected in Crete

Coastal Wildlife

The beaches west of Réthymno, west of Chaniá and around Mátala are important breeding grounds for the loggerhead sea turtle. These creatures lay their eggs in the sand at night and are greatly threatened by tourism development. The Sea Turtle Protection Society of Greece (PO Box 30, 74100 Réthymno, tel/fax: 08310-72288 or 08310-52160, email: stps@archelon.gr; www.archelon.gr) operates a conservation programme, with kiosks at these resorts to raise public awareness.

Most in danger of extinction, though, is the Mediterranean monk seal, which has been seen around islets off the coast.

Furious Cat

The Cretan wildcat, *fourokattos* (furious cat), was thought to be a myth until a team of students studying carnivorous animals accidentally trapped one in 1996. This astonishing find confirmed reports of shepherds in the Psiloreítis Mountains who claimed to have seen this elusive, nocturnal animal. Weighing 5.5kg, with a tawny coat and tiger-like growl, it is not in fact related to the cats of mainland Greece or Europe but to a North African species. The cat was radio-collared, studied and set free, but no-one knows if there are any more.

Gorge-ous!

Samariá is Crete's most famous gorge (► 140–141), but there are several others that offer rewarding – and less crowded – hikes. These include:

Ímpros Gorge (► 145): northeast of Chóra Sfakia
Kotsifoú Gorge: north of Plakiás
Kourtaliótiko Gorge: north of Moní Préveli
Arádena Gorge: west of Loutró

The Iron Gates of the Samariá Gorge

Just the Facts

Surface area: 8,300sq km
Length east to west: 250km
Width north to south: 60km (widest), 12km (narrowest)
Highest peak: Mount Ída (Psiloreítis), 2,456m
Longest gorge: Samariá, 18km
Longest river: Geropotamós, on the Mesará Plain, 45km

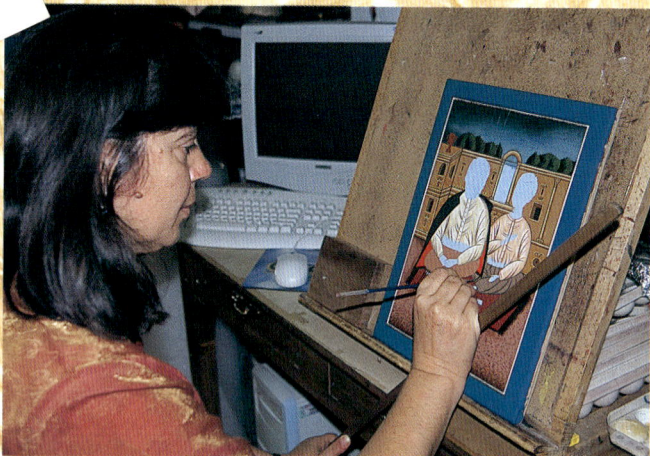

THE ICON

"There are still plenty of icon painters in Crete," says Yiorgia Petrakis, "but not many of them are painting with the heart." Yiorgia is taking a break from her work at the Petrakis Icon Workshop, which she runs with her husband, Ioannis, in Eloúnta. Standing at the back of the shop is her easel, specially adapted with wooden supports so that Yiorgia can rest her wrists while working for long hours.

Icon painting is a great Cretan tradition and the island's artists became renowned for the genre from the 15th to 17th centuries under the name of the Cretan School (▶ 32). Icons were being painted for many centuries before this, of course, but during that period Cretan artists were in great demand in Venice, the artistic capital of the western world.

Top: Yiorgia Petrakis at work in her studio/shop

It is a skill that is still highly respected on Crete, though few artists today create icons in the traditional way. Born in Thessaloníki, Yiorgia met Ioannis when they were both studying icon painting at the Painting School at Athens University. They married and moved to his home town of Eloúnta in 1992, where they opened their workshop.

"We studied for several years," Yiorgia says. "Icon painting is full of rules. You can't explain them, you must feel them. It must come from the heart."

The frame for an icon painting must be made from customers from all over the world. Most of the work that we do is to order, but we always have work in the shop for people to buy.

"It is not just the skill of the work, of course. It is the feeling for Mary, for Jesus, that affects the painting. Your love for them must come through."

As Yiorgia returns to her canvas, it is quite clear that her own love shines through every icon. The spirit of the Cretan School lives on, in this little shop in the holiday resort of Eloúnta.

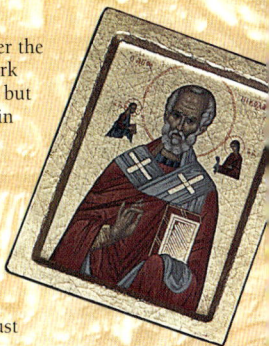

Below: Painting of the Madonna and Christ Child from the Petrakis icon workshop

PAINTER

a hard, dry wood like oak, chestnut or pine, not an oily wood such as the olive tree. The paper is handmade from cotton, egg and vinegar are used to make the egg tempura, and 23-carat gold leaf provides the background. Paints are also handmade in the traditional way, with dyes derived from minerals, plants and metals. Yiorgia and Ioannis buy their paints from the one factory in Greece that still makes them in this manner.

"Sometimes to make just one colour can take years," Yiorgia explains. "They bury a metal in the ground until it decays to the point where they get exactly the colour that they want. And it can take one month to make one of the larger paintings, which is why real icon paintings can be expensive. But we have

Writers & Artists

Homer, the 8th-century BC Greek epic poet, could be said to have "invented" literature when he began weaving his narrative tales that were ultimately written down in *The Odyssey* and *The Iliad*. The Greeks also spawned modern drama during the Golden Age of Pericles in Athens (5th century BC), when writers such as Sophocles, Euripedes and Aeschylus developed revolutionary new styles of drama never before seen on stage.

In more recent times, Greece has produced two winners of the Nobel Prize for Literature: poets George Seferis and Odysseus Elytis.

Elytis (1911–96) was born on Crete, and though he moved away to be educated in Athens and Paris he often returned to his Greek island home. He was one of the great Greek war poets, writing powerfully about his experiences fighting the Germans during World War II, and he was awarded the Nobel Prize in 1979.

Crete has produced many fine writers and artists, even though a lot of them are not known worldwide. Two notable exceptions are the painter El Greco and the writer Nikos Kazantzakis.

The Cretan School

From the mid-15th century, Crete was increasingly important as a trading centre under the Venetians. So much so that from the 15th to 17th centuries it had economic equality with Venice, although the islanders kept their own artistic traditions. They were influenced by Italian as well as Byzantine art: many artists from Constantinople moved to Crete. All forms blossomed, and so strong was the Cretan School that it began to exert an influence on its own masters in Venice, and throughout Europe.

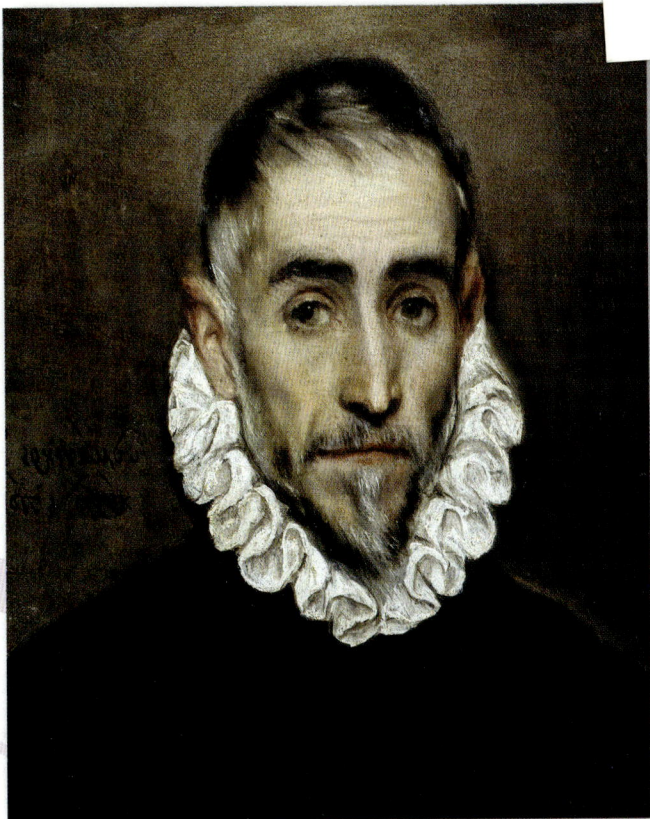

El Greco (The Greek)

El Greco's real name was Domenikos Theotokopoulos. He was born on Crete in 1541, supposedly in the village of Fódele (►88), although there is no documentary evidence to prove this. Theotokopoulos was an artist of immense talent and studied under one of the greatest Cretan artists of the day, Michael Damaskinos, whose best works can be seen in the Icon Museum in Irakleío (►60–61). At the age of 27, Theotokopoulos moved to Venice to further his studies and pursue the art of icon painting. There he successfully combined the Byzantine style that he had mastered on Crete with the Renaissance style that was prevalent in Italy. After almost ten years in Italy with limited commercial success, the artist moved to Toledo in Spain, where he lived for the most part until his death in 1614. It was there he achieved fame, as a sculptor and architect as well as an artist. Several of his paintings are in the National Gallery in Athens, but only one can be seen on his native island, in the Historical Museum in Irakleío (►58–59).

The face of El Greco, from the Prado Museum in Madrid

> "
> ...successfully combined the Byzantine style that he had mastered on Crete with the Renaissance style...
> "

Nikos Kazantzakis

Crete's other towering artistic figure is the writer Nikos Kazantzakis (1883–1957), and he called his autobiography *Report to Greco*, in a nod to his great forebear. Born in Irakleío in 1883, he is forever associated with the character he created for his 1946 novel – *Zorba the Greek*. Usually regarded as signifying the robust Cretan character, Zorba was in fact a mainland Greek who came to Crete and showed the locals how to live. The author's ambivalence to his fellow islanders is also shown in another of his great novels, *Christ Recrucified*, in which Cretan villagers tear each other apart while the Turkish ruler stands by.

Kazantzakis was proud of his island, though, and the island is proud of him. At his request, he was buried in Irakleío and his grave stands on top of the Martinengo Bastion on the city walls. His epitaph says a lot about the Cretan character: "I hope for nothing. I fear nothing. I am free."

Anthony Quinn was an unforgettable Zorba the Greek

The grave of Nikos Kazantzakis

Pandelis Prevelakis

Pandelis Prevelakis (1909–1986) was born in Réthymno and became a great friend of Kazantzakis, going on to write his biography. Although rather overshadowed by that towering figure, Prevelakis is nevertheless regarded as Crete's second greatest writer. His 1938 novel *Chronicle of a City* (sometimes translated as *Tale of a Town*) is a historical fiction about Réthymno and goes in and out of print, so you may need to hunt it down.

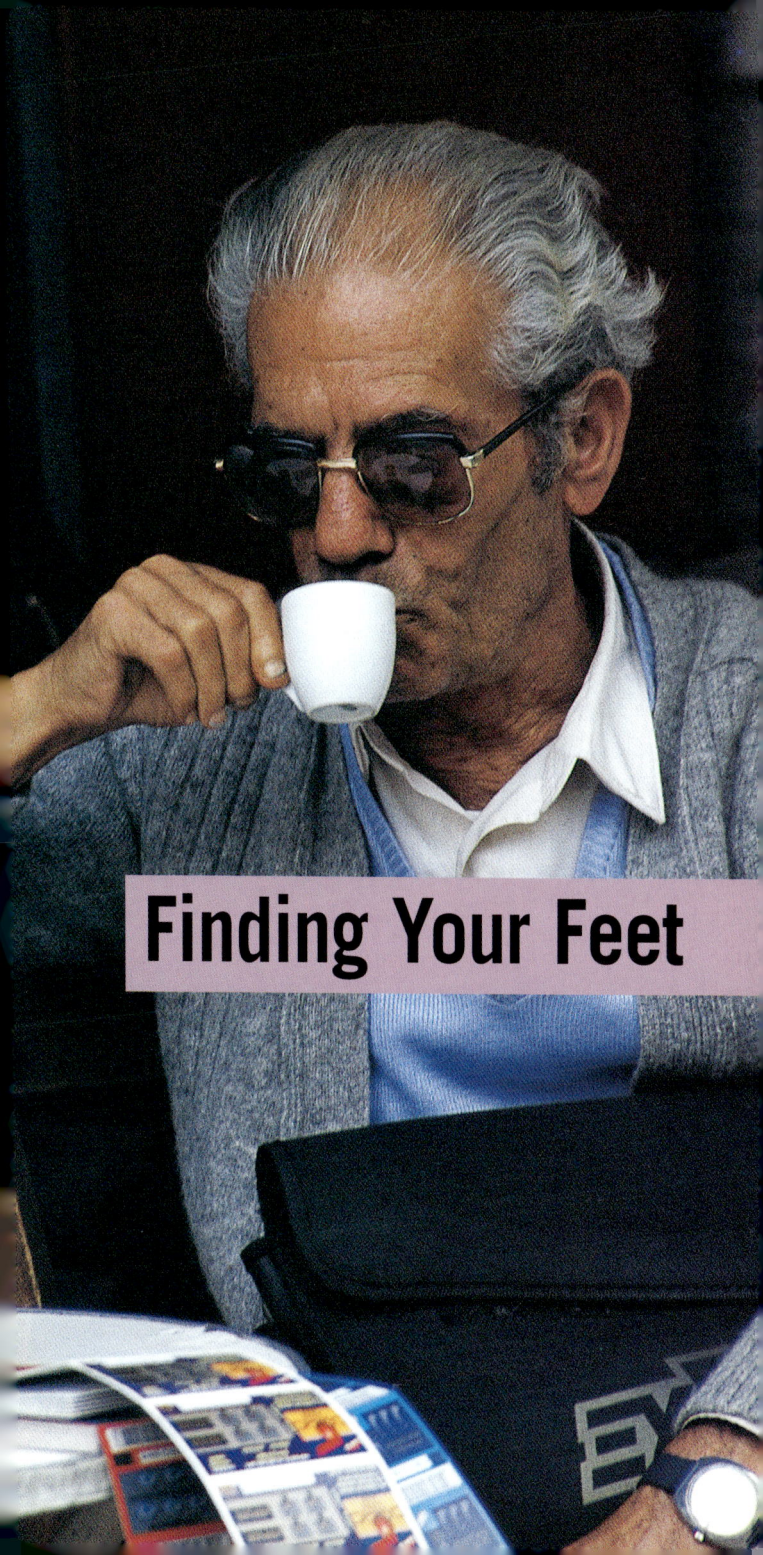

Finding Your Feet

First Two Hours

Arriving

The two main points of entry are both on the north coast of Crete. Irakleío, the capital, serves the centre and east of the island and Chaniá, the second city, serves the west. Both have ferry ports and international airports. Irakleío is served by more airlines and ferries so may be more convenient from that point of view, but if your main interest is in visiting the west of Crete, try and arrange to arrive at Chaniá.

A third airport capable of taking international flights is due to open at Siteía, but there is some uncertainty over the date. It would be worth checking if you wish to visit the less busy eastern end of the island.

It takes about two hours to drive the 160km between Irakleío and Chaniá along the good New Road (National Highway), which runs for most of the length of Crete's north coast.

Irakleío Airport

- The airport is **5km east of the city centre** (tel: 0810-245644).
- **Bus No 1** leaves from in front of the terminal for the city centre every few minutes from 6 am–11 pm. The fare is about €1.
- **Numerous taxis** can always be found outside the airport. Beware of touts and go to the official taxi rank.
- Check that the fare is **metered** and the meter switched on, or agree the fare beforehand. Take time to find the board at the taxi rank that lists the approximate fares to most popular destinations (another reason not to go with a tout).
- A **taxi into Irakleío** should cost about €8 (higher after midnight) with a small charge for baggage.
- **Money exchange facilities**, **car-hire offices**, plenty of **luggage trolleys**, **shops**, **bars** and **cafés** are available at the airport.
- If you are **hiring a car**, the airport is close to the New Road. Follow signs for Ágios Nikólaos if you are heading east, or for Irakleío and then Réthymno if heading west. Irakleío city centre is about a 15-minute drive away.
- If you need to **park** at the airport for any length of time, use the large and inexpensive public car-park directly opposite the terminal building on the far side of the dual carriageway.
- Unfortunately **delays** are common in summer on charter flights. There is far more room on land-side than air-side, so don't go through passport control until you need to.
- Depending on the season, there are as many as **15 flights a day** to Athens, a journey which takes just under one hour.
- There are **regular services** to Thessaloníki, Rhodes, Santorini (Thíra), Páros and Mýkonos.
- Most **domestic flights** are operated by the national carrier, Olympic Airways, but there is now also a number of competing smaller airlines, such as Air Greece, Air Manos and Aegean Cronus Airlines, so shop around. These airlines now offer more regular services.

Chaniá Airport

- The airport is **near Soúda**, about 15km northeast of the city centre (tel: 08210-63264).
- **Public buses** meet incoming flights but there is no regular service and most people take a taxi.

- **Taxis** are numerous and a ride into the city centre should cost about €9. See above for precautions to take when getting a taxi.
- **Money exchange** offices, car-hire desks, shops and cafés are all available at the airport.
- There are **several flights a day** connecting with Athens, from the national carrier Olympic Airways and from small independent airlines including Air Greece, Air Manos and Aegean Cronos Airlines.
- Aegean Cronos Airlines also operates **one flight per day** to Thessaloníki.
- If you are **hiring a car**, follow signs for Soúda to reach the New Road and avoid central Chaniá; otherwise follow signs for Chaniá to reach the city centre. When you reach the New Road, turn left to head east marked Réthymno and Irakleío and turn right to head west. This is marked Chaniá but bypasses the city centre.

Siteía Airport
- The airport is about **2km northwest of the centre** (tel: 08430-24666).
- **Taxis** meet incoming flights. The fare into Siteía should be about €4.

Irakleío Harbour
- The commercial harbour lies **slightly to the east** of the town centre.
- The walk between the two is not long, but if you have **heavy luggage** you would be advised to take a taxi.
- There are **daily ferries** to Athens and Santorini (Thíra), and frequent sailings to the Cycladic Islands, the Sporades and Thessaloníki.
- For **information** contact the Port Authority (tel: 0810-244956).

Chaniá Harbour
- **Ferries** dock at the harbour near Soúda, which is about a 20-minute drive east of the city centre. **Taxis** are available.
- There is a **daily ferry service** to Athens.
- For **information** contact the Port Authority (tel: 08210-43052).

Tourist Information Offices
Tourist offices can only be found in the large towns. Where there isn't one, try travel agencies for information.
National Tourist Office (Irakleío): Odós Xanthoudidou 1, tel: 0810-228225, opposite the entrance to the Archaeological Museum.
Chaniá: Kriari 40, near Plateía 1866, tel: 08210-92943.
Réthymno: Odós Venizelou, the waterfront, at the eastern end towards Plateía Iroon, tel: 08310-29148.
Ágios Nikólaos: north of the bridge in between lake and harbour, tel: 08410-22357.
Siteía: on the waterfront, tel: 08430-28300.

Telephone numbers
Telephone numbers in Crete are due to change. The initial "0" in the area code will be replaced with a "2" ("6" for mobile phones). The exact date for this is unconfirmed at the time of printing.

Admission Charges
The cost of admission to museums and places of interest mentioned in the text is indicated by price categories.
Inexpensive under €2   **Moderate** €2–€3.5   **Expensive** over €3.5

Getting Around

Travelling around Crete is easy provided you are not too ambitious. It is a big island, and if you want to spend some time relaxing then the best advice is to limit yourself to one region.

Bus Services

- Bus services are **generally good**. There are, for example, roughly 25 buses per day between Irakleío and Chaniá and a similar number between Irakleío and Ágios Nikólaos.
- The **best services** are between the major towns and major tourist resorts. Buses here are usually frequent and comfortable. In more remote places, you may find older buses in use, with a service restricted to an early morning bus into the main town, and an afternoon bus back again.
- Services are **operated by KTEL**, and buses are pale blue. In larger towns there is often more than one bus station, so check which one you need.
- **Tickets should be bought** in advance at the bus station. In smaller places where the "bus station" is merely a parking spot, the nearest shop will often sell tickets. Look for signs or ask.
- A **timetable** for the whole of Crete is produced each year, which is available from bus stations and travel agents. However, double-check times if possible, as services do change.
- You can check timetables in advance on the KTEL website: **www.ktel.org**

Taxis

- Taxis on Crete are **generally inexpensive** and many people use them for quite long journeys.
- Taxis are **metered** but it is common to agree a price for a particular journey. Always do this in advance.
- **Taxi ranks** should carry display a board showing price guides to the most popular destinations.

Ferries

- For travelling within Crete, ferries are **not usually the best option** as there are reasonably good roads and a good bus network.
- There is one exception: travelling along the south coast. In summer **a regular service operates** from Palaiochóra in the west to Agía Galíni further east, stopping at Soúgia, Agía Rouméli and Chóra Sfakia on the way. This is much easier than taking buses inland and around the mountains if you do not have your own transport.
- A ferry operates from Palaióchora to the **offshore island of Gávdos**.
- The **major ports are on the north coast** at Irakleío, Chaniá, Siteía, Ágios Nikólaos and Kastélli Kissámou. All except the last have ferry connections to Piraeus for Athens and to other Greek islands, while Kastélli Kissámou is the best for services to the Peloponnese.

Driving

- Most of the **main roads** are of a good standard, the best being the E75 highway, that links towns along Crete's north coast. This is invariably signposted as the New Road, but is also called the National Highway.
- Off the main road **standards vary enormously**, and even on major roads you should watch out for unexpected pot-holes or rock-fall.

- On many main roads the **right-hand "lane"** is actually a wide shoulder, used for pulling on to when a car wishes to overtake.
- It is always best to ask locally about **road conditions**, as roads which may appear to be good on maps can turn out to be rutted tracks. Greece has the second-worst record in Europe for deaths on the road.
- Many locals drive down **the middle of the road**. Keep well in to your side of the road. Reckless overtaking is common, even on blind bends.
- Another **driver flashing his headlights** at you means that he is coming through, NOT that he is giving way to you. Either that, or he is warning you there is a police speed trap around the corner.
- The **beeping of horns** is very common, but it can simply mean the driver has seen a friend walking by, or is tooting as he passes a relative's shop, so don't assume it is directed at you.

Driving Essentials
- Drive on the **right-hand** side of the road.
- Wearing **seatbelts** where fitted is compulsory, but many locals ignore this rule. Don't be tempted to copy them.
- **Children** under ten must not sit in the front seat.
- **Drink-driving** is a serious offence. A blood-alcohol level of only 0.05 per cent means a heavy instant fine, and over 0.08 per cent is a criminal offence and can lead to imprisonment. The police sometimes set up random breath-testing checkpoints.
- The **speed limit** is 120 kph on highways, 90 kph on other main roads and 50 kph in urban areas. These limits may vary slightly so watch for the speed-limit signs.
- **Vehicles coming from the right** have right of way, even on roundabouts.

Car Hire
- All main towns and tourist resorts, and airports, have several **car-hire companies** competing for business.
- **Rates** on Crete are higher than the European average, but local firms tend to under-cut the major international names.
- In theory, an **international driving licence** is required, but in practice a valid national driving licence will suffice.
- **Minimum age** varies from 21 to 25, depending on the company's policy.
- Rates usually include **third-party insurance** and **unlimited mileage**, but it is advisable to take out additional coverage for CDW (Collision Damage Waiver) insurance.
- Rental companies **usually ask for a deposit** by credit card or in cash.
- If hiring in **late summer or autumn**, it may be worth paying extra for a recognised name such as Hertz or Europcar, whose vehicles probably have a better service record.

Bringing Your Own Car
- You are allowed to take your own car to Crete for a period of **up to six months** or until the tax or insurance expires.
- EU citizens **no longer need a Green Card**.
- These rules change regularly on Crete so check with a **motoring organisation** such as the AA for up-to-date information.

Breakdowns
- Car-hire companies will **provide an emergency number** to contact.
- Alternatively, members of the AA and other motoring organisations are entitled to free emergency help from the Greek equivalent, **ELPA**. Dial 104 for emergency help anywhere on Crete, or 174 for information.

Accommodation

This guide recommends a carefully selected cross-section of places to stay, ranging from inexpensive but comfortable hotels to those offering international standards of luxury. Standards of accommodation are generally quite high, and prices comparatively low, so travelling around Crete need not be an expensive business.

Booking a Hotel

- It is quite common to **ask to see a room** before booking it.
- You will need to leave your **passport** at reception to enable the registration records to be completed and also to act as security against non-payment.
- **Booking ahead** in high season is highly recommended. Many hotels are block-booked by tour groups.
- Travelling without pre-booked accommodation is **easier in spring and autumn**.
- Many hotels are **family run** and usually kept spotlessly clean. Facilities may be simple, but there will probably be everything you need for a comfortable stay.

Rooms to Rent

- In addition to conventional hotel accommodation, you will also see "**Rooms to rent**" signs (*zimmer* in German and *domatia* in Greek). These will often be spare rooms in private accommodation, and usually very cheap. Standards vary so ask to see the room first.
- You may find yourself being made **one of the family**, and be treated to generous Cretan hospitality.

Rates

- All hotels are **inspected annually** by the tourist police, and the room rates and category of hotel agreed. These rates should by law be displayed in each room, usually on the back of the door.
- Out of season it **may be possible to negotiate prices**, but don't expect any leeway in summer. Room rates vary according to the season and according to the standard of the room; those with a sea view, for instance, command a higher price.
- The **price of breakfast** may or may not be included in the cost of the room, and this will also be indicated in the notice on the door. The quality of hotel breakfasts varies enormously, from the perfunctory to the generous – and usually the cost is the same. If breakfast is optional, you can always opt out and eat in a café.

Tips

- If unable to find accommodation yourself, try the **tourist office** (if there is one), any **travel agent**, or ask for the **tourist police**. In many places the latter will have a list of accommodation and can offer advice.
- Many hotels use **solar power** so take your hot shower in the early evening as small tanks can sometimes run out of hot water by the following morning.
- Greek **plumbing systems** are unique, and you must not flush toilet paper down the toilet as this blocks the pipes. Instead, use the basket that is provided. The only exceptions are some of the more modern luxury hotels. If in doubt, ask.

Food and Drink

Greek cooking does not have a great reputation but Crete can compete with any Mediterranean island and hold its head high. The Cretan Diet (► 20–22) has been proven to be one of the healthiest in the world, with lots of fresh fish, fruit and vegetables.

Specialities
While similar to conventional Greek cuisine, Crete does have its own specialities, including a good range of local cheeses and wines.
- Try the sweet *myzithres* **cheese** as a change from *feta*.
- **Snails** are quite common on Cretan menus, and have been since Minoan times, while **game** also features.
- **Rabbit** is more popular here than in the rest of Greece, often made into a *stifado* (stew).
- Try *loukanika*, too (delicious village sausages), **goat** or the local version of *kleftiko* – lamb and cheese in pastry baked in the oven.
- The nearest thing to a national dish is *dhakos*, which tastes better than it sounds: rusks soaked in oil and covered with tomatoes.

Eating Places
- There is a blurry distinction between **restaurants** and tavernas. Restaurants tend to be more up-market, and of course there are many smart restaurants in the major towns and tourist resorts. In a restaurant you will probably get a wine glass rather than a little tumbler, and a linen tablecloth instead of the paper variety.
- **Tavernas** are more down to earth, where service will be informal and you may be invited into the kitchen to take a look at the daily specials. The cooking in these family run affairs can be every bit as good as that in pricier places.
- *Psarotavernas* specialise in fish; *psistaries* feature grilled dishes, often over charcoal; and *ouzeri* are bars that specialise in ouzo served with the small plates of Greek starters known as *meze*, or *mezedhes*.
- **Dress code** in all but the smartest restaurants is very relaxed.
- You might wish to **book** in the more expensive dining places, although this is not the norm on Crete. Most people simply turn up and hope to be seated. Waiters will either produce an extra table or ask you to wait till someone has finished.

Eating Times
- **Breakfast** is usually served from an early hour in hotels, but cafés offering breakfast often don't open till about 8 am.
- **Lunch** and **dinner** are both eaten fairly late. Cretans have lunch from about 2 to 3 pm, although eateries open for business from the tourist trade from about noon onwards. In the evening, in busy resorts, some places may serve food as early as 6 pm; in fact some serve all day, so you may not be quite sure if a table of diners is having a very late lunch or an early dinner.
- **Cretans** don't dine in the evening much before 9 pm, and truly local restaurants only start buzzing as it gets towards midnight.

The Menu and the Bill
- Menus often show **two prices**, with and without tax, but you will pay the "with tax" price.

- Most places will have **menus** in Greek and English, and frequently other languages too, especially German.
- **Service** is usually included but it is common to leave an additional amount of about 5 per cent, or the small change from the bill.

Drinks

- Do taste the local **barrel wines**, made locally and sold direct from the barrel. The general standard is surprisingly good, although reds tend to fare better than whites.
- Central Crete and the Siteía region in the east have some of the best **wine-growing areas**.
- As in the rest of Greece, aniseed flavoured **ouzo** is a popular aperitif.
- The great Cretan tipple is *rakí*, also known as *tsikoudhia*. It is basically a stronger version of ouzo but without the aniseed taste. A complimentary glass is often served to customers after a meal.

Shopping

Crete is not a destination that attracts people with its shopping, but nevertheless while you are there you will have no trouble finding a good choice of souvenirs for family and friends, as well as gifts for yourself. This applies whether your taste is for the cheap and cheerful or for more expensive arts and crafts. Note that a lot of the cheap "local" souvenirs are actually made overseas and imported.

Crete has a wide range of traditional crafts that are kept alive thanks to its popularity as a holiday destination. These include:

Ceramics

- The familiar cheap and cheerful **blue and yellow plates** of the island are available everywhere.
- The village of **Margarítes** (➤ 142) is the centre for ceramics.

Icons

- Holy icons are still **made in the traditional way** on Crete (➤ 30–31) but check for the certificate on the back authenticating this.
- Icons can be found throughout the island in souvenir shops, but the **best quality examples** are to be found at churches and monasteries, and at places such as the Petrakis Icon Workshop in Eloúnta (➤ 30 and 123).

Jewellery

- All over the island there are jewellery shops selling **fine quality silver and gold**. Pieces are sold by weight and often represent good value.
- Look for the shops where you can **see the jeweller at work** in the back, then you know you are buying original handcrafted work.

Leatherware

- Life in the Cretan mountains is tough, and sturdy leatherware has long been made for practical purposes. Today the workshops also produce **handbags, purses, wallets and other items** for the tourist trade, but you can still buy local items such as the long-legged Cretan boots.
- **Chaniá** has the widest range (➤ 153).

Weaving

- This island tradition still flourishes, particularly in mountain towns such as **Kritsá** (► 104), **Psýchro** (► 123) and **Anógia** (► 88–89).
- Shop-fronts are festooned with **carpets and rugs**, far too many to have been produced by the one old lady who runs the shop. The better-quality handmade items will invariably be a lot more expensive, but worth it.
- **Chaniá** is also a good place to buy woven goods (► 153).

Woodcarving

- Many tourist resorts have their own **olive-wood workshop**, with souvenir shops selling attractive carvings of bowls, spoons, salt and pepper sets, plus many other items.

Food and drink

- If you have developed a taste for the local firewater, *rakí*, you might want to take some home. Both *rakí* **and ouzo** can be bought in elegant bottles that could be used afterwards as vases or shelf decorations.
- Almost all towns now have shops specialising in **Cretan herbs and spices**, which the chef of the family will want to investigate.
- **Cretan honey** is popular, being extremely pure and tasty, but is often far more expensive than at home.
- The real bargain is **olive oil**, as Crete produces some of the finest quality oil in Greece.

Entertainment

Arts and Festivals

- Art forms such as **dance and drama** tend to be concentrated in summer festivals, rather than performed all year round. At these times, old forts and monuments are turned into theatrical venues. Irakleío (► 70), Chaniá (► 154), Réthymno (► 154), Siteía (► 124) and Ágios Nikólaos (► 124) all have their own local arts festivals.

Bars, Clubs and Discos

- **Bars** are not particularly Cretan, as Greeks are not great drinkers and do most of their socialising in cafés. In recent years, though, fashions have started to change and young Cretans now hang out in stylish bars just like young people the world over. There are plenty of these establishments in the main towns, often crowded together, and it won't take long to find out where the local action is. Bars in resorts tend to be more tourist-influenced, often modelled on British-style pubs or German *bierkellers*, with big-screen TVs offering MTV or sports channels.
- **Clubs and discos** are usually synonymous, and the larger resorts will normally have a few competing for custom. Some places such as Mália have numerous nightspots thumping out music till the early hours. As with any tourist area, what's fashionable can change from one season to another and clubs, like bars, can change hands, name and style. Some have free entry, others charge an admission fee that buys you your first drink. Prices are not outrageously expensive, and most places don't get going till midnight...and then keep going till the last customers leave. With a lack of listings magazines, look out for flyers on walls and telegraph poles telling you what's on where.

Cinemas

- Cinema-going is a popular pastime on Crete and in many places summer sees the arrival of **open-air cinemas**. These can be great fun, but don't expect to be able to hear every word of the dialogue.
- Lots of **American films** are shown in their original language with Greek subtitles, but check on the posters around town or at the box office to be sure.

Outdoor Activities

- **Cycling** and **mountain biking** are not quite as popular as hiking on Crete, but in some resorts it is possible to hire bikes or join a guided tour. Ask at tourist information offices or in local travel agents.
- **Horse-riding** is a wonderful way of seeing some of Crete's remoter parts. There are several stables around the island, listed in the appropriate section.
- The best **tennis** courts usually belong to the large resort-hotels. Some are for guests' use only but others will let non-residents play on them for a fee, so make enquiries. There are public courts in Chaniá and Irakleío.
- **Walking** is one of the main reasons many people visit Crete. The mountains are spectacular and unspoilt, but even less energetic visitors feel compelled to take on the challenge of the Samariá Gorge (► 140–41). This trip can also be arranged from any resort remotely within reach of the gorge. Travel agents will often also offer walking tours to less well-known places, such as the Ímpros Gorge (► 145), and several towns have specialist walking companies, listed in the text.
- **Watersports** are popular throughout the island's resorts and all but the tiniest of places have a watersports centre of some kind. Activities range from banana boats through to jet-skis, water-skiing and scuba diving, although the last is restricted to certain areas due to the fact that there are still many unexplored underwater archaeological sites around Crete. Contact a local diving club for more information; there are several in Chaniá (► 154), Ágios Nikólaos (► 124), Réthymno (► 154) and elsewhere.

Publications

- The most comprehensive listings of what's going on are to be found in the free *Kriti Times*. Printed in both English and German, it is usually handed out at the airport to new arrivals, but is also widely available.
- *Cretasommer*, also free and printed in English and German, principally features life in Réthymno but includes a few articles on the island generally, too.

Gay and Lesbian Travellers

- There is **no particular gay scene** on Crete, and no resorts that cater especially to gay travellers in the way that, say, Mýkonos and Lésvos do elsewhere in the Greek islands.
- **Gay travellers are as welcome** as any other travellers, and Cretans are as tolerant as other Greeks. The more outrageously dressed gay and lesbian couples will probably be looked at with amusement rather than hostility.
- Be aware of a borderline, though. **Overt behaviour**, which includes public kissing, goes a step too far and may not receive the same amount of tolerance.
- **Homosexuality is legal** throughout Greece from the age of 17 (male homosexuality is far more common than female), but you will not find many Cretans who flaunt it.

Irakleío

Getting Your Bearings

A graceful Venetian fortress guards the harbour of Crete's capital, Irakleío, the fifth largest city in Greece and the main gateway to the island. Many visitors, however, do no more than make a quick trip to the wonderful Archaeological Museum, or use it as a convenient base for Knosós. But though it's often noisy, busy and clogged with traffic, the city has many charms and a number of excellent restaurants easily repay an overnight stay. The loggia, several churches and the Morosíni Fountain are among the attractions that reveal its proud history and character.

Page 45: The Turkish fleet in old Irakleío

Irakleío was heavily bombed during World War II, which accounts for the proliferation of drab, modern concrete buildings in what was formerly a handsome Venetian city. However, a few of the old mansions survive and the old city walls are still intact, running for 3km around the old town and separating it from the sprawling suburbs beyond. Apart from the Natural History Museum, everything of interest in the city lies within the walls. The central thoroughfare through the old town is Odós 25 Avgoústou, which runs from the harbour up past the street market. Most of the main attractions lie along this route, or on small squares near by. Odós Daidálos intersects with Odós 25 Avgoústou and leads to the Archaeological Museum. You can walk the short distance from one sight to another, and there are plenty of cafés and bars to stop at for a cool drink along the way.

3 Historical Museum

GIAMALAKI

CHANDAK

KALOKAIRINOU

Icon Museum (Agía Aikateríni)

Ágios Minás Church

PLATEÍA AG AIKATERINIS

4

Ágios Minás Cathedral

Martinengo Bastion

Statue in Plateía Kornárou

★ Don't Miss

1 **Archaeological Museum** ➤ 50
2 **Venetian Harbour & Fortress** ➤ 56
3 **Historical Museum** ➤ 58
4 **Icon Museum (Agía Aikateríni)** ➤ 60

At Your Leisure

5 Natural History Museum ➤ 62
6 Plateía Eleftherias ➤ 62
7 Ágios Títos ➤ 62
8 Venetian Loggia ➤ 63
9 Ágios Márcos ➤ 63
10 Plateía Venizélou ➤ 64
11 Plateía Kornárou ➤ 64

2 **Venetian Fortress (Rocca al Mare)**

2 **Harbour**

ODÓS ΟFOKLI VENIZÉLOU

AVGOÚSTOU

Arsenali

Arsenali

PLATEÍA KOUNTORYOTON

EPIMENIDOU

ODÓS 25

EPIMENIDOU

El Greco Park

PLATEÍA AGIOU TITOU

7 **Ágios Títos**

AG TITOU

MALIKOUTI

Plateía Venizélou 10

8 **Venetian Loggia**

MIRAMPELOU

MIRAMPELOU

rosíni ntain

9 **Ágios Márcos**

IDOMENÉOS

Archaeological Museum 1

BOFÓR

DAIDÁLOS

DIKAIOSÍNIS

Plateía Eleftherias 6

City Wall

IKAROÚ

PLATEÍA DAKALOGIANI

EVANS

0   200 metres
0   200 yards

Bembo Fountain

AVÉROF

DIMOKRATÍAS

Plateía Kornárou 11

Jesus Bastion

ODÓS PEDIÁDOS

Natural History Museum 5

You can just about fit Irakleío's main sights into one long day if you take advantage of early and late opening times. But check the hours for each attraction, as you may need to switch the Icon Museum and Archaeological Museum on certain days.

Irakleío in a Day

8:00 am

Get an early start at the **Archaeological Museum** (right, ➤ 50–55). If you haven't had breakfast yet, break your visit with a coffee and pastry in the museum coffee shop. Remember to keep your ticket as it is valid for re-entry to the museum on the same day and you may want to return later.

10:30 am

Walk down Odós Daidálos, the main shopping street, and turn right when you reach the end at Plateía Venizélou. Continue down Odós 25 Avgoústou, stopping to admire the **Venetian loggia** (➤ 63). Just beyond, peek into the lovely **Ágios Títos church** (➤ 62), set back on a small square. Continue to the end of the street, where it reaches the waterfront.

11:30 am

Walk out along the colourful **harbour** and visit the **Venetian fortress** (below, ➤ 56–57). Be sure to climb to the top for the city's best views.

12:30 pm

Have an early lunch by the waterside at Taverna Paralia (► 68), with lovely views of the fortress.

1:30 pm

Walk along the water-front to the **Historical Museum** (left, ► 58–59).

3:00 pm

Return to Plateía Venizélou and take a closer look at the Morosíni Fountain (right). If you've got some time to kill, there's no better spot for people-watching. Have a rest at Bougatsa Kirkor and try Crete's traditional custard pastry, the *bougátsa*, or relax in the nearby El Greco Park.

4:30 pm

Visit the **Icon Museum** (right, ► 60–61) and the cathedral and Church of Ágios Minás (► 61), both on the same square. Afterwards, take time for a last look at the Minoan treasures in the Archaeological Museum, or enjoy a pre-dinner drink in one of the bars behind Odós Daidálos (► 70).

❶ Archaeological Museum

Irakleío's Archaeological Museum is not only the major museum on Crete, it is the largest repository of Minoan antiquities anywhere and stands among the finest museums of the ancient world. This magnificent collection of pottery, frescoes, jewellery, ritual objects and utensils brings the Minoan world to life. Come here first before visiting the ancient palaces and your view of the ruins will be enlivened with a sense of the colour, creativity and richness of the fascinating culture that once flourished on this island.

The Archaeological Museum covers 5,500 years of Cretan history, from neolithic times (5000–2600 BC) to the end of the Roman era (4th century). The two-storey building was built between 1937 and 1940 and both the collection and the present-day summer crowds have outgrown this space. As there are plans to renovate the museum over the next few years to create new exhibition areas, some rooms may be closed or displays rearranged while work is in progress.

Buy your tickets at the kiosk in the courtyard. Beyond is a small garden and a coffee shop on the terrace behind the main building. Inside the entrance hall is a large desk where you can buy postcards and a museum guide. This is not essential, as most of the major exhibits are labelled in both Greek and English, though not in great detail.

A procession of figures on the sarcophagus from Agía Triáda

Timeline

Archaeologists categorise the museum's artefacts into the following periods:

Pre-Palace period: 2600–1900 BC
Old Palace period: 1900–1700 BC
New Palace period: 1700–1450 BC
Late Palace period: 1450–1400 BC
Post-Palace period: 1400–1150 BC
Sub-Minoan, Geometric, Oriental and Archaic periods: 1150–6th century BC
Classical, Hellenistic and Roman periods: 5th century BC–4th century AD

The collection is arranged chronologically from room to room, with finds from the major Minoan periods grouped according to the sites where they were discovered.

Museum Tour

Room I houses some of Crete's oldest artefacts, ranging from neolithic stone tools and crude idols to early Minoan pottery, figurines and jewellery from the Pre-Palace period (see **Timeline** panel). The ancient origins of bull sports, later an important ritual in palace life, are depicted by the small clay figures of bulls with acrobats grasping their horns (cases 12, 13 and 15). Look out, too, for early signs of Minoan craftsmanship in the Vasilikí pottery from eastern Crete, with graceful, elongated spouts and deep red and black mottling obtained by uneven firing. Also noteworthy are the early seal stones (➤ 53).

In **Room II** are Old Palace finds from Knosós and Mália. The painted and glazed earthenware plaques of the Town Mosaic (case 25) depict the multistorey dwellings of Minoan architecture. The many human and animal figurines were votive offerings found in peak sanctuaries. Clay *taximata*, representing diseased feet, arms or other parts of the body needing cures, are forerunners of the silver ones pinned to icons in churches today. Pottery is more elaborate, with the white and red polychrome decoration of Kamáres ware, and the delicate "egg shell" cups.

The style reaches its height in **Room III**, devoted to finds from the same period at Faistós Palace. Here large amphorae sport elaborate spirals, fish and other designs, while the royal banquet set (case 43) includes a huge fruit stand and a jug with relief decoration of large white flowers. However, the highlight of this

Europe's First Written Word

The earliest known written history in Europe began on Crete around 2000 BC. Known as Linear A, these inscriptions pre-date the documents of Mycaenean Greece, written in Linear B, by 600 years. Nearly 1,600 Linear A inscriptions have been found to date, and although they are not fully deciphered most are probably administrative records. Only 10 per cent are thought to be religious in nature.

áklềo

Minoan Motifs

Look for the major motifs that appear on artefacts from Minoan times: the double axe, the spiral and the horns of consecration were often painted or etched on pottery, while votive figurines took the shape of bulls, or goddesses with upraised arms.

room is the Faistós Disc (▶ 85) with its intricately carved hieroglyphic characters, possibly from a ritual text. It stands alone in a central case.

You'll find some of the finest artworks in the museum, dating from the New Palace period when Minoan art reached its peak, in **Room IV**. As you enter, in the left corner is an exquisite gaming board from Knosós, made of ivory with gold casing and inlaid decoration of rock crystal and lapis lazuli. Further along this wall in case 50 are two superb statues of the Snake Goddess, sacral relics from the temple repositories. Both figures are bare-breasted, one holding a pair of snakes in her upraised arms, the other with snakes coiled round her outstretched arms. They represent a major Minoan deity, or possibly a priestess engaged in ritual.

Above: Allow plenty of time to browse

Case 51 contains the bull's head *rhyton* from Knosós (a *rhyton* is a libation vessel used in religious ceremonies). Magnificently carved from steatite (a black stone), it has inlaid eyes of rock crystal, nostrils of white shell and restored wooden horns. Other life-like artworks are equally impressive, such as the alabaster head of a lioness, also a libation vessel, and a stone axe-head carved in the shape of a panther (both from Mália in case 47); and in case 56 the graceful ivory figure of an acrobat in mid-leap. The Jug of Reeds (case 49), with its dark colours and patterns depicting themes from nature, represents new developments in pottery.

A male figurine from the museum's vast collection

Room V, with Late Palace period finds from the

Small is Beautiful
Despite their tiny size, seal stones display an amazing degree of craftsmanship. Animals, people, imaginary creatures and hunting or religious scenes were carved in intricate detail on to hard stones such as agate or amethyst. These images were then impressed on to clay seals, which were used as a signature on correspondence or as a guarantee on shipments of goods. No two are alike.

Knosós area, has an interesting model of a Minoan house at Archánes. In case 69 are rare examples of Linear A script, the written language of the Minoans, alongside the Linear B script of mainland Greece.

Room VI contains a range of objects from cemeteries at Knosós and Faistós. In case 71 is a delightful clay statuette of men locking arms in a ritual dance between the horns of consecration, and another clay scene of ritual washing. Along the back wall are the bizarre remains of a horse burial, while case 78 contains a helmet made of boars' tusks. There are also several cases of jewellery and bronze objects.

Three enormous bronze double-axes erected on wooden poles guard the entrance to **Room VII**. The most outstanding piece of Minoan jewellery ever found – the intricate honeybee pendant with two gold bees joined round a honeycomb – is tucked away among the displays of jewellery in case 101 at the back of the room. Equally famous are three elegantly carved steatite vases from Agía Triáda (case 94–96):

Below: This gold bracelet was a find from Knosós

the harvester vase shows a procession of harvesters and musicians; the

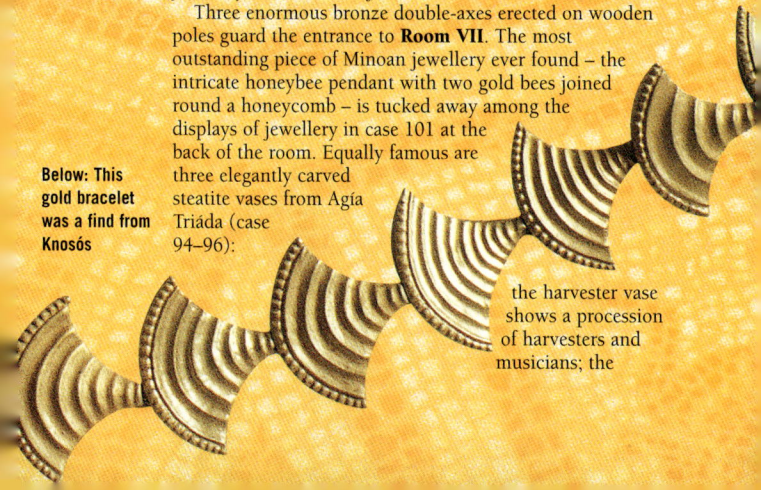

chieftain cup portrays an official receiving a tribute of animal skins; and the boxer *rhyton* depicts boxing, wrestling and bull-leaping.

Room VIII is devoted to treasures from the Zákros Palace (► 118). In case 109 along the wall is one of the triumphs of the museum – the stunning rock crystal *rhyton* with a green beaded handle, expertly reconstructed from over 300 fragments. The peak sanctuary *rhyton* in case 111 depicts scenes of Minoan worship.

Room IX houses finds from settlements in eastern Crete, including Gourniá, and has a marvellous collection of seal stones.

Rooms X to XII represent the Post-Palace period. Here, Minoan art is in decline, and the influences of Mycenaean Greece and Egypt are apparent.

Room XIII contains dozens of clay sarcophagi (coffins) painted with geometric designs. Many are shaped like bathtubs, and two are complete with skeletons.

Upstairs, **Room XIV**, the Hall of Frescoes, is the highlight of the museum. The long walls are lined with the famous frescoes from Knosós: the bull-leaper, the lily prince, the dolphins from the queen's bedroom. Only fragments of the original frescoes survive, with the paintings reconstructed around them, but the colour and detail in these few pieces reveal the remarkable skill of these early artists. In the centre of the room is the magnificent Agia Triáda sarcophagus,

Parting Gifts

Men were buried with bronze weapons and tools, while bronze mirrors were beloved offerings for female burials.

The famous
Snake Goddess

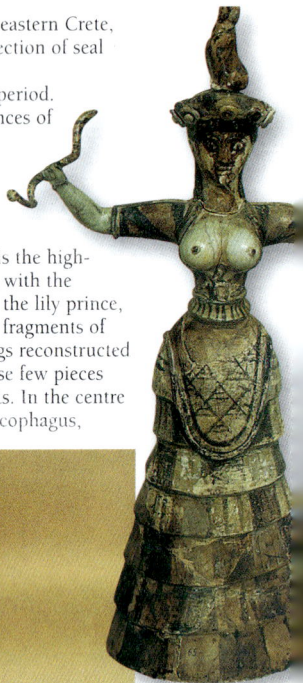

A bronze goddess found at Dréros, near Eloúnta

Right: This clay model shows a typical Minoan house

which survives intact. It is decorated with elaborate scenes of a funeral procession and an animal sacrifice.

Rooms XV and **XVI** have smaller frescoes, including the sensuous *La Parisienne* (No 27). Also notice the *Saffron Gatherer*, originally thought to be a boy picking flowers but later reinterpreted as a blue monkey.

At the end of the Hall of Frescoes a wooden scale model shows the Palace of Knosós in all its glory. Back on the ground floor, **Rooms XIX** and **XX** contain classical Greek and Roman sculpture.

TAKING A BREAK

Many tavernas line nearby **Plateía Eleftherías**, while the bars and restaurants of **Odós Koraí** are a short walk away.

🞢 183 D4 ✉ Odós Xanthoudidou 1 ☎ 0810-226092 🕐 Mon 12:30–7, Tue–Sun and holidays 8–7; reduced hours in winter 🍴 Café (€) 🚌 Bus stop near museum 💶 Expensive ❓ No flash photography

---

ARCHAEOLOGICAL MUSEUM: INSIDE INFO

Top tips Visit first thing in the morning, during lunchtime or in the late afternoon to **avoid the worst of the coach-party crowds**.
• You don't need to tackle all the exhibits at once. Your **ticket is valid for re-entry on the same day**, so take a break if you're feeling tired or overwhelmed.

Must sees Faistós Disc (Room III)
• **Snake Goddesses** (Room IV)
• **Bull's Head Rhyton** (Room IV)
• **Rock Crystal Rhyton** (Room VIII)
• **Hall of the Frescoes** (Rooms XIV–XVI)

Hidden gems Don't overlook the tiny gems, such as the **seal stones**, the **honeybee pendant** (Room VII) or the **ivory butterfly** (Room VIII).

One to miss The **classical Greek and Roman statues** seem anticlimactic after the Minoan art.

2 Venetian Harbour & Fortress

Irakleío's Venetian harbour is one of its most attractive features, and a stroll around here with a visit to the Venetian fortress that guards it is a relaxing treat. From the fortress you get an excellent view not only of the city but of the remains of the Venetian shipyards, or *arsenali*, across the water.

The graceful arches of Irakleío's *arsenali*

Below: The Lion of St Mark, on the fortress walls

Arsenali

Close up, the *arsenali* are none too impressive, surrounded as they now are by the modern city, but the view from the fortress shows something of their old scale and style. A look at the model in the Historical Museum (▶ 58–59) also helps re-create a picture of what life must have been like under Venetian rule. These 16th-century shipyards would have resounded to the noise of large boats being built and repaired, where today it is the bobbing of the small boats belonging to Irakleío's fishermen that sets the tone.

The Fortress

The fortress, which dominates the harbour entrance, was built between 1523 and 1540, though there had been several earlier forts on the site, one of which was destroyed in an earthquake in 1303. The Venetians rebuilt it and named it Rocca al Mare, Rock in the Sea, and the impressive name is appropriate for

St Mark's Lion

The winged lion of St Mark the Evangelist was the emblem of the Venetian Republic. It was depicted in all areas under the Republic's dominion, carved in limestone or marble above gateways or on public buildings and fortifications. Some 80 reliefs have been recorded on Crete.

VENETIAN HARBOUR & FORTRESS: INSIDE INFO

Top tip When an **exhibition** is on in the fortress the opening hours may change, so you may want to check in advance if planning a special visit.

Hidden gems Look for the **lions of St Mark** (see panel) above the entrance gate and on the seaward wall.

Above: Today the Venetian fortress guards only the fishermen's boats

the building you discover beyond the entrance gate.

Inside, you step into a huge dark vaulted room with various rooms and passageways leading off it. Ahead and to the right a long steep slope leads to the upper levels, where you can climb the walls for fine views of the harbour and city beyond, or out to sea. Some of the towers can be climbed, too.

While here, mull over the most significant episode in the history of the fortress. In 1647 the Venetian rulers of Crete retreated into the fortress under siege from Turkish invaders. That siege was to last until 1669 and so became one of the longest in history. Eventually the Venetians had to succumb, but only after a long and bloody struggle during which it is said that 30,000 Venetians and 118,000 Turks lost their lives.

The fortress has been extensively refurbished and some say it now looks more like a film set, but its scale remains impressive. It sometimes houses temporary exhibitions, and occasional plays and concerts are performed in the upper level.

TAKING A BREAK

You can enjoy good views of the fortress over a drink or a meal at the **Taverna Paralia** (► 68).

Venetian Fortress
🔲 183 D4 🕐 Daily 8:30–3 🎧 Inexpensive 📷 Photography allowed

3 **Historical Museum**

For an overview of the history of both Crete and Irakleío, a visit to this small but informative museum occupying an elegant Venetian town house is a must. Highlights of the collection include the study of Nikos Kazantzakis and the only work by El Greco still on the artist's native island.

At the ticket desk be sure to pick up one of the leaflets, available in Greek, English or German, which gives a map of the museum and a brief note of what is in each room. Most of the displays have information in both Greek and English, but in some instances the details given are fairly basic.

That said, in **Room I**, to your right as you enter, the information panels are anything but basic. They cover in some detail four of the major periods in Crete's history and correspond to four shelves of objects from those periods: the First Byzantine (330–824), the Arab occupation (824–961), the Second Byzantine (961–1204) and Venetian rule (1204–1669).

A typical Cretan house, displayed in the Historical Museum

Forming the major display in this room is a wonderful 1:500 scale model of Irakleío as it was in 1645. At that time it was still known as Chandax, the name given to the city by the Arabs when they made it the island capital in the early 9th century; it may derive from the Arabic words *Rabdh el-Khandak* (Fortress of the Moat). On the walls beside it maps show the development of the city over the years; note the buttons beneath the displays that illuminate the relevant parts of the model.

The museum tour continues beyond the ticket desk, with the rooms spread over several levels.

Room II is the Ceramics Room and has beautiful bowls and plates imported from Italy during the Venetian period. These are cleverly displayed side by side with locally made pottery from the same period, clearly showing the Italian influence on local designs. Lovely, delicate jugs and bowls from the Arab occupation of the island are also on display.

The rest of the ground floor has several rooms containing

Byzantine items, Venetian coats of arms and carvings (note the fountain from a 17th-century palazzo in Room VI), with stairs leading up to the second level.

The highlight of **Level B** is undoubtedly the small, dimly lit room containing El Greco's painting of the *Monastery of St Catherine Beneath Mount Sinai*. This, his only work to remain on Crete, was painted in 1570. Some background to it is given. Elsewhere on this floor are several icons, and at the rear one room is given over to the struggle for independence against the Turks.

The major display on **Level C** comprises the writer Nikos Kazantzakis's study when he lived in Antibes from 1948 to 1957, complete with manuscripts of his works, his library of books, and copies of his own books translated into many languages.

At the time of writing the museum's top floor was closed for renovation, after an accident, but when reopened it will contain a folklore collection based on the theme of the life cycle of birth, marriage and death. The museum's fine collections of weavings, embroidery, old costumes, household items, musical instruments and many other objects will contribute to the display, along with newly acquired pieces.

Manolis Kazanis, Cretan revolutionary leader

TAKING A BREAK

There is nothing outstanding in the immediate vicinity, but take a two-minute stroll towards the harbour to enjoy a drink or a meal at the **Taverna Kastella** overlooking the water.

Wall-painting showing the Turkish fleet in the harbour at Irakleío

183 D4 ✉ Odós Lysimahou Kalokairinou 7 ☎ 0810-283219/288708; fax: 0810-283754; email: info@historical-museum.gr; www.historical-museum.gr 🕐 Mon–Fri 9–5, Sat 9–2, Mar–Nov 💰 Moderate ❓ No flash photography

---

HISTORICAL MUSEUM: INSIDE INFO

Must see El Greco's painting *Monastery of St Catherine Beneath Mount Sinai*.

Hidden gems Cabinets in the centre of Room I, slightly overshadowed by the other displays, contain **fascinating glass and clay hand grenades** found on a galleon that sank in 1669.

One to miss The **Emmanuel Tsouderos room**, opposite the Nikos Kazantzakis room, is unlikely to appeal unless you have a deep interest in Greek politics.

4 Icon Museum
(Agía Aikateríni)

Cretan icon painters were considered to be the best in the world, and here in the small Church of Agía Aikateríni you can see some of the finest works by one of the greatest masters of the art, Michael Damaskinos. In addition, this excellent collection includes religious vestments, bibles, illuminated manuscripts, coins and frescoes rescued from or donated by churches and monasteries all over Crete.

The church that houses the collection was built in 1555, but the seating has been removed to expose the marble floors and provide space for the display cabinets in the aisles and around the sides. Icons grace the walls.

Just inside the door is the ticket desk, with six hugely impressive 16th-century icons, the work of Michael Damaskinos, hanging on the wall opposite. He was the only Cretan painter of his era to rival the talents of El Greco himself. Like the master, Damaskinos went to Venice to study, but he returned to his native island and the icons here are considered to be among his finest works. Depicting various biblical events such as the *Adoration of the Magi*, the *Last Supper* and the *Burning Bush*, they were all painted in between 1582 and 1591 for Moní

Detail from a work by Michael Damaskinos

ICON MUSEUM: INSIDE INFO

Top tips The museum's **opening hours do change** from time to time, so check in advance if you can.
• With **no air-conditioning**, the building can get very hot and stuffy, so visit early in the day if possible.

Hidden gem In what would be the south chapel of the church, look for the exceptional icon of the **Lady of the Kardiótissa** from Moní Kera. The Virgin, dressed in red, has sorrowful eyes that seem to stare right into your soul.

Vrontísiou (Vrontisiou Monastery) northwest of Zarós
(► 156–157). Their liveliness and depth of image and colour
make them seem as if they were done yesterday. They were
brought to Irakleio in 1800 to save them from destruction by
the Turks.

Other Byzantine Treasures

In the central aisle two cases contain Byzantine coins and
holy manuscripts. On the left aisle is a
series of large icons
saved from moun-
tain chapels and
monasteries; they
mostly date from
the 15th and 16th
centuries and are
anonymous. Note
the nearby case of
lovely 16th-century
illuminated
manuscripts from
Moní Epanosiphi and,
opposite these, the
ornately carved
wooden bishop's
throne from Moní
Kera.

You'll see more icons
as you approach the
high altar, including a
very vivid 17th-century
Last Judgement in which
naked souls are cast down
into hell where they are
being eagerly greeted by
devils throwing them into
the fiery furnace.

Round to the left of the
altar the collection broadens
out to include brightly
coloured frescoes and a large
stone iconostasis. Two cases
contain chalices, bible covers

*The Beheading
of St John the
Baptist,* an
18th-century
icon

and a holy cross.

On leaving the church, walk across the square to see the
small **Church of Ágios Minás**, if open, and the large 19th-
century cathedral of the same name with its elaborate metal
chandeliers, beautiful painted ceilings and vast stone pulpit.

TAKING A BREAK

Walk along Odós Karterou at the southeast corner of the
square to bring you to **Plateía Kornárou** (► 64), where the
Turkish well house now serves as a charming café.

✚ 183 D4 ✉ Platéia Agía Aikaterínis ⏰ Mon, Wed, Sat 9:30–2:30; Tue,
Thu, Fri 9:30–2:30, 4:30–6:30 💰 Inexpensive ❷ No photography

At Your Leisure

5 Natural History Museum

It's well worth going the extra distance to visit the Natural History Museum, housed in a modern air-conditioned building outside the city walls on the Knosós road. The museum provides a wonderful introduction to the wildlife, plants and natural environment of Crete, and if you are planning trips to the countryside or a drive around the island, it will certainly enhance your appreciation of the things you'll see. It lies about halfway between the town centre and Knosós, so you can easily stop off on your way to or from the Minoan palace. Look for the colourful banners waving outside.

The ground-floor rooms contain informative displays on the flora and fauna of Crete. Life-size dioramas re-create cave, forest, wetland and shoreline environments, and show the birds and animals that inhabit them. Both native birds of prey and migrating species are highlighted. Glass cases in the gift shop house live snakes, the curious ocellated skink and the Cretan spiny mouse. Other rooms are devoted to endangered species and to creatures of the high mountains, including the Cretan wild goat (*kri-kri*) and the magnificent griffon and lammergeier vultures.

To reach the upper level you walk through a lovely botanical garden,

especially aromatic in spring and summer when the many species of wild herbs are in bloom. Upstairs is an informative exhibit on the evolution of mankind, a re-created Minoan farm, and displays of fossils, rocks and minerals that illustrate Crete's geological evolution.

🔵 183 D4 ✉ Odós Knosou 157
☎ 0810-324711 🕐 Daily 9–7
🍴 Coffee shop (€) 🚌 2, 3, 4 💷 Free
❓ Photography allowed

6 Plateía Eleftherias

Its name translates as "Liberty Square", and this large open space at the top of Odós Daidálos, opposite the Archaeological Museum, provides freedom from the sometimes claustrophobic feel of the city. Traditionally this square was the centre of the city, and though the ring of rushing traffic around the edge has somewhat dampened its appeal, locals still frequent it for an evening stroll. There are shady benches beneath the palms and acacias, and a string of cafés and restaurants alongside.

🔵 183 D4

7 Ágios Títos

Ágios Títos sits back from the main road on a lovely square. With its sky-blue ceiling and dome, triple-tiered carved wooden chandelier and modern stained-glass windows, it has a light, airy feel in contrast to most of the churches you'll visit on the island. Built during the Second

Plateía Eleftherias – "Liberty Square"

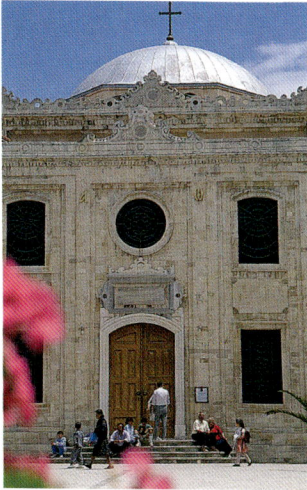

The lovely facade of Ágios Títos

Byzantine period (▶ 15), it was the seat of the Metropolitan (bishop) of Crete. During the Turkish occupation it was converted into a mosque but was entirely rebuilt following its destruction in an earthquake in 1856.

When the Turkish population left Crete in 1923 it was reconsecrated to St Titus, Crete's first bishop. His remains had been kept here for 700 years until the Venetians took them to Venice in 1669. They were returned in 1966, and the saint's skull now lies in a gold reliquary.

➕ 183 D4   ✉ Odós 25 Avgoústou
🕐 No set times, but generally mornings and evenings   🎟 Free

8 Venetian Loggia

After the fortress, this is Irakleío's second most handsome building. Built in the 1620s by Francisco Morosini, it was a place of meeting and recreation for the Venetian nobility. Its Palladian style combines Doric order on the lower floor with Ionic on the upper. Medallions of famous Cretans decorate the ground-floor porch, with its elegant arches. The loggia forms part of a larger building that once held the Venetian armoury and now houses the town hall. It stands opposite the Morosini Fountain (see Plateía Venizélou).

➕ 183 D4

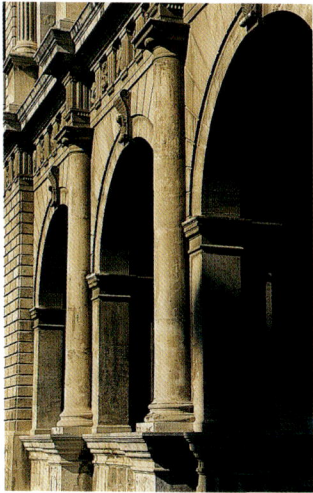

The elegant Venetian loggia

9 Ágios Márcos

The Church of Ágios Márcos (St Mark), first built in 1239, was the church of the duke, ruler of the island. It became a cathedral in Venetian times but, like most other Irakleío churches, was converted by the Turks into a mosque. Unlike the others,

however, it was not reconsecrated after their departure and in 1923 it became the National Bank. Now restored to its original form, with a striking colonnaded porch and marble doorway, it is used as a concert hall and art gallery. The arched ceiling, fat pillars and stone walls of the interior make a superb display space for changing exhibitions of contemporary art.

➕ 183 D4 ✉ Odós 25 Avgoústou
🕐 No set times, but generally evenings
💶 Free

The former church of Ágios Márcos

🔟 Plateía Venizélou

This small central square is one of the liveliest in the capital and a popular focal point for tourists and locals alike. It is named for the great Cretan statesman Elefthérios Venizélos, who became prime minister of Greece. Also known as Lion Square or Fountain Square, its centre-piece is the Morosíni Fountain. Francisco Morosíni, the Venetian governor of the city, built this regal work in

1628. A 16km aqueduct was constructed to bring water down from the mountains. The four stone lions supporting the central basin have great character and are even older; dating from the 14th century, they are thought to have come from another fountain. Carvings of mermaids, tritons and other marine figures decorate the curvaceous marble base.

The square has plenty of cafés and restaurants where you can have a coffee, an ice-cream or the custard-filled Cretan speciality, *bougátsa*. It's a perfect vantage point on the passing scene, but if you prefer a quieter retreat try the nearby El Greco Park, behind the yellow sub-post office. It has pretty gardens and a children's playground at one end.

➕ 183 D4

For Children
Venetian Harbour and Fortress (► 56–57)
El Greco Park (► above)
Natural History Museum (► 62)
A ride on the **Happy Train**, which follows the Venetian wall around the old city. Departures from the Archaeological Museum on the hour, 11 am–2 pm, and from the Venetian Harbour 6–9 pm; buy tickets on board (tel: 0897-33624).

🔟🔟 Plateía Kornárou

Irakleío's street market ends at Plateía Kornárou, a small, quiet square that makes a pleasant place to stop for a break. The stone kiosk in the centre, which once housed a Turkish fountain, has been converted into a small café. Beside it is the Bembo Fountain, named after the Venetian commander Zanne Matteo Bembo, who first supplied the town with running water. It was erected in 1588 and incorporates the torso of a Roman statue from Ierápetra (► 116), about 65km southeast of Irakleío.

➕ 183 D4

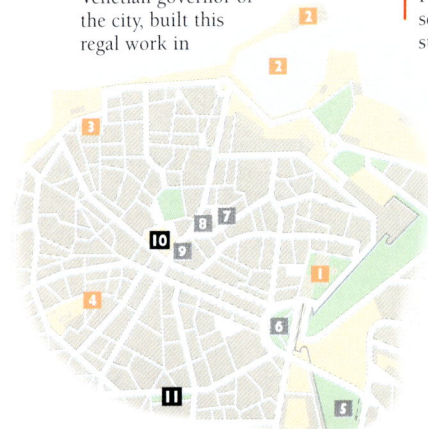

Where to... Stay

Prices

Prices are for a double room per night in high season including taxes

€ under €60   €€ €60–€100   €€€ over €100

IRAKLEÍO

Astoria Capsis €€€

Although right on Irakleío's main square, the Capsis is quiet inside and offers stylish, reasonably priced accommodation. All the rooms, bright and modern with a predominantly blue decor and lots of wood furnishings, have plenty of closet space, TV, phone, mini-bar, air-conditioning and en-suite facilities (baths not showers). The terrific rooftop pool has its own bar, and there are great views over the city. It stays open till 10 pm and is a very popular spot for an evening swim.

�︎ 183 D4 🖂 Plateía Eleftherías 5
☎ 0810-229002; fax: 0810-229078

Atlantis Grecotel €€€

This is the best hotel in the centre of Irakleío, and though it has some 160 rooms and suites you would still be advised to book ahead in high season as it is popular with tour groups and business conferences. Some rooms have views over the harbour, so ask if one of these is available when you book. Right by the Archaeological Museum and only a short walk to most other city attractions, the Atlantis has so many of its own facilities that you hardly need to leave it: gym, pool, laundry, bars, restaurant, shops and even a rooftop garden.

🚫 183 D4 🖂 Ygias 2 ☎ 0810-229103; email: atlantis@atl.grecotel.gr

Dedalos €

This very superior mid-range hotel is tucked away on a pedestrianised street, which makes initial access difficult if you have heavy bags to carry or are driving (park near the Archaeological Museum) but ensures peace at night. The air-conditioned rooms are bright and cheery with paintings and sketches on the walls, and all are en-suite with either bath or shower. Some have TVs.

🚫 183 D4 🖂 Odós Daidálos 15
☎ 0810-24481 2; fax: 0810-224391

El Greco Hotel €

Better than average for a moderately priced hotel, the El Greco is in the heart of the city, close by the busy market and the characterful Plateía Venizélou (▶ 64). Its 90 plain but pleasant and clean rooms are all en-suite with phone and heating. Most have balconies and some have TVs and air-conditioning, so if you are staying in high season try to book one of these. The bar/breakfast

room, spacious lobby and friendly staff all add to the relaxed atmosphere.

🚫 183 D4 🖂 Odós 1821
☎ 0810-281071; email:
elgrecohotel@her.forthnet.gr

Galaxy Hotel €€€

The Galaxy is slightly out of the city centre, about a kilometre along the Knosós road, but still within easy reach of the sights; a bus stops right outside the hotel. From the exterior it looks like any other modern concrete block, but inside there is luxurious marble decor and every amenity. It has a stunning swimming pool, the largest in the city, with a small sauna room, bars, shops and a restaurant.

🚫 183 D4 🖂 Odós Leofóros
Dimokratías 67 ☎ 0810-238812;
fax: 0810-2211211;
www.galaxy-hotels-com/galaxyhotel/

Hotel Kronos €

This clean, friendly, inexpensive hotel stands right on the waterfront road, which does mean some traffic noise at night in the front rooms. That aside, it offers excellent value accommodation in the centre of town. Downstairs a lounge doubles as the breakfast room, and there is a bar with a soft-drinks cabinet. The 32 rooms are a good size and have everything needed for a comfortable stay: balconies, phone, TV, en-suite facilities.

Lato Hotel €€

Space and marble decor make the modern lobby to this stylish hotel immediately welcoming and a wall of water at one end is very eye-catching. You'll find a lounge, a bar, and a restaurant with an old-fashioned fireplace off the lobby. Ask for one of the rooms on the upper floors as some of these have impressive views of Irakleío, but all have phone, TV, mini-bar, air-conditioning and bathroom with both bath and shower. The hotel is near the bus station and it's a short walk to the centre and the Archaeological Museum.

➕ 183 D4 ✉ Odós Epimenídou 15 ☎ 0810-228103; email: info@lato.gr; www.lato.gr

➕ 183 D4 ✉ Odós Sofokli Venizélou 2/Agaráthou ☎ 0810-282240; fax: 0810-285853

AROUND IRAKLEÍO

Apollonia Beach Hotel €€€

Standing just 10km west of the centre of Irakleío, the luxury Apollonia has its own beach and the local bus stops right outside the entrance. The 321 rooms, bunga-lows and suites, all with either a balcony or terrace, are spread around the large gardens and there are two outdoor pools, a children's pool and a heated indoor pool, as well as numerous sports facilities including watersports, cycling and horse-riding. With two discos, it's also ideal for children of all ages.

➕ 182 C4 ✉ Linoperámata ☎ 0810-821602/821624; fax: 0810-821433 ☉ Apr–Oct

Candia Maris €€

About 5km west of the city centre but with a quick and regular bus service into Irakleío, the Candia Maris makes an ideal base if you want to explore the city but also enjoy the beach. Its facilities include a fitness centre, tennis and squash courts, three swimming pools (plus one for children), watersports, an indoor games room, three restaurants and four bars. The rooms are spacious and bright, and the rates very reasonable for a mid-range hotel.

➕ 183 D4 ✉ Ammoudára ☎ 0810-377000; email: candia@maris.gr; www.maris.gr

Minoa Palace €€

The Minoa Palace exudes class yet offers a very reasonable room rate. Half-board and full-board options are available. All rooms have balconies with sea views, and the hotel boasts its own private beach as well as a large pool. Close to the airport, it would make the ideal base for the first or last night's stay. A car is advisable, though there is a public bus service into Irakleío, 6km west.

➕ 183 E4 ✉ Amnisos Beach ☎ 0810-380404/380006; email: minoaplc@iraklio.hellasnet.gr ☉ Apr–Oct

Santa Marina Beach Hotel €€

With Irakleío just 6km to the west, this 210-room hotel complex is the perfect base for anyone wanting to combine sightseeing with sunbathing, though there are plenty of sports facilities here. Away from the main block, many of the rooms are bungalow-style and laid out in the manner of a Cretan village. All have balconies or terraces, air-conditioning, TV, phone, fridge and safe. There are bars and restaurants both inside and out, a pool, a chil-dren's pool, tennis, mini-golf, volleyball and watersports.

➕ 183 D4 ✉ Ammoudára Beach ☎ 0810-261103; fax: 0810-261369 ☉ Apr–Oct

Where to...
Eat and Drink

Prices

Prices are for a two-course meal for one person, excluding drinks and tips

€ under €9   €€ €9–€14.5   €€€ over €14.5

IRÁKLEÍO

Garden of Deykaliola €€

This bright and busy restaurant stands behind the Historical Museum, off a small courtyard with an old stone fountain. It has smart green paintwork outside and a miniature ship's anchor for a door knocker, while all the seating is in a cheerful room with yellow walls and stone arches. Artificial vines hang from the roof and accordions and guitars decorate the walls – although only till the owners take them down to play music for the customers into the wee small hours. Snails with a Cretan sauce is one speciality on a menu that's stronger on meat dishes than fish.

➕ 183 D4 ☒ Odós Kalokairínou 8 ☎ 0810-244215 ⓒ Mon–Sat 8 pm–late

Giovanni's €€€

Despite the Italian name, this up-market restaurant has a very Greek menu. A speciality of the house is feta cheese baked in the oven with olive oil, tomato and oregano, but a mixed seafood platter also features regularly, as does fresh fish – which can be expensive. Outdoor and indoor seating, a good Greek wine list and a generally smart look tend to attract a well-to-do Irakleio crowd.

➕ 183 D4 ☒ Odós Korai 12 ☎ 0810-246338 ⓒ Mon–Sat 12.30 pm–2 am, Sun 5 pm–1.30 am

The Ice-Factory (Pagopoleion) €€

This bar/restaurant is more what you might expect to find in London or New York than on Crete. The bar is lined with fake fur, the bar stools brightly painted, there's upbeat music (sometimes live bands) and the walls are hung with photos of 1950s movie stars and film stills. Fun more than food is the emphasis, but the menu offers a good choice of simple Greek dishes, mostly as inexpensive set three-course meals. Good choice of Cretan wines. And yes, it was once an ice factory. Today it's just cool.

➕ 183 D4 ☒ Plateía Ágiou Títou ☎ 0810-346028 ⓒ Daily 9.30 am– 3 am

Ionia €€

Founded in 1923, when it played host to the archaeologists from Knosós, the Ionia claims to be the oldest restaurant on Crete. There are a few seats outside but most are indoors in a fairly nondescript modern room decorated with old archaeological photos on the walls. Filled more with Greeks than with tourists, it serves up plain but excellent dishes such as grilled chicken, grilled lamb chops and sardines. "Whatever is fresh in the market," says the manager, "that is what we cook. Seasonal food."

➕ 183 D4 ☒ Odós Evans 3 ☎ 0810-283213 ⓒ Mon–Fri 7 am–9.30 pm, Sat 7–4

Ippokampos €€

This is one of the liveliest places in town, so get there early or expect to wait for a table. There are two floors indoors but the place to be is on one of the pavement tables, picking up the sea breeze. It specialises in *meze* and fresh fish, from tiny whitebait to fillets of mako shark, though there are a few vegetarian and meat dishes too.

**+ 183 D4 ⊠ Odós Mitsotaki 13
☎ 0810-280240 ⏰ Mon–Fri 1–3:30 pm, 7–late**

O Kyriakos €€€

The Kyriakos has been around for 50 years and is where visiting dignitaries tend to be taken. There is a relaxed outdoor seating area shielded from the street by lots of greenery, and a slightly more formal dining-room inside with white walls and more plants. Service is very friendly and the restaurant prides itself on its range of good *meze*. Aubergines stuffed with feta is a simple dish but deliciously done.

+ 183 D4 ⊠ Odós Leofóros Dimokratías 53 ☎ 0810-224649 ⏰ Daily noon–5, 7–midnight

Loukoulos €€€

With its charming courtyard beneath a spreading lemon tree and views right into the kitchen, this

stylish Mediterranean restaurant offers the very best cuisine from Greece and Italy, with other flourishes too. The wine list is excellent and the service, by knowledgeable staff who can describe each dish in mouthwatering detail, impeccable. One superb speciality is veal with a sauce of dried figs.

+ 183 D4 ⊠ Odós Korai 5 ☎ 0810-224435 ⏰ Mon–Sat noon–1 am, Sun 6.30 pm–1 am

New China €€

Along busy Odos Korai, where there are numerous bars, is something a little bit different, the New China. It offers Chinese food with a Greek accent, although lovers of Chinese food will find it pretty authentic fare. There is seating outside in a relaxing shady courtyard set slightly off the main street, and inside where the decor is Chinese. The menu is extensive and there are choices of set meals too, but it is a little pricey by Cretan standards.

+ 183 D4 ⊠ Odós Korai 1 ☎ 0810-245162 ⏰ Daily 7 pm–midnight

Pantheon €€

With outdoor seating on both sides of the covered side street, the Pantheon couldn't be closer to the butchers and the greengrocers of Irakleío's market. It serves plenty of conventional dishes such as chicken and moussaka, but take a look in the kitchen to see the day's more unusual specials, such as lamb cooked in a clay pot in the oven with artichokes and peas, or aubergine stuffed with lamb and topped with cheese.

+ 183 D4 ⊠ Odós Theodosáki 2 ☎ 0810-241652 ⏰ Mon–Sat 11 am–late

Taverna Paralía €

Set right on the waterfront, the Paralía's tables look out over the occasionally crashing waves and across to the Venetian fortress. On breezy days you can choose the sheltered seating indoors, where the

style is typically Greek – blue and white décor with checked tablecloths. The menu includes many standard Greek dishes, plus pasta and pizza, but the speciality is fresh fish such as swordfish or sea bream, simply grilled.

+ 183 D4 ⊠ Odós Venizélou 5 ☎ 0810-28475 ⏰ Daily 10 am–midnight, Apr–Oct

Terzakis €€

One of the down-to-earth ouzeries in Irakleío that the casual visitor never finds. It specialises in *meze*, the small mixed dishes of Greek favourites that go to make up a meal. The waiter brings a list in Greek and English and you check off what you want. Try three or four to start with, and see how you get on. Leave some room for the little bottle of *raki* that usually appears at the end of the meal, along with some fruit or other small offering.

+ 183 D4 ⊠ Odós Marinéli 17 ☎ 0810-221444 ⏰ Mon–Sat lunch and dinner

Where to...
Shop

Like any major city, Crete's capital has no shortage of shops. Most cater for the locals so if you're after traditional crafts you'll find more choice elsewhere on the island. That said, Irakleio can offer a selection of all Crete's popular souvenirs.

Odós Daidálos, a pedestrianised thoroughfare, is the main tourist shopping street. These days it's mainly given over to fashion, with top names such as Hugo Boss, Zara for men and women, Timberland, Nautica, and a number of shoe shops.

The more touristy shops are towards the top end of the street, approaching the Archaeological Museum.

For unique Cretan gifts, try **Galerie Dedalou** at No 11, where you'll find replica coins and Byzantine crosses, repro watches, jewellery, silverware, icons and worry beads.

Aerakis, at No 35, specialises in contemporary and traditional Greek music; also on this street are **Virgin Records** and **Metropolis**, for international artists.

In Irakleio you are especially likely to see gold and silver jewellery with Minoan spirals and motifs, or replicas of famous pieces such as the honeybee pendant from the museum. The shops opposite the Archaeological Museum have a fine selection.

You could also try **Vassilakis** at 28 Odos 25 Avgoustou, a family-run shop with good prices. **Kassotakis** jewellery workshop, 14 Odos Katechaki, specialises in historically inspired Byzantine and archaic jewellery.

The square opposite the Archaeological Museum is lined with shops catering for tourists, with pottery, statues, icons, decorative Cretan daggers and replicas of the Faistós Disc and other Minoan treasures. There are also many rugs, textiles and woven goods, but these are often imported or factory made. True handmade goods will have rough stitching on the back and are more expensive.

Although **Odós 25 Avgoústou** is mainly flanked with travel agents and car-hire companies, there are a few shops worth browsing for gifts. **Emika**, at No 15, has a good selection of wines from local wine co-operatives as well as gift bottles of ouzo, herbed olive oils in pretty bottles, Cretan honey and packets of herbs. Further up the street, next to the loggia, **Cretan Nature** has a similar selection of gift items, including olive-oil soap and creams.

The most colourful place to shop is the market (open weekdays) on **Odós 1866**, also known as Market Street, which is always packed with both locals and tourists. There are stalls selling fresh fruit and vegetables, honey, olives, spices, nuts, dried fruit and sweets, bakers, and butchers with skinned lambs and rabbits. Cheese shops will let you sample cheese from different villages before you buy. This is the place to find Cretan wedding loaves – the wreath-like bread topped with flower decoration – for a kitchen ornament. One shop sells lace table-cloths and embroidered linens, and you can also buy sponges, T-shirts, leather bags, belts and sandals, as well as tourist tat.

There is also a large market on Saturday morning near the bus station, opposite the port.

Odós Chandákos, behind Plateía Venizélou, has some nice little shops with handcrafted jewellery and other gifts.

Busy **Odós Kalokairinou** is Irakleio's high street, with Body Shop, Benetton, Max Mara and other fashion and shoe shops. There are also shops selling embroidered goods along this street.

Where to...
Be Entertained

Nightlife in Irakleío is generally not the raucous affair you find in the beach party towns. If that's what you're after, head for the clubs along the coastal strip at Ammoudara, west of the city, or to Chersonisou or Mália (▶ 124) to the east. Also note that while bars are open all day until late, clubs and discos don't start up until 11 pm or midnight.

NIGHTCLUBS

Nightclubs in town are geared for the locals, and it can be hard to find the "right" one unless you go with someone who knows the scene. Many are around the harbour, such as **3/4** and **Portside** along the port promenade. Two long-time favourites on Odós Bofór are **Yacht Club** and **Privilege**.

BARS

The bars on **Plateía Venizélou** can't be beat for people-watching but are pricey. **Café Aktaríka**, opposite the Lion Fountain on the corner with Odós Daidálos, is a large, busy bar with a big-screen TV. Off Daidálos, **Odós Ioánnou Perthíkari** leads to Irakleío's trendiest nightlife area. Clustered around the intersection with Korai are several popular bars: **Irithanos**, **Ideon Antron**, **Rebels**, and **BestSeller**. Turn right on Odós Korai for **Koraís**, a huge open-air cafe-bar with music, video screens and a smart young crowd. **Plateía Korai** at the end of this street is also lined with bars and cafes.

Another area for nightlife is **Odós Chandakos**, running south of Plateía Venizélou.

TRADITIONAL MUSIC

Most top-class hotels hold Greek nights during the high season where you can get a taste of traditional Greek music and dancing. Two good clubs are **Sordina**, about 5km southwest of town, and **Aposperides**, on the road to Knosos, both reached by taxi.

ARTS FESTIVAL

Irakleío's summer arts festival is held from late June to mid-September and features Greek and international artists in music, dance and theatre productions that range from ballet to Greek drama. Performances take place on the roof of the **Venetian fort** or in the **Nikos Kazantzakis Open-Air Theatre** at Jesus Bastion (tel: 0810-242977, box office). In summer the latter is also used as an open-air cinema. In the town centre, the **Alpha Odeon cinema** at Plateía Eleftherías shows English films with Greek subtitles.

INTERNET CAFÉS

Good central internet cafés include **Sportcafé**, off Odós 25 Avgoustou on Kosma Zotou; **Netclub** and **Mitsotaki 2**, both near the waterfront; and **GG** at Odós Korai 6.

SPORTS

Most sports facilities are located out of town. To find a good tennis court, contact the **Tennis Club of Irakleío** at Odós Bofór 17 (tel: 0810-344545).

The **Mountaineering and Skiing Club of Irakleíon** organises weekend excursions to various locations. Visitors are welcome (tel: 0810-227609, daily 8:30 pm–10:30 pm).

Central Crete

Getting Your Bearings

Visitors who fly into Irakleío then head east or west along the coast in search of sandy beaches often overlook central Crete. But turn south instead and you'll find mountains, caves, gorges, monasteries and churches, craft villages and hill villages, Minoan sites and, at the end of your journey, beautiful beach resorts like Mátala and Agía Galíni.

Central Crete claims the number-one attraction on the island, the ruins of ancient Knosós, but it also has smaller, equally fascinating sites. Faistós, near the south coast, has an attractive setting overlooking the Mesará Plain. Here you can see the spot where archaeologists found what is perhaps the island's single most important historical item: the Faistós Disc.

Those fascinated by history will also revel in two other sites close to Faistós. One is the Roman site at Gortýs, the other the Minoan villa of Agía Triáda. Both gloriously demonstrate that small can be beautiful, their human scale really bringing history alive.

Details from the dolphin fresco at Knosós

The mountain village of Zarós is a gateway to some wonderful walking, but central Crete is also ideal for those who want to combine history with sunbathing. The south coast resorts of Mátala and Agía Galíni both have good beaches, good eating and nightlife, and make great bases for exploring the whole area. From south to north is little more than an hour's drive…or more like a week if you want to explore every nook and cranny.

Making sense of Agía Triáda

★ **Don't Miss**

At Your Leisure

0   20 km
0   10 miles

Órmos Fódele

Síses

E75/90

7 **Fódele**

Akrotíri Panagía

Kólpos Irakleíou

Kouloúkonas

Márathos

IRAKLEÍO

Arolíthos 4

Kályvos

Anógia
8

Tílisos 5

99

Knosós

1

Knosós

Goniès

97

Stavrákia

1584m
▲ Sítaras

N í d a

Krousónas

Choudétsi

Mount Ída 9

9 **Ídaean Cave**

1860m
▲ Koudoúni

Avgenikí

Parthéni

Psiloreítis

Nithavris

Kamáres

Gérgeri

97

...ampes

97

Zarós

Lethéos

Agía Varvára

Laráni

13 **Agía Galíni**

Museum of Cretan Ethnology

Tefélí

Tympáki

Vórol

10

Moíres

Gortýs
2

Agíoi Déka 6

Órmos Mésaras

Agía Triáda 11

3

Pitsídia

Geropótamos

M e s a r á

Asími

Faistós

Vagioniá

Chárakas

12 **Mátala**

Pómpia

Loúkia

Asteroúsia

Akrotíri Lithíno

Kaloí Liménes

Léndas

Weaving is a popular Cretan craft

Enjoy the beaches of both the north and south coasts, the mountain villages of the interior, the major Minoan sites including Knosós and Faistós, and – perhaps – the birthplace of Zeus: a true Cretan experience.

Central Crete in Three Days

Day One

Morning

Try to get to **Knosós** (right, ► 76–80) by opening time, to have any hope of beating the crowds and heat, and allow a good hour or two at the site. Afterwards, head back towards Irakleío and take the New Road west towards Réthymno, but turn off towards the craft village of **Arolíthos** (► 87). The restaurant at Arolíthos is surprisingly good, but don't linger too long.

Afternoon

The ancient site of **Tílisos** (► 87) closes at 3 pm so try to arrive by 2 pm to enjoy it before continuing on the winding mountain road to **Anógia** (► 88). If time and daylight allows, drive on to visit the **Ídaean Cave** (left, ► 89), though you'll need to allow at least two hours.

Evening

Spend the night in **Anógia**, where there is a hotel and rooms to rent. A good dining spot is the simple Taverna Skalómata on the right as you leave the village on the road to the cave, which has great views.

Day Two

Morning

Visit the Ídaean Cave if you didn't manage it the night before, then head back through Tílisos to reach the New Road. Head west towards Réthymno but look for the turning to **Fódele** (► 88). Have lunch at one of the simple tavernas here.

Afternoon

Head back towards Irakleío on the New Road but as you reach the city look for the right turn marked to Míres. This is a fast road but makes a pleasant drive as it eventually heads up into the hills. In Agía Varvára watch carefully for the almost hidden little right turn to Zarós.

Evening

After another lovely drive, relax by the pool and later dine at the restaurant of the Idi Hotel (► 92) in Zarós.

Day Three

Morning

Explore **Zarós** (► 156–157) and go for a short walk up the gorge before heading south on the road to Moíres, turning left to reach **Gortýs** (right, ► 81–83).

Lunch

East of Gortýs is the **Church of Agíoi Déka** (► 87). The village has several authentic tavernas where few tourists venture.

Afternoon

Allow plenty of time for visiting **Faistós** (below, ► 84–86) before deciding where to spend the night: in the small resort of Mátala, or the bigger but prettier **Agía Galíni** (► 91).

Evening

The Lions Restaurant in Mátala (► 93) has excellent food, while Agía Galíni offers numerous choices, including Madame Hortense (► 93) and the Onar Restaurant (► 94).

❶ Knosós

Historical wonder or archaeologist's fantasy? The Minoan palace of Knosós is Crete's biggest attraction, and its excavation yielded the most important remains of this ancient civilisation. Even if you find its reconstructed rooms and columns a travesty, they are none the less fascinating and help to make sense of the sprawling maze of stone. Unlike traditional "bare" archaeological sites, Knosós provides an intimate glimpse of the lives that might have been lived here.

Covering a vast area of 75 hectares (only a portion of which is open to the public), Knosós is the largest of the Minoan palaces. It was built on five levels and had over 1,200 rooms, providing accommodation for a huge court. It is thought that more than 100,000 people lived in and around the palace when the Minoan civilisation was at its height.

Shade is not easy to find at Knosós

Neolithic remains found at Knosós suggest that there were settlers here as far back as 6000 BC. The first Minoan palace was constructed around 2000 BC, but was destroyed in an earthquake three centuries later. What you see today are the remains of the even grander palace that replaced it. Even after this palace was destroyed in the great cataclysm of 1450 BC (▶ 10–13), Knosós remained an important settlement for newcomers to the island well into Roman times. Afterwards it fell into obscurity until a Cretan archaeologist, Minos Kalokairinos – coincidentally named after the ancient priest-kings – discovered the storerooms in 1878.

On the Royal Way at Knosós

A Reconstruction

A few years later, a young Englishman, Arthur Evans (▶ below), became intrigued by the site and bought up the land, and by 1900 a full-scale archaeological dig was under way. In just two years he uncovered most of the palace area, but his hasty methods caused important information to be lost or poorly documented. Of greater controversy was Evans' reconstruction of parts of the palace, which he claimed was necessary to preserve and understand it. There was some truth to this, as the original pillars and beams had been made of wood and as he unearthed room after room, the entire structure was in danger of collapse. Evans incorporated original fragments into new concrete pillars and supports, and restored rooms according to how he believed they would have looked during the Minoan era. Later archaeologists have been highly critical of his romantic re-creations, but Evans' work does give visitors a glimpse of the splendour of the Minoan world, and a means to visualise the frescoed walls, ceremonial staircases and red pillars that supported this multi-storey complex.

Seeing the Palace

With its narrow passageways, connecting rooms, raised walk-ways and L-shaped steps leading to dead-end landings, Knosós can be confusing. No wonder it has been linked with the mythical labyrinth of King Minos. Rooms are not labelled, and can be hard to identify even with a map, but you will eventually come across all the interesting areas, sometimes

Sir Arthur Evans

Sir Arthur Evans

At the entrance to Knosós is a bust of Sir Arthur Evans (1851–1941), excavator of the site. He was a man of many talents, working as a journalist and war correspondent before becoming director of the Ashmolean Museum in Oxford at the age of 33. Ten years later, in 1894, his job led him to Knosós for the first time and he became intrigued by speculations of an ancient palace buried here. Evans was a wealthy man – and a tenacious one. It took him five years to purchase the land from its Turkish owners. Though his autocratic methods drew much criticism, his findings rewrote the history of the ancient world. He was knighted for his achievements in 1911 and continued to work on the site until 1935, when he was 84 years old.

when you least expect it.

Sadly, Knosós has suffered from its own popularity. The sheer number of tourists treading its ancient walls has caused structural problems, and many areas and paths are now roped off. False walkways have been built over the natural stone paths to cater for the tour groups on a beaten trail, but they spoil the character of the site and make it difficult for individual travellers to escape the crowds. The best way to enjoy Knosós is to take your time and use your imagination.

> ## Waterworks
>
> A drainage system of terracotta pipes, ingenious for its time, ran below the palace and incorporated a means to stop or control the flow of water. You can still see parts of this system under grilles and around the edges of the royal chambers.

The entrance is through the **west court**, passing the circular pits where devotional objects were placed at the end of sacred rituals. Turn right, and follow the Corridor of Processions, where you have the first sight of the palace frescoes. These show a party of men and women carrying gifts and ceremonial vessels. Evans hired French artists to repaint all of the frescoes on site, once the originals were moved to the Archaeological Museum in Irakleio.

The Priest King fresco

Inside the palace walls, on your left is the **south propylaeum** with its tapering white columns and fresco of a cup-bearer. On your right is a reproduction of the enormous Horns of Consecration, standing where the original fragments were found. Just ahead, in an upper chamber, is the famous fresco of the priest-king.

Evans gave the frescoes and rooms their names, such as the *piano nobile*, taken from the Italian Renaissance. A staircase behind the south propylaeum leads up to it, where there is a good view over the central court and the storerooms with their giant storage jars, called *pithoi*.

The colourful griffin frescoes of the Throne Room

Detail from the
Ladies in Blue
fresco

Below, in the northwest corner of the court, is the **throne room**, decorated with frescoes of griffins. The gypsum throne is thought to be the oldest in Europe. Opposite is a sunken lustral basin, used for purification. If you can't resist the impulse to pose for a photo, there is a wooden replica for that purpose in the antechamber. The throne room is one of the highlights of the palace and long queues often form as people wait to peer over the threshold.

What's in a Name?

The notion of Knosós as the labyrinth of King Minos may be more than just myth. In pre-Hellenic times the word *labrys* meant "double axe" and the ending *nthos* meant "house of" – thus, "house of the double axe". Giant double axes were found at Knosós, and were thought to be a symbol of religious and political power.

The heart of Knosós is the **central court**, measuring approximately 55m by 28m. Originally surrounded by high walls, it is where the bull-leaping rituals and athletic contests depicted in the frescoes took place.

On the east side of the court, the grand staircase leads down to what Evans believed were the **royal chambers**. This is now also blocked off, but you can descend via a corridor to your left. These are the best-preserved rooms, and though they are built into the slope of a hill, they are lit by a

The royal
chambers lay
east of the
central court

clever system of large light wells. Look out for the king's chamber, whose ante-room is marked with shields and the sign of the double axe. The queen's chamber is adorned with a delightful fresco of dolphins. Sadly, the adjacent rooms, which held a clay bathtub and flush toilet, are no longer on view.

To the north of the royal chambers are the **palace workshops** and the magazines of giant *pithoi*, used to store olive oil and wine. A **theatre** with some 500 seats lies northwest of the palace. The royal road, with original paving stones dating from the third millennium BC, leads north and may once have run all the way to the sea.

TAKING A BREAK

As an alternative to the site café you could try any one of the number of **tavernas** lining the road **outside Knosós**, most of which are touristy and unremarkable but fine for a drink or light meal.

The Dolphin Fresco adorns the Queen's chamber...

✚ 183 D4
✉ 5km south of Irakleío on Odós Knosou ☎ 0810-231940 ⏰ Daily 8–7
🍴 Café (€) 🚌 Bus 2, 4 💰 Expensive ❓ Photography allowed

KNOSÓS: INSIDE INFO

Top tips Knosós is Crete's most popular attraction and it is always busy, especially in summer. **To avoid the worst of the crowds**, try to be there when the site first opens in the morning, or in the early evening. Midday can also be quieter, when large tour groups leave for lunch.

• The **summer heat** is intense and there is little shade; bring water and sun hat.
• Allow two hours to **see the highlights**, more if it is very crowded.
• You'll find **pay-parking areas** on the main road just before Knosós and immediately past the entrance.

2 Gortýs

On an island full of Minoan remains, the ruins of this ancient Greco-Roman city give a glimpse of a later era. The core site is small but impressive, with the enormous basilica of Ágios Títos and the law code – the first such code to be written down in Europe – inscribed on massive stone blocks. If time allows, you can wander through the surrounding fields and olive groves to discover the scattered remnants of this important city.

...and spring flowers adorn the fields around Ágios Títos at Gortýs

The settlement of Gortýs dates back to Minoan times. Built along the River Lethéos (also known as the Mitropolitanos) on the fertile Mesará Plain, it prospered and grew under the Dorian Greeks and by the 8th century BC had become the most important city in southern Crete. When the Romans conquered the island in 67 BC, they made Gortýs the capital of their province Cyrenaica, which encompassed not only Crete but much of North Africa. A century later, St Titus (► 82) made his base here and set about converting the population – which numbered some 30,000, the largest on Crete – to Christianity. It became the religious as well as the political centre of the island.

Gortýs flourished throughout Byzantine times until Saracen raiders sacked the city in 824. It never recovered and was soon abandoned. Today its ruins cover a large area, much of which has not yet been excavated.

Ágios Títos

The major ruins of Gortýs lie within a fenced site on the north side of the road. As you enter, the massive shell of Ágios Títos draws you to the left. Built in the 6th century, it is the best-preserved early Christian church on Crete, and was the seat of the archbishops until the Arab invasion. The vaulted central apse gives you an idea of its former magnificence, and there is a small shrine in one of the side aisles. The holy relics of St Titus were kept here until 962, when they were moved to a new church in Irakleío (➤ 62). A service is held here once a year on 23 December, the saint's feast day.

St Titus the Apostle

According to tradition, Titus was a descendant of a noble Cretan family. He was well educated and journeyed to Jerusalem, where he became a devoted disciple of St Paul the Apostle and travelled with him on his apostolic missions in Asia and Europe. Paul brought Christianity to the island in around AD 59, and left Titus to establish the Cretan Church. He became Crete's first bishop, and died at the age of 94 in about AD 105.

The Law Code

Beyond the church is an area thought to be the ancient agora, or forum. Here, overlooking the remains of the Roman *odeon* (a small theatre used for musical performances and poetry recitals), is a modern building sheltering Gortýs's greatest find: the law code. Carved by the Dorian Greeks around 500 BC on to massive stone blocks, it represents the earliest known written laws in Europe.

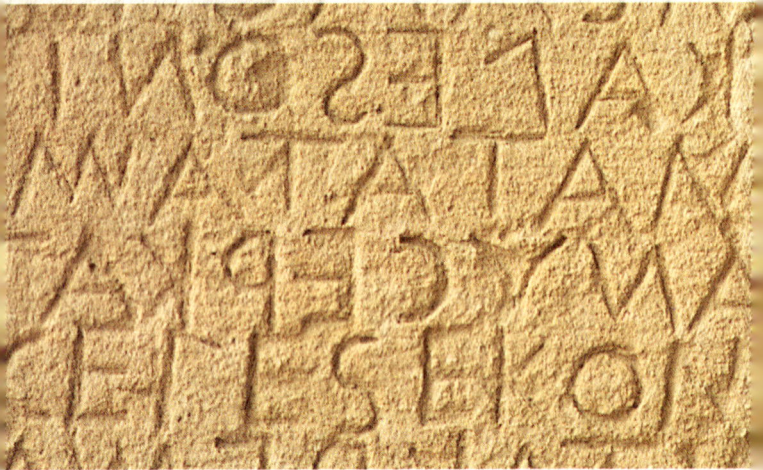

The tablets are arranged in 12 columns standing 3m high. The 600 lines of archaic inscription are read alternately left to right and right to left – a style known as *boustrophedon*, a word which describes the pattern made by an ox plough. They provide invaluable insight into this period of Greek history, particularly its social organisation. The code is actually a series of rulings clarifying laws that pertain to marriage, divorce, adoption, property and rights of inheritance. It also laid down penalties for adultery, rape, assault and other offences. Gortýs's population was divided into a distinct hierarchy of rulers, citizens or freemen, serfs and slaves, and the rights and penalties varied greatly among the classes.

Gortýs's code of law, in clear detail

The ancient fortress at Gortýs, with the Roman odeon and the building sheltering the law code

The Acropolis and the Roman City

On the opposite bank of the river you can see the remains of a larger theatre. Above, on the hilltop, are the ancient acropolis and the ruins of a Greek temple, a Roman hall (the *kastro*) and ramparts.

Dotted throughout the open fields on the south side of the main road, stretching back to Agíoi Déka, are various remains of the Roman city. Many are little more than scant walls and piles of stone, but it's good fun to seek them out in this atmospheric setting among giant gnarled olive trees. Several of the main sites lie along a track, including the Temple of Isis and Serapis, dedicated to the Egyptian gods. To the south, the Temple of Apollo Pythios with its stepped monumental altar was the main place of worship in pre-Roman times. To the east is the *praetorium*, the Roman governor's palace. Through the fence you can see its paved courtyards, carved columns and capitals and brickwork walls, and the *nymphaeum*, or bath suite.

TAKING A BREAK

On site is an unremarkable but adequate **café**. Otherwise, head back to **Agíoi Déka** or press on to **Faistós**.

✚ 182 C2   ✉ 36km southwest of Irakleío
☎ 08920-31144   🕐 Daily 8–7   🍴 Café (€)   🚌 Buses to Faistós stop at Gortýs   💷 Moderate   ❓ Photography allowed

GORTÝS: INSIDE INFO

Top tip It's a **steep, hot climb** to the top of the acropolis, but you'll get a great overview of the site.

Hidden gem Near the Temple of Apollo Pythios is a small **Roman theatre**, the best preserved on Crete.

Ones to miss The **amphitheatre** and **stadium**, both southeast of the *praetorium*.

❸ Faistós

The Minoan palace at Faistós is felt by many to be a far more enjoyable site to visit than the better-known Knosós. It stands on a hill overlooking the fertile Mesará Plain, and the fact that it has not been reconstructed allows visitors to view the palace in the best possible way: in the imagination. To see the large central court, the royal apartments, the grand staircase and the nondescript spot where the fabulous Faistós Disc was found all make for a memorable experience.

Faistós looks out over the Mesará Plain

The approach to Faistós is part of its charm, especially if you have already seen Knosós. There are no parking attendants here trying to lure you into their parking lots, just a small car park at the end of a zigzag climb up a little hill. You then walk along the approach to the site to buy a ticket. After entering the site beyond the very good bookshop, souvenir store and café, you are greeted with a good overall view of the layout.

It is thought that the views were part of Faistós's original attraction for the Minoans, with the palace built in a way that makes the most of them. Prior to their settlement, it seems others enjoyed the setting, as deposits have been found going back to neolithic and early Minoan periods (3000–2000 BC).

The first palace here, dated from about 1900 BC, is known as the Old Palace and some of its remains can still be seen on

The Faistós Disc

Only about 15cm in diameter, the Faistós Disc, now in the Archaeological Museum in Irakleío (► 50–55),is one of the most important and intriguing items ever found on Crete. It dates from between 1700 and 1600 BC and was uncovered in 1903. Baked in clay, the disc has spirals of pictograms on either side, including flowers, people and animals. No one has ever cracked the code, but the most favoured theory is that it was a religious object of some kind, with the symbols perhaps being the words to a prayer or hymn.

the western edge of the site. Destroyed and repaired twice before its ultimate destruction in an earthquake in 1700 BC, it was replaced by the New Palace, which remained in use until the end of the Minoan civilisation.

Exploring the Palace

The first open space you come to, the **west court**, is a good place to try to picture the palace as it would have been. Go down into the court and look towards the easily recognisable grand staircase. To the right of this are the remains of the western façade of the palace, built to bask in the glow of the setting sun. To the north of the court is the theatre area, and to the south some large storage pits, used principally for grain.

If you climb the grand staircase you'll see to the right the storerooms within the palace itself, where grain and oil were stored in the type of vast storage jars or *pithoi* that can be seen in almost every museum on Crete. It is not known for sure if the commodities stored at the palace were given to the royal family by way of a tithe, or if the building acted as a secure storage area for everyone to use.

To the east of this you enter the impressive central court, a vast open area whose paving dates from 1900 to 1700 BC. If you walk to the southern end of this there are good views over the plain, still a source of grain and oil today. It is the largest and most fertile of all the plains on Crete, producing

The royal apartments surround a small court

huge crops of olives, citrus and other fruit, and many types of vegetable.

To the north of the central court the area becomes a little confusing, as the remains are on two levels, but beyond the small south court, which you may be able to identify, are the **royal apartments**. There are many chambers and antechambers here, one set of rooms belonging to the king and another to the queen.

If you continue walking past these almost to the edge of the site, you can turn right and see on your right the walls and foundations of a row of small buildings. These were the palace archives, where the **Faistós Disc** (► panel, 85) was found, a small object that preserves its secrets, just as the palace of Faistós preserves its own air of mystery and beauty.

TAKING A BREAK

The **on-site café** is the only place to get something to eat for miles around, but fortunately it serves plenty of snacks and simple meals and has a lovely dining terrace with views of the surrounding countryside.

A well provided water for the palace at Faistós

➕ 182 B2 ☎ 08920-91315 ⏰ Daily 8–7 🍴 Café (€) 🚌 From Irakleío take the Faistós or Mátala bus 💰 Moderate ❓ Photography allowed

FAISTÓS: INSIDE INFO

Top tips As Faistós is open till late, visit the nearby site of **Agía Triáda** (► 90) first, which closes at 3 pm.

• Faistós has plenty of **benches and shady spots**, making it a pleasant place to relax as well as sightsee.

Hidden gem If you walk beyond the archives and then turn right, you will reach an open area, the **east court**, in which the remains of a pottery kiln can be seen.

In more depth The leaflet for the site is useful up to a point but the map is rather confusing. Buy a more **detailed site guide** in the excellent little bookshop, and make use of those shady trees to do some reading and take in the full story.

At Your Leisure

4 Arolíthos

Although this "traditional village" was purpose-built for tourists, it is nevertheless charming and has become a centre for the folkloric traditions of Crete. Its name means "a natural hole in a rock which collects rainwater". You can watch weavers, potters, icon painters and other artisans producing traditional crafts, enjoy Cretan food and music or learn how *raki* is made in the agricultural history museum.

✚ 182 C4 ✉ 10km southwest of Irakleío ☎ 0810-821050 🕐 Mon–Fri 9–8, Sat–Sun 10–6, Apr–Sep; Oct–Mar, Mon–Fri 9–5, Sat–Sun 10–6, rest of year 🍴 Café (€) 🎫 Free ❓ Photography allowed

5 Tílisos

The remains of this ancient Minoan town sit right within the village of the same name, a delightful example of the continuity of life through the ages. This small peaceful spot beneath shady pines is little visited and makes a refreshing change from the larger archaeological sites. It centres on three Minoan villas, which are thought to have been part of a larger community. Tilisos was one of the first Minoan sites to be excavated, prompted by the discovery of three giant bronze cauldrons; these and other finds are now in the Archaeological Museum in Irakleío (► 50–55). The ruins are well preserved, and you can wander among the stone walls and through doorways into small rooms and courtyards. Olive groves and vineyards, where sweet, dark Malmsey wine has been produced since Venetian times, surround the village.

✚ 182 C4 ✉ 14km southwest of Irakleío ☎ 0810-831241 🕐 Daily 8:30–3 🚌 Irakleío–Anógia bus stops at Tílisos 🎫 Inexpensive

6 Agíoi Déka

The name of this village translates as the "Holy Ten" and refers to ten early Christian martyrs who were beheaded here in AD 250 by order of the Roman Emperor Decius. They are still highly revered today and two churches in the village are dedicated to them. The Old Church, 14th-century but Byzantine in origin, is a lovely stone building with a tiled roof; it is sign-posted off the main road, a five-minute walk. Inside are frescoed arches and beautiful woodcarvings, including one of Christ with the martyrs' heads. Two painted icons depict their decapitation, and there is a stone block said to have been used for the execution. The New Church, at the west end of the village towards Gortýs, is a simple chapel. Below is a crypt, visible from the outside, where you can peer through an iron gate to see six of the martyr's tombs.

✚ 182 C2 ✉ 35km southwest of Irakleío 🕐 Daily 🚌 From Irakleío take the Faistós or Mátala bus 🎫 Free

The bell tower at Agíoi Déka

7 Fódele

This pleasant village, surrounded by orange groves, claims to be the birthplace of El Greco (▶ 33). A memorial plaque to the painter is on display in the shady town square, and across a small bridge spanning the river is the church, which has many copies of El Greco's works.

To see his alleged birthplace, continue along the path (signposted) out of town beside the orchards for about a kilometre. The house is greatly restored and contains a few displays on the painter's life.

Domenikos Theotokopoulos, better known as El Greco (inset) and his home village, Fódele (above)

Opposite the house is the delightful Church of the Panagía. Built in the early 14th century, it incorporates the nave of an earlier 8th-century basilica. The baptismal font beside the church – set in the floor for total immersion – also dates from this period. Partially restored frescoes depict angels, saints and scenes from Christ's life.

🕂 182 C5 ✉ 25km west of Irakleío ☎ 0810-521500 (museum) 🕐 Museum and church Tue–Sun 9–5 🚌 Direct bus from Irakleío 🎟 Inexpensive

8 Anógia

The mountain village of Anógia has suffered greatly at the hands of foreign invaders over the years. The Turks destroyed it twice after rebellions in 1821 and 1866, and in August 1944 German troops shot every male in the village and burnt every house to the ground in retaliation for the abduction of General Kreipe (▶ 19). A statue commemorating the freedom fighters stands

Washing day in Anógia

in the square in the upper part of town.

Anógia is best known though for its woven goods and embroidery. Brightly coloured textiles drape the streets of the lower town and you can often watch the local women at work inside their shops.

Behind the café tables in Plateía Livádhi notice the odd wooden sculpture of Elefthérios Venizélos (► 6). It is the work of the late local artist Alkibíades Skoúlas, whose son has opened a museum (open daily 9–7) to display his father's works. Anógia is also renowned as a centre of *lyra* music; many top musicians have come from here.

➕ 182 B4 ✉ 35km southwest of Irakleío 🚌 Buses from Irakleío and Réthymno

9 Mount Ída (Psiloreítis) and the Ídaean Cave

At 2,456m, Mount Ída is the highest summit on Crete. The locals call it Psiloreítis, "the high one". Its twin peaks, capped with snow late into spring, are often hidden in cloud, but on a clear day when the powerful granite bulk is revealed you can understand why it is thought to be Zeus's birthplace (► 91).

From Anógia a good paved road winds up through the stark, rocky landscape to the Ídaean Cave, 22km away. The trip takes about half an hour each way. Birds of prey circle overhead, and you pass round stone shepherds' huts, or *mitáta*. Most are now abandoned but were once used as summer dwellings and for making yoghurt and cheese from sheep's milk. The drive is especially pretty in late spring, when the rugged land-scape is ablaze with wild flowers.

The twin peaks of Mount Ída

As you climb higher you may find you are driving through low-lying clouds.

The road opens out with fine views over the fertile Nída Plateau far below. An unfinished visitor centre sits forlornly at the road's end, but there's a cheerful taverna inside.

From here, a 15-minute walk brings you to the Ídaean Cave. A place of pilgrimage and cult worship since Minoan times, it yielded a wealth of artefacts from throughout Greece and is mentioned in the works of Greek philosophers Plato and Pythagoras. Steps lead down into the cave but you may find its history the most exciting part – it is relatively shallow and has no impressive natural features.

➕ 182 B3 (Ídaean Cave), 182 A3 (Mount Ída) ✉ 50km southwest of Irakleío 🕐 Always open 🍴 (€) 🚌 No public transport 🎫 Free

10 Museum of Cretan Ethnology

Located off the beaten track in the village of Vóroi, near Faistós, this excellent folk museum, founded by a local man, is one of the best of its kind on the island. The items are attractively laid out, with information panels in English. Among the ground-floor exhibits are agricultural and domestic items, such as terracotta

Displays at the Ethnology Museum in Vóroi

beehives used since Pharaonic times, furniture, pottery and architecture. Another beautiful collection consists of woven blankets and textiles, and there is an interesting study of door patterns and their relation to status.

The highlight upstairs is a fascinating display of 25 types of baskets, made with different techniques and for different purposes. You can also see musical instruments and wonderful photos of people and festivals.

🔁 182 B2 ⊠ 3km north of Faistós at Vóroi (park on the main street and follow signs to the museum) ☎ 08920-91112 (to view in winter tel: 91110/91111) ④ Daily 10–6, Apr–Oct 🚶 Moderate ❓ Photography allowed

11 Agía Triáda

This Minoan site is small-scale after nearby Faistós, but its intimate nature is the very reason it should be visited. The main ruins consist of a small palace or large royal villa, built in about 1600 BC and destroyed, like many other Minoan sites, by a huge fire around 1450 BC. Staircases show that the palace had several levels. Fabulous mosaics, jewellery, pottery and other finds have been made here, all now on display at the Archaeological Museum in Irakleio (▶ 50–55). There is also a cemetery, and the remains of the small town that built up around the palace: a market, shops, houses and workshops. Part of Agía Triáda's delight is that no one is quite sure what it was or who lived here, as there are no references to it in existing Minoan records.

🔁 182 B2 ⊠ 3km northwest of Faistós ☎ 08920-91360 ④ Tue–Sun 8:30–3 pm 🚌 Bus to Faistós 🚶 Inexpensive ❓ Photography allowed

The harvester vase found at Agía Triáda

12 Mátala

Mátala's days as a hippie haven are long gone, but its famous caves continue to draw scores of visitors. The caves are man-made, cut into the sandstone cliffs by Romans and early Christians and used as catacombs. Local people inhabited them down the centuries until the 1960s, when foreign hippie troglodytes moved in. The caves are now fenced off to discourage overnight stays, but it's worth the small charge to see them during the day. Some have carved doorways, windows and benches.

The caves form a honeycomb backdrop to Mátala's fabulous beach, wide and curving round the bay with taverna balconies jutting over the sand. Otherwise, it's a small, slightly tacky town with one touristy strip of restaurants and shops, tending to attract a young and boisterous crowd.

⊞ 182 A1 ⊠ 59km southwest of Irakleío ⊙ Caves open daily 10–4, Apr–Sep 🚌 Several buses daily from Irakleío 🎟 Inexpensive

13 Agía Galíni

Agía Galíni is arguably the prettiest resort on the southern coast, if not the entire island. Nestled into the surrounding mountains, its white-washed buildings, dripping with bright bougainvillaea and jasmine, rise up the steep streets from a picturesque harbour. It's now pretty much given over to tourism, and the traffic-free streets in the centre of this former fishing village are lined

Agía Galíni rises up from the harbour

with shops and good restaurants. The long strip of beach has more rocks than sand, but is pleasantly fringed with tavernas. Though the town can get busy, it is a real delight out of season.

⊞ 182 A2 ⊠ 45km southeast of Réthymno 🚌 Buses from Réthymno

The Birthplace of Zeus

Mythologists argue over whether the god Zeus was born in the Idaean Cave or the Diktaean Cave (▶ 114). His mother, Rhea, had to bear the child in secrecy because his father, Kronos, Lord of the Titans, had devoured his other offspring, fearing they would someday dethrone him. Guardian warriors, the Kouretes, hid baby Zeus's cries with the clashing of their shields. When Kronos finally tracked Rhea down, she fooled him by giving him a stone wrapped in swaddling clothes to swallow. Zeus grew up with the shepherds on Mount Ída, protected by his grand-mother Gaia.

Where to... Stay

Prices

Prices are for a double room per night in high season including taxes

€ under €60   €€ €60–€100   €€€ over €100

Armonia Hotel €

This delightful small hotel is a real find. As you approach Matala on the main road look for it on the left, a white building (covered in bougainvillaea) with a pool. It is well outside the town so you will need a car, but it makes a perfect getaway for nature lovers and walkers. Most of the 27 rooms are in small blocks behind the hotel.

➕ 182 A1 ⊠ Mátala ☎ 08920-45735; fax: 08920-45758; www.armonia-matala.com
🕐 Apr–Oct

El Greco Hotel €

Ideally placed halfway between the town centre and the town beach

(on the right of the main road as you first enter Agia Galini), this is an excellent, inexpensive hotel with its own car park opposite. The blue and white frontage matches the bright rooms, those at the back being slightly more expensive because of their balconies and great sea views. The buffet breakfast varies each day and can be taken on the terrace at the back.

➕ 182 A2 ⊠ Agia Galini ☎ 08320-91187; fax: 08320-91491

Fevro Hotel €

This 50-room hotel can be found on the right after the road into Agia Galini descends almost to sea level, where there is a sharp turn left towards the harbour – that's if you can see the hotel name, as the entire building is almost obscured by the most wonderful cascade of bougainvillaea. The clean and simple rooms are a reasonable size, with white walls and dark wood furniture. Some have views of the town, and those lower down have "no views but not so many stairs"! It is open in winter by prior arrangement only.

➕ 182 A2 ⊠ Agia Galini ☎ 08320-91275 (winter: 08920-22865); fax: 08320-91475 (winter: 08920-23848)

Hotel Zafiria €

The main hotel in Matala is the 70-room Zafiria, easily found on your left as the main road enters the town centre. The rooms are typically mid-range – simple and clean – but all have a shower, a radio and a balcony. Some look out towards the sea, others to the hills behind. The hotel has its own bar and restaurant, and owns the mini-market across the street. Although

nothing fancy, this makes a good, reasonably priced base.

➕ 182 A1 ⊠ Mátala ☎ 08920-45112/45747/45366; fax: 08920-45725; email: info@zafiria-matala.com 🕐 Apr–Oct

Idi Hotel €

Situated on the edge of the mountain town of Zarós and popular with walkers, the Idi Hotel is an unexpected treat. With its swimming pool and tennis court, bar and Votomos Taverna (▶ 94), it represents excellent value for money. Some rooms are in the original small hotel block, while others occupy separate buildings in the beautiful gardens. Rooms are pine-panelled with telephones and air-conditioning and, unusual for Greece, are comfortably carpeted. The staff can advise on walking in the Zaros Gorge (▶ 156–157) and other walks in the area.

➕ 182 B2 ⊠ Zarós ☎ 08940-31302; fax 08940-31511; email: votomos@otenet.gr

Where to...
Eat and Drink

Prices

Prices are for a two-course meal for one person, excluding drinks and tips

€ under €9   €€ €9–€14.5   €€€ over €14.5

Charlie's Place €€

Charlie's Place is a popular spot with great character. Plain wooden tables are crammed together in one room, spilling over into the street outside. The kitchen is at the back, a tiny place where the owner cooks, grills meat, prepares drinks and writes out bills in a whirr of frenetic activity. The menu is small and traditionally Cretan, but with some creative twists. It is one of the busiest places in Agia Galini, so arrive early or be prepared to wait for a table.

🏠 182 A2 ✉ Agia Galini ☎ No phone 🕐 Daily 7 pm–late

Corali €€

The bright yellow paintwork of the Corali stands out on Matala's little square. Here food is served from breakfast time until the last customers leave. You'll have to wait till lunchtime if you want hot dishes though; these include a good range of the usual Greek fare and fresh fish, but there are pizzas too if you fancy a change.

🏠 182 A1 ✉ Mátala ☎ 08920-45744 🕐 Daily 10 am–late, Apr–Oct

Fish Taverna Faros €

This unpretentious little fish taverna is run by a fishing family serving whatever they catch that day. It is a world away from the several swish restaurants to be found in Agia Galini, but don't let that put you off. The tables on the pedestrian street are waited on by the friendly father or his cheerful son, who will invite you into the kitchen to choose your fish. They also offer boat trips, including the chance to catch your own fish and have it cooked for you the same evening.

🏠 182 A2 ✉ Agia Galini ☎ 08320-91346; fax: 08320-91346 🕐 Daily 6:30 pm–late

Lions Restaurant €€

Looking right over the beach, Lions has an upper taverna/bar where you can have coffee, drinks and snacks, or choose from the full menu in the slightly smarter restaurant downstairs. The chef lived in Australia for 30 years and as a result the menu here is more eclectic than in many Crete restaurants: it's one of the few places on Crete where you'll see Coquilles St Jacques, for example, while another speciality is sole stuffed with crabmeat.

🏠 182 A1 ✉ Mátala ☎ 08920-45108 🕐 Daily 9 am–late, Mar–Nov

Madame Hortense €€

Climb the flight of wooden stairs and pass a large collection of evocative black and white photos of Cretan characters and scenes to reach a large room with wooden flooring and great open views over the harbour. There are plenty of Greek and Cretan specialities on the menu, which has an extract from *Zorba the Greek* on the front explaining the restaurant's name. Chicken with peas and olives is one speciality, as is the house version of *kleftiko*: lamb wrapped in filo pastry and baked in the oven. The service includes an aperitif of ouzo served in a beautiful little bottle of coloured glass and a small plate of hors d'oeuvre.

🏠 182 A2 ✉ Agia Galini ☎ 08320-91215 🕐 Daily 6 pm–late

Onar Restaurant €€

This large, two-storey restaurant has an upstairs roof garden and a lower floor, both of which have good views out over the bustling harbour. Inside is modern and spacious with brick half-walls and lots of timber, plus attractive murals and wall hangings. Excellent food and wonderfully friendly service are the hallmarks here, with food grilled over charcoal a speciality. One excellent dish is barracuda fillet with a tomato and garlic sauce.

⊞ 182 A2 ⊠ Agia Galini ☎ 08320-91121 ⊗ Daily 8 am–1 am, Mar–Nov

Potamida Restaurant €€

Standing right by the beach, the Potamida is one of the biggest restaurants in a row of cafés and tavernas, distinctive with its bright blue and white décor. It is open all day and has sunbeds and umbrellas on the beach. The menu offers a huge choice of dishes, particularly salads and pastas, but fresh seafood is the speciality. Indeed, you might see the chef wading into the sea in the morning with his harpoon gun in his hand to catch the fish of the day.

⊞ 182 A2 ⊠ Agia Galini ☎ 08320-91121 ⊗ Daily 9 am–11:30 pm, Mar–Oct

Skala €

To find Skala, go to the very far end of the waterfront to the south and walk through what seems like the last taverna and up some steps; the restaurant is perched on top of the rocks beyond. Family owned, it's a very simple but very popular place, with a great view across the water to the beach. The large open dining terrace with cheerful blue and white walls and doors fills quickly, so arrive early. Fish is the speciality on the menu, and depending on the season might include red mullet, red snapper, perch, lobster, octopus and mussels.

⊞ 182 A1 ⊠ Matala ☎ 08920-45489 ⊗ Daily 9 am–late

La Strada €€

The cheery blue and white tables on the street contrast with the rustic Italian décor inside, where there is more seating, as well as on the roof terrace. Outside a blackboard lists the day's specials, while the menu has a whole page devoted to pizzas and other Italian dishes, although the wine list is resolutely Greek. La Strada is always busy but the service is brisk and efficient.

⊞ 182 A2 ⊠ Agia Galini ☎ 08320-91053 ⊗ Daily noon–3, 6–midnight

Taverna Giannis €

This is a real family taverna, found on the right just beyond Matala's small main square. It's as simple as you could get, with a few tables inside and out, serving barrel wine only. You could try one of their specials, such as a Cretan plate of octopus, squid, potatoes and vegetables, or opt for one of the simple Greek dishes, including grilled fresh fish (according to the day's catch). While the choices may be unsurprising they are very well prepared and the standard of cooking is excellent, with friendly service.

⊞ 182 A1 ⊠ Matala ⊗ Daily noon–late, Apr–Oct

Votomos Taverna €€

This rural restaurant, situated next to the Idi Hotel (▶ 92) by a stream and small watermill, specialises in trout from the nearby hatchery. Options include plain trout, salmon trout and smoked trout, along with a range of other fish and meat dishes, with wine from the barrel or from the short list of Cretan wines. There's both indoor and outdoor seating, as well as a large stage used for occasional live music. In the summer months it's advisable to book to avoid waiting for a table.

⊞ 182 B2 ⊠ Zarós ☎ 08940-31302 ⊗ Daily 11 am–midnight, Mar–Oct; Sat–Sun 11 am–midnight, rest of year

Where to...
Shop

VILLAGE CRAFTS

You'll find the usual tourist shops and stalls at the entrance to **Fódele**, but for something special try **Atelier Keramos**, the ceramic studio of Manolis Grammatikakis and Paraskevi Laskari-Grammatikaki (tel: 0810-521362), whose family has been making pottery for four generations. They incorporate new designs into traditional styles to create both useful and decorative pieces. Many designs are available, or you can design your own piece.

Anógia is one of the best-known villages on Crete for textiles, but don't overlook the handicrafts in smaller villages. At **Tílisos**, for example, right next to the archaeological site, a woman and her

daughters have a tiny shop where they sell beautiful handmade embroidered pieces at very good prices.

Colourful blankets, wall hangings, bags and other pieces made on the loom, or handstitched embroidery or lacework, such as tablecloths or curtains, are the things to look for, but be aware that more and more textiles are imported these days. One way to tell if an article is handmade is to look on the back. If the stitching there is rough and uneven, it's probably hand-done, whereas perfectly smooth stitches indicate a factory-sewn item. Another tip is to look for shops where the proprietor herself is working on a piece of embroidery or on a loom. You are welcome to watch, but be prepared for a sales pitch afterwards.

At **Arolíthos**, where there is a small row of workshops, you can watch potters, weavers, jewellery-makers, silversmiths, icon painters and other artists create beautiful

pieces using time-honoured methods and designs.

AGÍA GALÍNI

Among the many shops in Agía Galíni a few stand out. **Labyrinth** (tel: 08320-91057), in the tiny pedestrianised centre, is where Savas Tsimpouras makes beautiful gold and silver jewellery, as well as rings and necklaces adorned with rose quartz, tourmaline and other precious stones. He also makes replicas of the honeybee brooch in Irakleío's Archaeological Museum (▶ 50–55) and other Minoan works, and will create pieces to order. A few doors away, next to the Blue Bar, is Eli, an artist who creates outstanding pottery in her workshop at the back of the shop. Her work, from female figures to cheery mobiles to beautifully shaped vases in shades of blue, white and beige, many etched with dolphins or sun motifs, is unique and has a special quality about it.

You will also find lots of olive-wood souvenirs in Agía Galíni. Try **Wood Shop Maria** in the pedestrianised centre for a good selection of handmade items. **Le Shop**, just round the corner from La Strada restaurant (▶ 94), sells a nice range of quality leather items, silver jewellery and books and newspapers in several languages, including novels and books about Crete.

MÁTALA

Mátala has a covered market area lined with souvenir stalls, but nothing outstanding is to be found here. The nicest shop is **Natura Minoika**, on the main street, which sells natural Cretan products such as herbed olive oils, soaps and sponges, and popular art made from olive wood. Here you can buy mortar and pestle sets, unusual coffee and sugar measures, candle holders, wine holders, honeypots and beautiful wooden bowls of various sizes.

Where to...
Be Entertained

NIGHTLIFE

Agia Galini is the hotspot for nightlife in central Crete. Young Cretans from the Mesará area meet at the **Alibi Bar** by the waterfront to stop for a drink and exchange information. **Paradiso (Paradise Bar)**, a roof-garden bar up the steps from the waterfront, is a favourite for dancing and has a happy hour from 10 pm to midnight.

Also good for dancing are **Zorba's, Juke Box** and **Escape**, all located near each other by the harbour. Here the music hots up after 11 pm. Smaller, atmospheric spots for socialising over good music include **Blue Bar**, opposite Faros taverna, and **Miles Tone Blues & Jazz Bar** at the top end of the central pedestrianised area.

In **Matala**, on the road heading south parallel to the beach, the place to be is the famous **Rock Bar**, and it is not unusual to find young people from Irakleio who have come for the evening. Despite the name, a range of music is played. **Marinero** next door is another option. For a Latin beat and world music over good cocktails, try **Kantari** on the main square.

Club opening hours vary widely, with some (particularly those that are also cafés) being open all day, others opening early evening and some not till 10 pm or so. Clubs and discos seldom open before 10 or 11 pm and don't really get going till midnight. During high season in summer, clubs and discos are open nightly, but in low season they are often open only on weekends.

GREEK MUSIC

If it's Greek music you're after, there are Greek nights in **Arolithos** on Tuesdays, Wednesdays and Fridays in summer. Travel agencies in **Agia Galini** can also book Greek nights for you.

INTERNET CAFÉS

A good internet café is the **Alexander Bar**, at the east end of the waterfront in Agia Galini. **Café Bar Christos** in the pedestrianised centre has internet access as well as pool tables and a games arcade.

SPORTS

A host of **watersports** is available at Agia Galini, including waterskiing, paragliding, jet skis, banana boats and paddleboats. Enquire at the **Watersports Café** at the start of the beach.

Tour operators in town can book **boat trips** to more remote beaches, such as Agios Geórgios and Agios Pavlos, and to the sandy beaches of Paximádia Island, 12km offshore. There are also trips to the Samariá and Impros gorges (➤ 140–141 and 145), or Préveli Beach and Monastery (➤ 144). The **Argonaut**, operated by the owners of the Fish Taverna Faros (➤ 93), will take you on dolphin-spotting cruises, fishing trips or excursions to Gavdos Island.

For boat trips from Matala to nearby Red Beach and elsewhere, tel: 08920-45027 from 7 to 10 pm, or check with a travel agent. Some of Matala's beaches are spawning grounds for sea turtles, an endangered species.

The **Melanouri Horse Farm** (tel: 08920-45040) is signposted from the village of Pitsidia, northeast of Matala. Here the riding centre caters for all ages, including children, and offers rides along Kommos Beach and full-moon rides – a chance to explore the beautiful and fertile Mesara Plain.

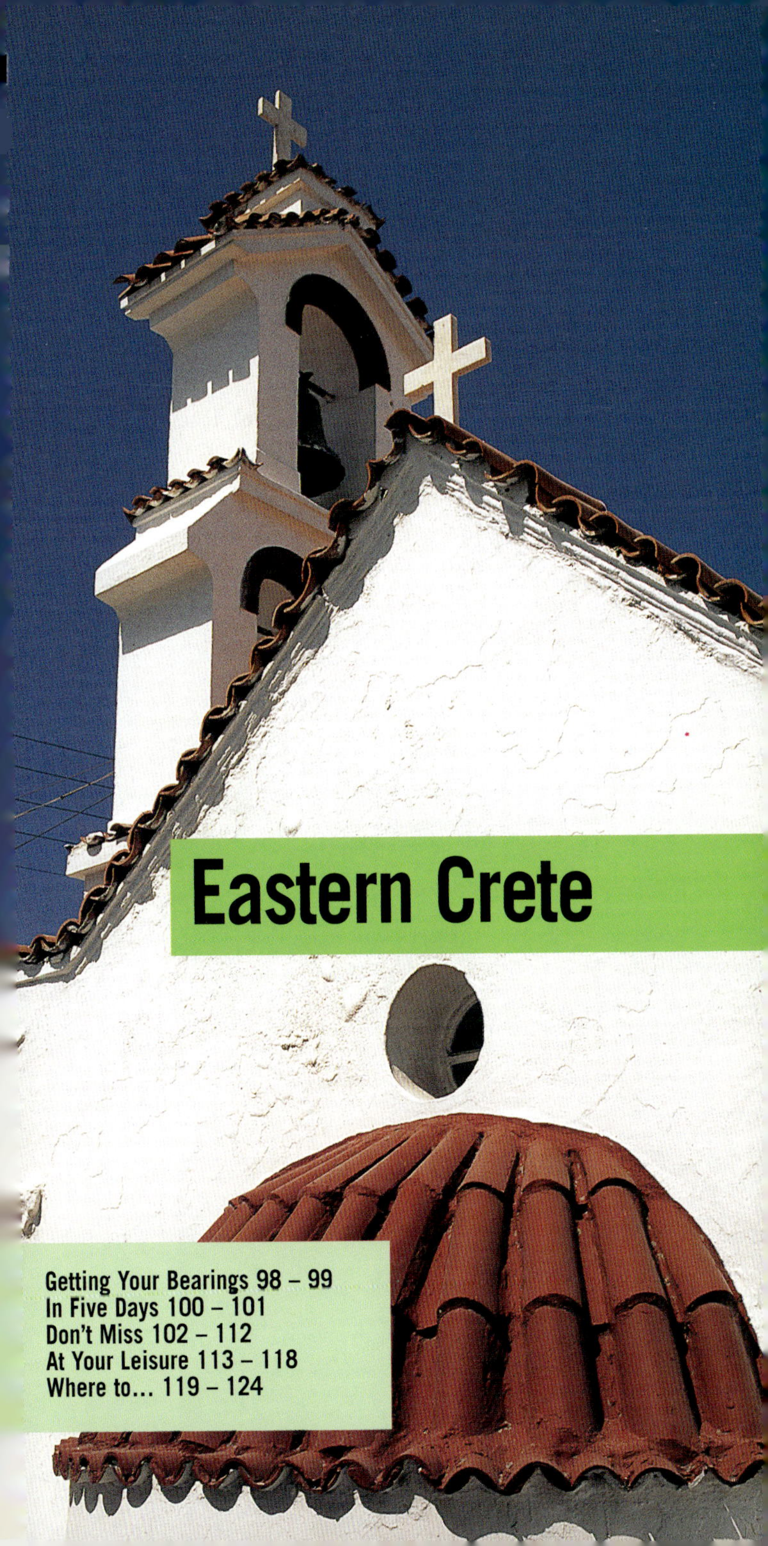

Eastern Crete

Getting Your Bearings

Eastern Crete has seen some of the densest tourism development on the island, particularly in the north between Irakleío and Kólpos Mirampellou (Gulf of Mirabello), where bustling resorts have gobbled up the coastal landscape. Beyond the bay, however, the far eastern region holds some of the most stunning scenery on the island, from rugged mountains to an unexpected palm beach.

Crete's main centre of package tourism lies east of the capital, stretching along the north coast to Mália. Here a string of burgeoning resorts have all but usurped the old villages with cheek-by-jowl hotels, apartments, restaurants, bars, travel agencies and souvenir shops. Ágios Nikólaos, set prettily around a little lake, is another bustling centre. Amid this hedonistic coastal strip, the ancient palace of Mália and the Minoan town of Gourniá anchor this changing landscape to the past.

A short drive inland takes you into another world. The provincial town of Neápoli is a gateway to the windmills and timeless farming villages of the Lasithiou Plateau. High in the Dikti Mountains is the birthplace of the Greek god Zeus. At Kritsá, the fresco-covered Church of Panagia Kerá is an artistic jewel.

A stunning coastal drive, not to be missed, brings you further east to Siteía, with its attractive waterfront and relaxed pace. From here you can strike out across a starkly beautiful mountainous landscape to reach Moní Tóplou, the palm-fringed Vái Beach and the Minoan palace at Zákros.

Ierápetra, Europe's southernmost town, is the largest on the south coast, with more fine beaches at small resorts to either side.

Káto Goúves · Limín · Chersónisou · M. Pa
Kokkíni Hani · Stalída · 6 · I
North Coast Resorts · Mália · Mochós · Kr S
Kastélli · Tzermiado · Lasíthic
Thrapsanó · Diktaean Cave · 7 · C · 2 1
Panagia
Áno Viánnos
Demáti · Chóndros · Ár
Tsoútsouros

Page 97: Church in Ierápetra

Left: Boats at Eloúnta

The village of Kritsá

0   20 km
0   10 miles

Akrotiri
Ágios Ioánnis

Váltos

Mílatos

10 **Spinalógka Island**

Fourni

Spinalógka

Váï Beach 14

Moní Tóplou 13

8 E75/90

9

Eloúnta

Órmos
Siteías

Órmos
Grántes

Neápoli

Zénia

3 **Ágios Nikólaos**

Siteía 5

Skopí

Petrás

Palaíkastro

Latό

Kólpos
Mirampéllou

Piskoképhalo

Azokéramos

2

**Kritsá and
Panagía Kerá**

Ístro

E75/90

Sfáka

Ornó

Néa
Praisós

Áno
Zákros

15

4

**Zákros
Palace**

Máles

Gourniá

Káto
Chorió

Ziros

Kalamáfka

Lápithos

Anatolí

Aglasménos

Schinokápsala

Agía
Fotiá

Makrýgialos

Goúdouras

2

11 **Ierápetra**

Mýrtos

The ideal way to
scoot around town

From beach resorts to ancient Minoan palaces and timeless villages and churches, eastern Crete is one of the most varied regions, with spectacular mountain and coastal scenery.

Eastern Crete in Five Days

Day One

Morning/Lunch

Get an early start from **Mália** (right, sacrificial altar, ➤ 102–103) or **Neápoli** (➤ 114). Follow the drive around the **Lasíthiou Plateau** (➤ 160–162) and visit the **Diktaean Cave** (➤ 114). The Kali Mera taverna just west of Psýchro is the closest place to the cave to eat, or drive on to the Platanos taverna, set around Krasí's giant plane tree.

Afternoon

Reach Mália Palace by 2 pm to explore the ancient ruins, then hit the beach for a swim.

Evening

You can stay in Mália and have dinner at one of the tavernas in the old village, or return to Neápoli for the night and have a pizza at Il Palazzo (➤ 122).

Day Two

Morning/Lunch

Visit **Kritsá** (left, typical blue pottery) and **Panagía Kerá** ➤ 104–105) early to beat the crowds. Have lunch by the lake at La Casa (➤ 121) in Ágios Nikólaos.

Afternoon

Drive to **Eloúnta** (➤ 115) and take the boat trip to **Spinalógka Island** (➤ 115).

Evening

Stay in Eloúnta and dine by the waterfront at the Ferryman Taverna (➤ 121) or Vritomartes (➤ 122), or head for Ágios Nikólaos.

Day Three

Morning/Lunch

Drive to **Agios Nikólaos** (left, Kitro Plateia Beach), and visit the Archaeological Museum (► 106–107) and other sights, then have lunch in the pretty courtyard of the Pelagos restaurant (► 122).

Afternoon/Evening

Explore the Minoan ruins at **Gourniá** (► 108–109) then make the short drive south across the isthmus to **Ierápetra** (► 116). From here, continue west to **Mýrtos** (► 116) for a relaxing drink beside the sea. Stay the night here and have dinner at Taverna Akti (► 121).

Day Four

Morning

Return via Ierápetra to the north coast and take the spectacular cliff road to **Siteía** (right, ► 110–112).

Lunch/Afternoon

Have lunch at one of Siteía's waterfront tavernas, but tear yourself away by 2 pm to visit the town's Archaeological Museum (► 111). Afterwards, sun yourself on the town beach.

Evening

Visit the Folklore Museum (► 111) and return to the waterfront for dinner at O Mixos (► 122).

Day Five

Morning/Lunch

Get an early start from Siteía for the winding drive to **Zákros Palace** (► 118). Relax over an early lunch at Káto Zákros Bay Restaurant (► 122).

Afternoon

On the return through Palaíkastro continue north for a swim at **Vái Beach** (► 117). Leave by 4:30 pm to reach **Moní Tóplou** (► 116), which is open until 6 pm.

Evening

Return to Siteía for dinner at The Balcony (► 121).

Mália Palace

Set on a flat plain along the northern coast, the island's third largest Minoan palace may lack the grandeur of Faistós or Knosós, but the beautiful reddish hues of its substantial stone walls give it an evocative beauty of its own. It is also less crowded and easier to fathom than its bigger sisters, making for an enjoyable place to wander back in time.

First built around 1900 BC, Mália Palace was destroyed by earthquakes and rebuilt around 1650 BC, after which it stood for another 200 years. The ruins date from the latter period. After its discovery in 1915 excavations were taken over by the French Archaeological School in Athens. These are still continuing, and the remains of a substantial town are being unearthed to the north and west of the main site. Some areas that were built of mud brick have been placed under canopies to prevent them being eroded by rain and wind.

Exploring the Ruins

The entrance to the palace is through the west court. You can weave your way through the thick stone walls of the west magazines (storerooms). Alternatively, turn right and head to the southwest corner where there are eight round granary pits. Follow the south side to a wide stone-paved passage that leads into the central court, a huge space measuring 48m by 22m.

The **west wing** held the most important sections of the palace, including the loggia, an elevated room looking on to the court, reached by the grand staircase alongside. Below this a hall leads into the pillar crypt, a place of religious ritual. In the court's southwest corner is another large staircase, and beside this is Malia's famous *kernos*. This circular slab of limestone with 34 depressions set around a central hollow is thought to have been a kind of altar in which seed or grain offerings were placed. It may also have been a gaming board.

One of Mália's more curious features is the large number of storage areas throughout the palace. The entire east wing was given over to more magazines used for storing liquids in giant *pithoi* (storage jars) placed in sunken pits, complete with drainage channels for spillage.

Giant *pithoi* (storage jar) standing in the grounds at Mália

Protection for the precious remains of Mália Palace

On the north side is the hypostyle, or pillared hall, and north court. To the west of this were the royal apartments. Two magnificent giant *pithoi* stand guard along the palace's northern edge. Mália yielded some outstanding artefacts, now in the Archaeolgial Museum in Irakleío (► 50–55). The famous honeybee pendant was discovered at the grave complex called Chryssólakos (pit of gold), to the northeast of the palace.

TAKING A BREAK

You can buy **drinks and snacks** from a van in the car park, but you'll have to return to **Mália town** for more substantial refreshment.

✚ 184 B4 ☎ 08970-31597 🕐 Tue–Sun 8:30–3 🚌 Buses to/from Mália town stop at the palace 💶 Moderate 📷 Photography allowed

MÁLIA PALACE: INSIDE INFO

Top tip For the best **photographs**, visit in the late afternoon when the light brings out the warm colours of the red stone.

Getting there The palace is **3km beyond Mália village**, signposted off the New Road.

One to miss The **museum is very small** with only a site model and some photos and diagrams on the wall.

2 Kritsá and Panagía Kerá

The tiny Byzantine Church of Panagía Kerá is one of the most famous on Crete, renowned for the 14th- and 15th-century frescoes that cover almost every inch of its interior walls with vivid religious scenes. It stands just outside the traditional village of Kritsá, as does the archaeological site of Lató, and a visit combining all three makes for a fascinating and contrasting few hours.

Kritsá

Said to be the largest village on Crete, Kritsá sits in the low hills about 10km inland from the busy resort of Ágios Nikólaos. It can be very crowded when coach parties descend and hundreds of people wander the steep streets searching for the best of the local handicrafts. Weavings, embroidery, lace and leatherware are all here in abundance, and with better prices than you will pay in shops in the resort towns on the coast. When the visitors depart, Kritsá reverts to being an ordinary Cretan village, and an attractive one, too, with its backdrop of mountains and views in places down to the coast.

Above: Just one of many frescoes in the Panagía Kerá

Lató

Signposted from Kritsá, 3km north, is the site of ancient Lató. It is well worth visiting both for the drive along the zigzag-ging valley road up to the site and the magnificent views over the valley when you get there. Lató is one of Crete's lesser-known sites, with comparably fewer visitors, and is all the better for that.

   It dates from the Dorian period, which followed the

Minoan and Mycenaean eras, when the Dorian people originally from northern Greece ruled Crete and much of the
Greek mainland. This began in about 1100 BC and lasted until
the arrival of the Romans in 69 BC. Lató was an important city,
as can be seen by the extent of the remains spread along the
hillside. Excavations did not begin until 1957 and much work
still needs to be done. Areas uncovered so far include the
agora, or market-place, steps that formed part of a theatre, the
foundations of shops and artisans' workshops and what was
probably the original entrance gate to the old city. The best
part of the experience is simply being there, however, as the
site exudes its own unique charm.

Panagía Kerá

The undoubted highlight of eastern Crete is the delightful
Church of Panagía Kerá, a little domed white building with
just three tiny aisles. It is reached by a path from the main
road. With the exception of the stone floors, the church inte-

**Below: Walking
through history
at Lató**

rior is covered in frescoes. Some of the colours now are a little
dulled with time, but the details are as clear and as beautiful
as when they were first painted during the 14th and 15th
centuries. The sheer volume of images, including
icons of the saints, biblical scenes such as the Last
Supper and graphic depictions of the punishments
that sinners can expect in Hell, is overwhelming.

TAKING A BREAK

There are several cafés and tavernas in **Kritsá**, and
the **Paradise Taverna** opposite Panagía Kerá is
open all day for everything from coffee to full
meals.

Lató
➕ 184 C3 ✉ Kritsá 🕐 Tue–Sun 8:30–3 💶 Free
❓ Photography allowed

Panagía Kerá
➕ 184 C3 ✉ Kritsá 🕐 Daily 8:30–3 🚌 Buses to Kritsá from
Ágios Nikólaos 💶 Moderate ❓ No photography allowed

KRITSÁ & PANAGÍA KERÁ: INSIDE INFO

Top tips Early morning and late afternoon are the quietest times to visit Kritsá.
Check the opening times of Lató and Panagía Kerá, and plan the visit accordingly.
• Don't even think about **parking** in Kritsá. Follow signs to the official car parks.

Hidden gem In the central aisle of Panagía Kerá, on the right-hand side near
the door, is a delightful and moving portrait of the **Virgin and Child**; the two
figures are exchanging the most loving of looks.

Getting there The **Church of Panagía Kerá** is on the right as you approach
Kritsá from Ágios Nikólaos, but the signposts are very small. Easier to spot is
the Paradise Taverna, on the left-hand side of the road.

3 Ágios Nikólaos

The town of Ágios Nikólaos with its twin harbours is one of the most attractive on Crete. Its popularity means that it is also one of the busiest, but if you don't mind the crowds you can enjoy its restaurants and nightlife. It also has an excellent archaeological museum with fine Minoan treasures.

Life centres round the two harbours, although the inner one is actually a small lake, linked to the main harbour by a narrow channel. Lake Voulisméni is also known as the Bottomless Lake, a slight exaggeration but it does have very steep sides and a middle depth of some 64m. Bars, cafés, restaurants and souvenir shops line the lake and harbour, and the area buzzes from morning till night.

The town has always been a port, in ancient times for the inland city of Lató (► 104–105), and later for the Venetians. They named the town after a 10th-century church dedicated to St Nicholas, and they also dubbed the gulf on which it stands Mirabello, or Beautiful View.

Along the waterfront north of the harbour is a small **aquarium**. Although housed in just one room, it is well laid out with lots of displays and information panels, mostly in English. The many tanks contain a host of creatures, from endearing little red-eared turtles and starfish, to octopuses and eels, to the ugly and dangerous scorpion fish and other inhabitants of the local waters.

The cathedral of Agía Triáda

Archaeological Museum

It's a steep climb, but one worth making, up to the town's excellent Archaeological Museum. Take the rooms, arranged around a small interior courtyard, in a clockwise direction.

After various displays of unusual objects, such as the earliest known fish-hooks on Crete and the longest early-Minoan dagger, you come to the museum's star attraction: the **Goddess of Mýrtos**. This exquisite piece, dating from around 2500 BC, depicts an unusual bell-shaped figure holding a jug in her stick-like arms. It was probably used for some kind of fertility ritual. Further on are ceramics, coins, votive figures and many unique objects,

A craftsman makes a museum copy in Ágios Nikólaos

Lakeside dining in Ágios Nikólaos

such as a late Minoan burial *pithos* from Krya with the skeleton inside. In Room IX, a local Roman 1st century tomb was found to contain the skull of an athlete crowned with a golden laurel and a silver coin resting in his jaw – to pay the ferryman to the Underworld.

TAKING A BREAK

Several places to eat fringe the **harbour and the lake**, but one of the established favourites for visitors and locals is **La Casa** (► 121), open from breakfast till late.

Ágios Nikólaos 🚩 185 D3

Archaeological Museum
✉ Palaiologou 68 ☎ 08410-24943
🕐 Tue–Sun 8:30–3 🅿 Parking in streets and car park near by 🏷 Inexpensive
❓ No flash photography

Aquarium
✉ Akti Koundourou 30 ☎ 08410-28030

🕐 Daily 10–9, Mar–Oct 🅿 Parking opposite along the waterfront 🏷 Expensive
❓ No photography

Folklore Museum
✉ Palaiologou 2 ☎ 08410-25093
🕐 Sun–Fri 10–1:30, 6–9:30 🅿 Parking further on around the waterfront
🏷 Inexpensive ❓ Photography allowed

ÁGIOS NIKÓLAOS: INSIDE INFO

Top tip Traffic is bad, so **avoid driving into the centre** if you can. One option is to park in the streets on the hill where the Archaeological Museum stands.

Hidden gem The 12th-century **Church of Panagía Vrefotrófou**, near the town beach at the western end of the marina, is said to be the oldest church on Crete. Some of the frescoes are thought to date back to the 8th and 9th centuries, with the building itself going back to the 7th century. If it is closed, ask at the nearby Minos Palace Hotel for the key.

Must see The **Goddess of Mýrtos** in the Archaeological Museum.

One to miss The **Folklore Museum** by the channel between the lakes is not bad, but could be skipped if time is short.

4 Gourniá

Crete's great Minoan palaces tend to get all the glory, overshadowing the other surviving remnants from the civilisation, which was widespread, particularly in the east. Gourniá is the largest town yet uncovered and its superbly preserved ruins give a fascinating insight into everyday life in Minoan times. This was a real work-a-day town, where tradesmen such as potters, bronzesmiths and carpenters went about their daily affairs.

Though Gourniá was settled in early Minoan times, the ruins you see today date from around 1500 BC, when the town was at its peak. It flourished because of its splendid position above Kólpos Mirampellou (Gulf of Mirabello), making it commercially as well as strategically important. It had its own harbour and traded with Ierápetra on the south coast via an over-land route across the isthmus (at 12km the narrowest point on the island), thus avoiding the dangerous sea journey round the eastern shores.

Destroyed in the cataclysm of 1450 BC (► 10–13), Gourniá rose from its ashes during Mycenaean times but was finally abandoned in 1200 BC. A young American archaeologist, Harriet Boyd Hawes (1871–1945), excavated it around the same time that Faistós and Knosós were being excavated (1901).

Exploring Gourniá

On entering the site, you immediately notice how well preserved it is. The foundations of hundreds of houses, up to a metre or more high, spread up the hillside; these were the basements, used as store-rooms or workshops, with living areas in the upper storeys that have long since vanished. Tools found in some of these buildings identified various tradesmen and craftsmen, farmers and fishermen, providing great insight into domestic life in Minoan times. Cobbled streets, wide enough for pack animals but not wheeled carts, wound through the town, dividing it into seven neighbourhoods. Even today, mountain villages on Crete follow this layout.

You can take the path straight ahead up the stone steps, or turn left along what was formerly a main street, still with its original paving. Both lead to the town centre at the top of the hill. At its heart was the palace, smaller than but similar in style to Knosós and Mália. It was probably the seat of the local governor.

To the south, L-shaped stairs lead to a large courtyard that was the agora, or market-place. The large stone slab next to the stairs may have been a sacrificial altar (or simply a

butcher's block). To the north was the sanctuary, where a shrine with snake-goddess figures and other cult objects was found.

As you survey the site from the top of the acropolis remember that Gourniá was four times larger than what you see today. Imagine it stretching northward all the way to the sea, as it did in antiquity.

TAKING A BREAK

There are **no refreshments** at Gourniá, so bring your own water and snacks.

A maze of streets and steps at Gourniá

➕ 185 D3 ☎ 08420-93028 🕒 Tue–Sun 8:30–3 🚌 Buses from Ágios Nikólaos to Siteía and Ierápetra can drop you near the site 💷 Inexpensive ❓ Photography allowed

GOURNIÁ: INSIDE INFO

Top tips Save for a couple of small trees, **there is no shade**. Wear sunblock, hat and sunglasses for protection.
• Gourniá is **delightful in springtime** when colourful wild flowers blossom amid the stones.

Getting there The **turning off the National Highway** (New Road) is easy to miss. Driving east, a few kilometres beyond Ístro you'll pass a large cement factory. The sign for Gourniá is just beyond, a sudden right turn on to a gravel road.

5 Siteía

If for no other reason, visit Siteía for the magnificent drive that takes you there through some of the finest scenery on Crete. Beyond Ágios Nikólaos the National Highway becomes a high cliff road that winds up and down the mountainsides with tantalising glimpses of the sea. Once in Siteía, you'll be delighted by its atmosphere. Set around a beautiful bay, it's more laid-back town than tourist resort and makes an excellent base from which to explore the attractions of the far eastern end of the island.

Crete's fifth largest town sits on the western side of the pretty Bay of Siteía, its sun-bleached houses climbing up the hillside above the waterfront. A wide promenade curves along the harbour, shaded by squat palms and backed by a ring of pleasant tavernas that provide the perfect spot to chill out and watch the colourful fishing boats bobbing on the water. East of the marina, just beyond the tourist office, is the sandy town beach. Although tourism is growing – and the new airport will guarantee that – locals still outnumber the tourists here.

There is much history here. Remains of a substantial Minoan settlement were discovered in the southern suburb of Petrás, and more Minoan villas and peak sanctuaries were found in this region of Crete than anywhere else. West of the harbour towards the ferry port are the remains of Roman fish tanks. On the eastern outskirts of town the

The ancient Hellenistic site of Tripitos

ruins of Hellenistic Siteía are under excavation. Earthquakes destroyed the town's Venetian-era buildings, save for the fortress that stands out on the hilltop. It is now used as an open-air theatre, particularly during the town's cultural festival, the **Kornaria**, held in July and August (➤ 124).

Archaeology Museum

This small but excellent museum contains many treasures from eastern Crete dating from neolithic to Roman times. The first section contains finds from various sites in Minoan Siteía. More than 80 excavated sites indicate the density of settlement in this region. Many beautiful pieces of pottery were discovered in cemeteries and their decoration is outstanding both in quality and preservation. In case 7 an exquisite figure of a bull comes from the cemetery at Móchlos. Crete's best-preserved hieroglyphic archive was discovered at Petras and there are examples in case 27.

Next come exhibits from the Zákros Palace (➤ 118), which yielded many unusual finds. The decoration on the large *pithoi* (storage jars) is superb. There are rare fragments of Linear A tablets, remarkably well preserved due to a cataclysmic fire that acted like a kiln and baked the clay. Another case holds beautiful rounded pitchers, three-legged pots, tiny vases and curious kitchen utensils, including a terracotta grill.

Erotókritos

Vitsentzos Kornáros, author of the epic poem *Erotókritos*, was born in Siteía in the 17th century. Standing on the waterfront by the tourist office is a monument to him, with scenes from his work, which is still sung today (➤ 23).

Post-Minoan-era finds complete the collection. Case 22 holds odd votive objects from an archaic sanctuary: the clay Egyptian-style heads were inserted into phial-shaped bodies, and may have been associated with fertility rites. In the last room a water tank contains a mass of vases compacted in a Roman shipwreck.

Peace by the harbour at Siteía

Folk Museum

Siteía also has a charming little folk museum, set in a former upper-class house. There are displays of agricultural tools, kitchen implements and a century-old loom, plus fine examples of traditional bedspreads, embroidery and other handiwork. Be sure to go upstairs to see the decorative 1890 bridal bed with silk canopy and coverings.

On the Outskirts

Siteía is one of Crete's best wine producing regions and a **wine co-operative** on the main road into town gives wine tours in summer. This includes a video on the wine-making process, a look around the museum and a tasting of local wines and olive oil, both of which are for sale.

About 2km along the beach road heading east towards Vái, a signposted track on the left marked "Archaeological Site" leads to the ancient Hellenistic site of **Tripitos**, which dates from the 3rd century BC. Park beside the farm building and walk up to the fenced site, which you can enter. The site is still under excavation, but the foundations of many buildings, rooms and streets are visible, and there's a grand view over the sea.

TAKING A BREAK

You're spoiled for choice along the waterfront. **Kolios** is a good spot for breakfast; **O Mixos** (➤ 122) for a meal.

Restaurants line Siteía's waterfront

SITEÍA: INSIDE INFO

Top tip Siteía's **waterfront** is so pleasant and relaxing that you may find yourself spending an extra day in the town.

One to miss The **ruins of the Roman fish tanks** are largely submerged and almost impossible to make out.

Siteía
✚ 186 B4

Archaeology Museum
✉ Odós Eleftherias Venizélou, opposite the bus station ☎ 08430-23917 ⏰ Tue–Sun 8:30–3 💰 Inexpensive ❓ No flash photography

Folk Museum
✉ Kapetan Sifi 26 ☎ 08430-22861 ⏰ Mon 9:30–1:30, 5–8, Tue–Fri 9:30–2:30, 5–9, Sat 9:30–2:30, Apr–Oct 💰 Inexpensive
❓ Photography allowed

Wine Co-operative
✉ Missonos 74 ☎ 08430-25200
⏰ Mon–Fri 8:30–2:30 💰 Free

At Your Leisure

6 North Coast Resorts

Chersónisou (▶ 184 A4) is the biggest and brashest of the northeast coast resorts. It's synonymous with raucous, alcohol-fuelled nightlife and most people come here to party.

For Children
Diktaean Cave (▶ 114)
Spinalógka Island (▶ 115)
Gourniá (▶ 108–109)
Makrýgialos and **Vái beaches** (▶ 114, 117)

The 2km-long main road and parallel beach road are packed solid with bars, shops and services, joined by narrow side streets crammed with hotels. But where's the beach? The narrow patches of sand are largely hidden among the hotels and the rocky coastline. A port (*limín*) in antiquity, the resort is also called Limín Chersónisou to distinguish it from the village of "Old" Chersónisos that lies slightly inland. A few kilometres east is **Mália** (▶ 184 B4), the

A quiet stretch of the beach at Mália

north coast's other famous party resort. It's just as busy and noisy but mildly more attractive. The sandy beaches, about a kilometre from the main road, can get crowded – those to the east are quieter. Mália Palace (▶ 102–103) lies just beyond Tropical Beach. The old village is uphill on the opposite side of the main road, with good traditional tavernas along its winding streets and in its pretty square.

In between the two is **Stalida** (▶ 184 A4), or **Stalís**, a burgeoning, tightly packed resort with a sandy beach and quieter nightlife. West of Chersónisos you'll find the smaller resorts of **Kokkíni Hani** (▶ 183 E4) and **Káto Goúves** (▶ 183 F4).

7 Diktaean Cave

Located high in the Díkti Mountains above the village of Psýchro, this is the most famous and impressive cave on Crete. In mythology it is said to be the birthplace of the god Zeus (► 91), and its importance as a cult centre since Minoan times was confirmed by the discovery of a huge number of votive offerings. It remained a place of religious ritual for the Dorian Greeks long after the Minoans' demise.

From the car park it's a 15-minute uphill walk to the entrance, but donkey rides are on offer if you don't fancy the climb. The 65m descent into the depths of the cave has been made easier, if less mysterious, by concrete steps and lighting. The path circles around the bottom, alongside a dark pool, with views of the great stalactites and stalagmites. It takes a little imagination to pick out such features as the "nipples" where the baby god suckled, but with the cave's mouth a mere slit of light far above, you can sense the mystical wonder it held for the ancient Cretans. This is especially true if you beat the crowds by visiting early morning or late afternoon.

➕ 184 B3 🕐 Daily 8–7 🍽 Café (€) 🎫 Moderate; additional parking fee

The market town of Neápoli

8 Neápoli

Tourists largely overlook this market town, but it has much local charm. The roads end at the main square next to the large, modern church. On the south side of the square a small **folklore museum** has local artefacts recalling the traditional way of life. Opposite the war memorial, the café **I Driros** is the place to sample the local speciality – a sweet, milky drink called *soumadha*, made from pressed almonds. It's also a pleasant spot from which to observe the passing scene.

Neápoli makes a good base for exploring the Lasithiou Plateau (► 160–162). Odós Ethnikis

South Coast Beaches

There are several beaches along Crete's southeast coast. **Makrýgialos** and **Análipsi** have merged into one large, rather unattractive resort, but the beach is sandy and the water very shallow. Further west, **Agía Fotiá** is a small, somewhat hidden place with a fine beach.

Antistasis leads from the square to the town's only hotel, the Neapolis (► 120).

➕ 184 C4 🚌 Buses from Ágios Nikólaos and Mália

9 Eloúnta

Situated about 7km north of Ágios Nikólaos, on the western shores of the Gulf of Mirabello, Eloúnta is a pretty and much more low-key resort than its neighbour. The long main road through town leads to a large square set around the harbour, which, lined with cafés and restaurants, is the focal point of activity. Boat trips to Spinalógka Island leave regularly from here. Just beyond the parking area is the sandy town beach.

From boat to table – Eloúnta's catch quickly makes its way to your plate

On the southern edge of town – reached by a small road along the shore that passes Venetian salt pans – is a causeway. It runs above a submerged isthmus that once connected the mainland to Spinalógka Peninsula. From here, when the waters are calm, you can see a few remains of the sunken city of **Oloús**. Behind the taverna on the causeway a fenced area protects the black and white mosaic floor of a 4th-century church. There are good beaches and birdwatching on the peninsula.

➕ 185 D4 🚌 Bus from Ágios Nikólaos 🍴 Small kiosk by the car park at the harbour square

Spinalógka Island's Venetian fortress

10 Spinalógka Island

A short boat ride from Eloúnta brings you to the eeriest place on Crete, tiny Spinalógka Island, commanding the entrance to the bay. The Venetians built a fortress here in 1579 to defend the gulf and it remained one of the island's most formidable strongholds long after the Turkish invasion, only handed over by treaty in 1715. Turkish settlers built homes here and refused to leave after Greece won independence. The government persuaded them to go by designating Spinalógka a leper colony in 1903. It was the last of its kind in Europe, and existed until it was evacuated in 1957.

The approach to the island is stunning, with the reflections of the round keep of the fortress and its walls gleaming in the bay. Guides meet you on shore to tell the sad tale of life on the"'island of the living dead", as it was locally known. There are wonderful views from the ramparts.

➕ 185 D4 🕐 Boats daily in season, every 30 minutes 9:30–4:30 💶 Expensive (for boat)

11 Ierápetra

With Africa just 300km away, Ierápetra is Europe's southernmost city. Though it gets the most sunshine, too, its prosperity comes not from tourism but from the region's farmers who grow year-round crops of tomatoes and peppers in masses of plastic greenhouses along this coast.

The only attractive part of this sprawling town – the fourth largest on Crete and the biggest on the south coast – is the waterfront area near the Venetian fort. You can wander around inside its restored ramparts though there's not much to see. Near by is a bell tower and the red-tiled domes of a 14th-century church, Aféntis Christós. Some characterful houses still stand in the winding lanes of the old Turkish quarter, behind the waterfront. Seek out the small square with an ornate Ottoman fountain and a restored Turkish mosque.

The small Archaeology Museum has two particular treasures: a 2nd-century statue of Demeter, goddess of fertility, holding an ear of corn; and a Minoan *larnax*, or lidded clay coffin, with superb decoration depicting a wild goat hunt and other figures. A morning fruit market is held near the museum.

Ierápetra looks south to Africa

A long, sandy beach stretches west of town, or you can take a boat trip to the more appealing beaches of **Chrýsi Island**, 12km offshore.

🔲 185 D2 (Archaeology Museum)   🕐 Tue–Sun 8:30–3   💷 Inexpensive

12 Mýrtos

The appeal of this charming south coast village far outweighs its small size. There are no sights, save a two-room local museum, and its pebbly beach is not outstanding, but it's the

Getting the daily bread at Mýrtos

sort of place where people drop in for a day and end up staying for months. Perhaps it's because Mýrtos remains a village, rather than a resort, and the tourists who come here prefer to blend into the local scene.

The pleasant tavernas along the waterfront make a delightful stop.

🔲 184 C2   🚌 Bus from Ierápetra

13 Moní Tóplou

Alone on its windy hilltop, Moní Tóplou looks more like

a fortress than a monastery. In reality, it was. Its name means "cannon" in Turkish, and artillery was installed here in Venetian times after it was sacked by pirates in 1498. Thus began its long history as a centre of resistance (➤ 16).

Tóplou owns much of the surrounding land and is said to be one of the richest monasteries in Greece. Its grounds and buildings have been greatly restored. Outside the entrance is an old stone wind-mill; look inside to see how the huge wooden millstones were turned by the sails to grind flour.

Inside the walls, the pretty cobbled courtyard – bright with flowers and greenery – is surrounded by the monks' cells and the bell tower. The church holds the monastery's great treasure: an 18th-century icon by Ioánnis Kornáros entitled *Lord, Thou Art Great*. It comprises 61 intricate biblical scenes, each illustrating a line from this Greek Orthodox prayer, and is considered a masterpiece of Cretan art. More icons can be seen in the museum and one room highlights the monastery's role in the battle for Cretan independence and during World War II.

➕ 186 C4 ☎ 08430-61226
🕐 Daily 9–1, 2–6 💶 Moderate
❓ Photography limited

🔟 Vái Beach

Although the crowds that flock to Crete's famous palm beach can mar the idyllic environment they've come to see, it's still worth a visit. For the most scenic approach, take the road that passes Moní Tóplou rather than the one through Palaikastro. As you descend through the stark landscape reminiscent of North Africa, a forest of date palms suddenly rises up oasis-like before you. *Phoenix theophrasti* is unique to eastern Crete, the last of an ancient palm species that was widespread in the southeast Aegean in antiquity, but today exists in such numbers only at Vái. Some say the grove grew from date stones spat out by Egyptian soldiers who camped here, others that the date-eaters were pirates. The grove, with boardwalks providing a path through, covers 20 hectares in a narrow valley stretching down to the beach. Tour buses call in here too, so the wide sandy beach is generally packed for much of the day. It quietens down again around 4 pm, however, so try to come early or late in the day to best appreciate its exotic beauty.

➕ 186 C4 🍴 Café (€) 🚌 Buses from Siteía and Makrýgialos 🅿 Parking inexpensive, beach free

Looking down at Vái Beach

🔢 Zákros Palace

If you make time to visit the fourth of Crete's great Minoan palaces, at the remote eastern reaches of the island, you'll be well rewarded. From Siteía the winding road takes you across a starkly beautiful high plateau ringed by mauve-coloured mountains. Allow an hour (minimum) to get to the ancient site, which lies 8km beyond Áno Zákros (the upper town) at sea-level Káto Zákros. Here a string of pleasant tavernas faces an idyllic pebble beach.

Built around 1900 BC, Zákros had a fine harbour and was the island's main naval base, flourishing on trade with Egypt and the Middle East. Like the other great Minoan palaces, it too was destroyed by catastrophic events around 1450 BC.

However, because the site was so isolated it had never been looted and when it was excavated in the 1960s more than 10,000 artefacts were found, many of them unique. Magnificent ivory, bronze and stoneware, including elaborate vases and chalices, are now in the museums at Irakleio and Siteía.

The dig yielded another remarkable find: in a ritual well filled with spring water the archaeologists discovered a votive cup of olives some 3,000 years old. Before the olives could disintegrate, the crew bravely tasted them – and found them as delicious as if they had just been picked.

Though Zákros is similar in design to the other palaces, it is far more peaceful and atmospheric. To the west of the central court and banquet hall is the central shrine, an archive where hundreds of Linear A tablets were stored, and the treasury where

Surveying the Palace from Áno Zákros (the Upper Town)

the famous rock crystal *rhyton* (► 54) was found.

The large round cistern, like the other wells, is full of terrapins. Beyond this, under a canopy, is a bathroom where visitors might have washed before entering the court. You can see the basins and traces of red fresco.

Large stone steps lead to the exit, which was the original entrance to the palace from the harbour road. Rising up the hillside are the ruins of the Upper Town, which afford great views over the entire site.

➕ 186 C3 ☎ 08430-61204
🕐 Tue–Sun 8:30–3 (last entrance 2:30) 🚌 Bus from Siteía 💶 Inexpensive

Where to... Stay

Prices

Prices are for a double room per night in high season including taxes

€ under €60   €€ €60–€100   €€€ over €100

Bay View Apartments €

You'll find this wonderful set of rooms on the left between the town of Zákros and Káto Zákros below. Easily spotted by the profusion of plants around, they command stunning views of the surrounding area and the sea. The rooms have bright, white walls and although extremely simple are clean and comfortable with TV, fridge, en-suite facilities and lovely verandas to relax on: a terrific bargain.

✚ 186 C3 ☒ Káto Zákros
☎ 08430-26887; fax: 08430-93205

Coral Hotel €€

The Coral, right on the waterfront, is the slightly less expensive sister hotel to the Hermes (see below), which has a fitness centre that guests here can use. Try to get one of the sea-view rooms, although all have bath, fridge, air-conditioning, phone and radio. The hotel has its own restaurant, with a sea view, and a rooftop swimming pool. It lays on a substantial breakfast buffet.

✚ 185 D3 ☒ Akti Koundourou,
Ágios Nikólaos ☎ 08410-28363;
fax: 08410-28754; email:
ermis1@ath.forthnet.gr;
www.hermes-hotels.gr ◉ Apr–Oct

Eloúndha Mare €€€

One of the best hotels on the island, this deluxe resort overlooks the Mirabello Gulf. In addition to its regular rooms, it has luxury villas, each with its own private swimming pool. Rooms are decorated in a style that mixes traditional wooden furniture with lots of marble and, of course, all modern amenities. There are three restaurants, golf, tennis, watersports galore, and it is well placed for visiting both Eloúnta and Ágios Nikólaos.

✚ 185 D4 ☒ Eloúnta ☎ 08410-41102; fax: 08410-41307; email:
info@eloundahotels.com;
www.eloundahotels.com ◉ Apr–Oct

Eloúnta Beach €€€

This small, luxury resort, with some 260 rooms including de luxe suites that each have their own private little swimming pool, can claim to be the best hotel on Crete. Needless to say, the rooms have everything, including lots of space. If the TV is not enough you can borrow a video. There are numerous restaurants and bars, every indoor and outdoor facility you could wish for, and a breakfast buffet that could see you through the day.

✚ 185 D4 ☒ Eloúnta ☎ 08410-41412; fax: 08410-41373; email:
elohotel@eloundabeach.gr;
www.eloundabeach.gr ◉ Apr–Oct

Elysée €€€

Perfectly located right on the waterfront, the mid-priced Elysée is just a short stroll from the beach and the town centre. The rooms are clean and simple; those at the front have balconies with great views over the harbour, and all have lots of closet space, fridge, TV and phone. There is a breakfast room and a small lounge, plus ample private parking behind the hotel.

✚ 186 B4 ☒ Karamanli 14, Siteia
☎ 08430-22312; fax: 08430-23427

Hermes Hotel €€€

Along the waterfront from the Coral (see earlier), this smart hotel has a stylish lobby with a shop, flagstone floors and a wall lined with large copies of frescoes from Knosós. Here all the 200 rooms and six suites are spacious and have satellite TV, radio, phone, fridge and hairdryers, making it one of the most comfortable bases in the centre of town. In addition, the Hermes has two restaurants, a rooftop pool, a fitness centre and easy access to a diving club just across the road (▶124).

🏨 185 D3 ⊠ Akti Koundourou, Ágios Nikólaos ☎ 08410-28253; fax: 08410-28754; email: ermis1@ath.forthnet.gr; www.hermes-hotels.gr 🕐 Apr–Oct

Istron Bay €€€

One of the best hotels on the island, the Istron overlooks its own beach some 12km east of Ágios Nikólaos. Built into the cliff, it is all but invisible as you approach and all rooms have large balconies with sea views. They are also good-sized and decorated in traditional blue and white. The restaurant has won awards for its gourmet cooking, and with its own pool and friendly service the hotel is rightly popular, so book ahead.

🏨 185 D3 ⊠ Istro, Ágios Nikólaos ☎ 08410-61303/61347; fax: 08410-61383; email: istron@agn.forthnet.gr; www.istronbay.com 🕐 Apr–Oct

Itanos Hotel €

This family hotel is bigger than it looks, with 72 rooms in a building right by the main town square and overlooking the waterfront. The rooms are standard fare for a hotel in this price range, and all have phone, satellite TV, radio, bath, air-conditioning and balconies with soundproof doors. Try to get a room at the front for the sea views. Facilities include a large dining room and bar, and, right in the lobby, a rather tempting patisserie.

🏨 186 B4 ⊠ Siteiá ☎ 08430-22901; fax: 08430-22915; email: itanoshotel@yahoo.com; www.forthnet.gr/internetcity/hotels/itanos

Minos Beach €€€

This luxury hotel is well placed with easy access to both Ágios Nikólaos and Eloúnta. Striking sculptures stand in the lush gardens and the guest rooms occupy bungalows dotted around the grounds. Several restaurants and bars, a pool, tennis courts, watersports, a TV room and a baby-sitting service are all on offer, too. Car hire and tours can be booked from the hotel. Service is excellent. There are good sandy beaches close by.

🏨 185 D3 ⊠ Ammoudára ☎ 08410-22345; fax: 08410-22548; email: mamhotel@otenet.gr 🕐 Apr–Oct

Hotel Mýrtos €

Probably the best of a limited range of accommodation in Mýrtos, this inexpensive hotel is right in the packed centre of this little town, with its own restaurant attached. The rooms are a decent size with basic facilities, and a small balcony runs around the outside of the building, which all rooms can enjoy.

🏨 184 C2 ⊠ Mýrtos ☎ 08420-51227; fax: 08420-51215; www.myrtoshotel.com

Neapolis Hotel €

An eye-catching art deco-style building, the Neapolis has 12 rooms fitted with stripped-pine furniture and lemon-coloured walls. All the rooms have very small balconies overlooking the street (though noise is not a problem in this charming hill town) and some have air-conditioning. The breakfast is generous, often with fresh fruit added for good measure. You may return at night to find old men playing cards in the lobby, or the local priest watching the TV. Charming and well maintained, the hotel offers excellent value.

🏨 184 C4 ⊠ Evagelistrías Square, Neápoli ☎ 08410-33966 ; fax: 08410-33967

Where to...
Eat and Drink

Prices
Prices are for a two-course meal for one person, excluding drinks and tips

€ under €9   €€ €9–€14.5   €€€ over €14.5

Taverna Akti €€

At the far eastern end of the string of waterfront tavernas, the Akti is one of the oldest and best restaurants in Mýrtos. Outdoor tables with blue and white checked tablecloths overlook the beach, and there is indoor seating in a spacious room. The very friendly owner offers various specialities, including charcoal-cooked meats and a range of fresh fish, which he will bring to the table for you to choose from. One special dish is the octopus *stifado*.

➕ 184 C2 ✉ Waterfront, Mýrtos
☎ 08420-51584 🕒 Daily 10 am–late, Apr–Nov

The Balcony €€€

An hibiscus plant stands outside the pleasant back street entrance to this stylish but friendly little place where a blackboard lists the daily specials. Upstairs is the one indoor dining room, with stone walls and stained glass. The unusual menu specialises in a trio of cuisines: Cretan, Mexican and Asian. If you want to sample a mouthwatering Cretan treat, go for the pork tenderloin and mountain greens cooked in filo pastry and served with a sage sauce.

➕ 186 B4 ✉ Kazantzáki/Foundalídou, Siteiá ☎ 08430-25084

🕒 Daily noon–3 pm, 7 pm–midnight in summer; Thu–Sun, in winter

La Casa €€

One of the entrances to this café-restaurant is on a pedestrianised shopping street, the other by the lakefront where most of the seating is to be found. Being open all year, it's as popular with local youngsters as with visitors. Simple meals such as spinach pies and toasted sandwiches are served throughout the day. The more elaborate meals available at lunch time and in the evening include chicken, fish, *souvláki* and so on; one tasty and filling favourite is turkey stuffed with ham, bacon and eggs and baked in the oven.

➕ 185 D3 ✉ 28 Oktovriou 31, Agios Nikólaos ☎ 08410-26362 🕒 Daily 9 am–midnight

Ferryman Taverna €€

An imaginative menu distinguishes the Ferryman, one of several restaurants in a row at the southern end of the Eloúnta waterfront. In appearance it is much like the others, with outdoor seating overlooking the water and an indoor room across the quiet street. However, the cooking here is far more ambitious, and among the most popular dishes are Cretan lamb in red wine and a pork dish cooked with bacon, mushrooms, garlic, white wine and fresh cream. The restaurant takes its name from the BBC television series *Who Pays the Ferryman?* which was filmed in Eloúnta and nearby Ágios Nikólaos in the 1970s.

➕ 185 D4 ✉ Waterfront, Eloúnta ☎ 08410-41230 🕒 Daily 10 am–late, Apr–Oct

Itanos €€

This place near the cathedral lacks the relaxing views of those restaurants around the harbour. In fact, it lacks any kind of view, other than the passing traffic, but it attracts a mix of locals and more adventurous visitors. It's a bit basic, with outdoor tables on the pavement in summer, and a roof garden. People come for the food, which is traditional Cretan fare at reasonable prices. Its noted for its good grilled meats and local wine from the barrel.

🌐 185 D3 ✉ Kyprou 1, Ágios Nikólaos ☎ 08410-25340 🕐 Daily 10 am–midnight

Káto Zákros Bay Restaurant €

This family taverna is right by the sea in tiny Káto Zákros, a place for those who really want to get away from it all. In addition to the indoor seating there are pleasant tables outside overlooking the beach, beneath shade trees. The restaurant owners have a farm where they breed rabbit, quail and grouse; the vegetables come from their own garden; and all meals are cooked in extra-virgin olive oil…and it shows. Good local wines are on offer, too.

🌐 186 C3 ✉ Káto Zákros ☎ 08430-26887; fax: 08430-93205 🕐 Daily all day, Apr–Oct

Meltemi €€€

Hotel restaurants sometimes disappoint, but the Meltemi at the Istron Bay (▶ 120) is exceptional. It is one of the best eateries on the island and has won awards for its imaginative cuisine ranging from seafood to hearty but subtle meat dishes. You can also opt for the nightly buffet, which allows you to choose from a selection of hot and cold Greek dishes. There is an extensive wine list, too. Non-residents are welcome in the stylish dining room that overlooks the sea through a wall of windows. Booking is advised.

🌐 185 D3 ✉ Istro, Ágios Nikólaos ☎ 08410-6103/61347 🕐 Mon–Wed and Fri–Sat 7 pm–10.30 pm. Apr–Oct

O Mixos €€

Here waiters race back and forth with orders and dishes between the main seating area down on the waterfront and the backstreet kitchen. The quality of the food is superb, with an emphasis on meat and fish grilled on charcoal, cooked outside in the traditional way. Oven-baked dishes also feature, with lamb and artichoke casserole one speciality of the house.

🌐 186 B4 ✉ Kornarou 117, Siteiá ☎ 08430-22416 🕐 Daily 10 am–late

Il Palazzo €

It is surprising to find an Italian restaurant in a Greek hill village, let alone one as enjoyable as this. This is very much a family affair. The pizzas, cooked in the oven in the dining room, are excellent. There is a lovely covered patio area out front, with a flagstone floor and potted plants along the outer wall.

🌐 184 C4 ✉ Sergaki 14, Neápoli ☎ 08430-34180 🕐 Daily 6 pm–late

Pelagos €€

A fishing boat and a beautiful shady palm-filled courtyard where the tables stand on a stone floor identifies Pelagos. Inside there are several small, intimate rooms with bright blue and yellow paintwork. Food is served all day although you are welcome to sit just for a drink and a nibble. Seafood is the speciality, including octopus, mussels and of course the catch of the day, but meat-lovers and vegetarians are also well catered for.

🌐 185 D3 ✉ Koraka/Katechaki 10, Ágios Nikólaos ☎ 08410-25737; email: doxan45@hotmail.com 🕐 Daily noon–midnight, Apr–Oct

Vritomartes €€

This unmissable seafood restaurant stands out on the breakwater with its name emblazoned on the side in letters several feet high. A pleasant seating area overlooks the water, and before you get there you will pass the water tank containing live fish and lobsters. The menu is vast, and not confined to seafood, but it would be a shame not to try the more imaginative dishes, even if they push the price up a little.

🌐 185 D4 ✉ G Sfiraki waterfront, Eloúnta ☎ 08410-41325 🕐 Daily 10 am–11 pm, Apr–Oct

Where to...
Shop

Ágios Nikólaos has the most varied shopping in eastern Crete. Pedestrianised Odos 28 Oktovriou is largely geared for tourists, with restaurants and souvenir shops. There are more shops along Roussou Koundourou and Stakiaraki streets. All round the harbour and lake area numerous jewellery shops sell both modern and antique designs.

TEXTILES AND LOCAL CRAFTS

Just 10km away from Ágios Nikólaos, the mountain village of **Kritsá** is famous for its textiles. Here the streets are literally draped with rugs, wall hangings, woven bags, embroidered tablecloths and other traditional handicrafts. Make sure you purchase genuine hand-made articles (▶ 95). These will usually be more expensive but higher in quality.

The villages around the **Diktaean Cave** on the Lasithiou Plateau, particularly **Psychro**, also have a lot of textiles for sale. On the outskirts of Zenia (▶ 160) look for the elderly spoon-carver selling his wares outside his house. They're not the cheapest spoons around, but they make a unique and authentic gift and it's a charming place to stop and watch him work.

Surprisingly for a provincial town, **Neapoli** has several contemporary gift shops with unusual and attractive items. These are on Odós Ethnikis Antistasis, the main street into town between the Neapolis Hotel and the main square. The shop at No 56 sells traditional Cretan items, such as bells for goats and sheep in various sizes with or without the leather collar; also baskets, knives, carved walking sticks, wooden spoons and forks, and traditional high boots.

ICONS

Eastern Crete is a good area to shop for traditional Greek icons. The gift shop opposite **Panagia Kera**, just outside Kritsá (▶ 104–105), has some lovely and authentic hand-painted icons. They're not inexpensive, but the price reflects the skill and time involved in producing high-quality artwork. Beautifully painted icons, at better prices, can be found at the **Petrakis Icon Workshop** (▶ 31) in Elounta (tel: 08410-41669/41461). It is open daily 10 am–11 pm, Apr–Oct; phone for hours in winter.

BOOKS

Opposite Petrakis, tucked between the waterfront and the main road in Elounta, is **Eklektos**, an excellent bookshop which sells not only maps and guides but also fiction, poetry and essays on all things Cretan – and in several languages. If you can't find a publication here then it is probably not in print. There is also a huge second-hand section for paperbacks, plus top-quality gifts such as stationery, crystals and clothing (open daily 10 am–10:30 pm, Apr–Oct; tel: 08410-41641).

MARKETS

Every Wednesday morning an outdoor market next to the main hospital at **Ágios Nikólaos** sells food, produce and clothes. **Ierapetra** has a street market on Saturday mornings by the Próto Γymnásio (first high school) and **Siteia** on Tuesdays on Odós Plastira. Markets generally close around 1 pm. Cheese from the **Lasithiou** and **Katharó plateaux** is especially good; try the *graviera*. Siteia is a major wine-producing area – the red wines are very popular.

Where to...
Be Entertained

NIGHTLIFE

Eastern Crete's north coast resorts are the nightlife capital of the island. In **Limin Chersónisou** and **Mália**, bars and nightclubs buzz all night long. Among the most popular venues in Chersónisou are **Aria**, one of the biggest discos on Crete; and **Status**, **New York** and **Camelot Club** near the waterfront. On the main road is the **Fame Bar**, with soul, funk and jazz music; **Palace of Dance 99**; and **Hard Rock Café** and **Cheers**, both of which often have live music.

Mália's current rave is **Zoo**. Other hotspots on the beach road include **Zig Zag's**, **Apollo** and **Babylon**. The **R&B Dance Club** has the edge with the latest music.

The only large dance club in Ágios Nikólaos is **Lipstick**, along the harbour, but there are plenty of lively music bars in the town centre.

Along Siteía's waterfront are popular music bars such as **Nea Glyfada**, **Scala**, **Club Porto** and **Albatros**. Larger discos include **Hot Summer** on the beach road, and **Planitarion**, west of the ferry port.

TRADITIONAL MUSIC AND FESTIVALS

The tavernas around the square in **Mália** old town often stage live Greek music, and in summer frequent performances of Cretan music and dance take place at the **Lychnostatis Open-Air Museum**, on the eastern edge of Chersónisou.

Siteía is also the site of several cultural events. The main festival, the **Kornaria** (June or July to mid-August), features folklore dances, popular music, village feasts and exhibitions. Performances take place in the old Venetian fortress, or in the town square. Details available from the tourist office (▶ 37).

The **Sultanina** (Wine Festival) follows the Kornaria, a four-day event marking the beginning of the grape harvest in mid-August with traditional music and dance. In winter, the **Carnival** is held at the fortress on the last Sunday before Lent. A bulletin listing events is distributed around town in summer.

Ágios Nikólaos holds a cultural festival, the **Lato** (from June to September), with theatre, concerts, dance and traditional festival events. Details available from the tourist office (▶ 37).

SPORTS

The north coast beach resorts offer a wide range of **watersports**. Crete's biggest waterpark, **Water City** (tel: 0810-781386), is just inland from Kokkini Hani. Limin Chersónisou has two more water-parks: **Aqua Splash** (tel: 08970-24950) and **Star Beach** (tel: 08970-24434). All are open daily in summer (times vary). You can try **go-karting** at **Kartland** (tel: 08970-32769), adjacent to Star Beach.

Ágios Nikólaos is good for **scuba diving**. Dive centres are strictly controlled and offer lessons and equipment rental. PADI-certified centres include **Creta's Happy Divers** (tel: 08410-82546) opposite the Coral Hotel; **Pelagos Diving Centre** (tel: 08410-22345/24376) at Minos Beach Hotel; and the diving centre at the **Istron Bay Hotel** (▶ 120). Diving is also offered at **Vai Beach** (July–September).

The **Municipal Beach Club** at Ágios Nikólaos (daily 9 am–late) has mini-golf, billiards, table tennis, life-size chess and a basketball court, as well as watersports.

RiX Outdoor Activities (tel: 08970-32985) offers **bicycle** and **skate** rentals and numerous **tours**.

Western Crete

Getting Your Bearings

From the two loveliest cities on the north coast to the biggest gorge in Europe, which plunges down from the central mountains to the southern sea, western Crete has some of the island's best features. These include the two most historically interesting monasteries on Crete, Arkadíou in the north and Préveli in the south, both of which played immense roles in the island's battles for independence.

Chaniá and Réthymno, Crete's second and third largest cities respectively, have fine restaurants, museums and Venetian history. But if your only view of western Crete is of these busy parts of the north coast, you'll see just a fraction of what the area has to offer. The beaches here are bustling, and some resorts such as Plataniás and Balí are packed with summer sun-worshippers. But head south into the White Mountains (Lefká Óri), the island's highest and most dramatic range, and that world immediately disappears, to be replaced by quiet villages and breathtaking views.

Many people undertake the day-long trek through the Samariá Gorge, one of the most exciting experiences on the island, but other gorges, such as the Ímpros Gorge, also make for great walks. These are largely found along the south coast, which is much more rugged than the north. Options here range from hidden backwaters like Sougia to growing resorts such as Palaióchora.

To the west are inland hill villages surrounded by orchards, while down by the sea you'll find remote beaches, including the popular but still gorgeous sands of Elafonísi. Spend at least a day driving around this region to take in some of western Crete's spectacular beauty.

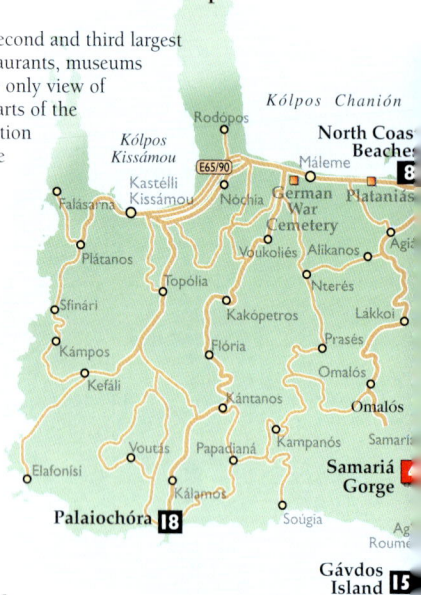

Kólpos Chanión

Kólpos Kissámou

Rodópos

North Coast Beaches 8

Máleme

E65/90

Kastélli
Kissámou

Nochia

German War Cemetery

Plataniás

Falásarna

Voukoliés

Alikanos

Agía

Plátanos

Topólia

Nterés

Sfinári

Kakópetros

Lákkoi

Flória

Prasés

Kámpos

Omalós

Kefáli

Kántanos

Omalós

Voutás

Papadianá

Kampanós

Samariá

Elafonísi

Samariá Gorge

Kálamos

Palaiochóra 18

Soúgia

Ag Roume

Gávdos Island 15

Museum mosaic, Chaniá

★ Don't Miss

At Your Leisure

Page 125:
Detail from a fresco at Moní Arkadíou

Right: Monks still live in the monastery of Préveli

Even five days in this large area will be rushed, but it does allow time to explore Chaniá and Réthymno, see some of the north and south coast beaches, and visit the Samariá Gorge and the monasteries at Préveli and Arkadíou.

Western Crete in Five Days

Day One

Morning
Explore **Moní Arkadíou** (icon, right, ➤ 130–131) then take the pleasant country road (signposted at the end of the car park) to the ancient site of **Eléftherna** (➤ 142). Continue on to the potters' village of **Margarítes** (➤ 142). Have lunch in Margarítes. Taverna Gianousakis at the upper end of the village is a pleasant place with good home-cooked food.

Afternoon
Drive northeast to visit the **Melidóni Cave** (➤ 142), then continue north to the coast road, perhaps stopping for a swim at one of the north coast beaches on your way west to Réthymno.

Evening
Spend the night at **Réthymno** (left, ➤ 132–135). For dinner, try the house special at Kyria Maria (➤ 152).

Day Two

Morning/Lunch
Explore Réthymno, perhaps spending the morning at the museums and art gallery, or at the Fortezza. Don't miss a meal at the Avli (➤ 151).

Afternoon
Explore the narrow streets of the old town, see the loggia, stroll around the Venetian harbour and visit the public gardens.

Evening
Enjoy a relaxing meal by the sea, but instead of choosing one of the touristy restaurants by the inner harbour, go to the Fanari (➤ 151).

Day Three

Morning/Lunch

Drive south to **Moní Préveli** (➤ 144), the last stretch through dramatic gorge scenery. Head west through **Plakiás** (➤ 144) and along the narrow, winding coastal road to **Fragkokástelo** (➤ 145). Dine by the lovely little harbour at **Chóra Sfakia** (➤ 146). The Livikon Restaurant, the town's oldest, serves good Cretan specialities.

Afternoon

Drive north past the **Ímpros Gorge** (➤ 145). You can occasionally glimpse the chasm from the road, even if you have no time to walk it. Head for Chaniá, stopping off at the Allied War Cemetery near **Soúda** (➤ 147–148) if time permits.

Evening

Spend three nights in **Chaniá** (lighthouse, right, ➤ 136–139). For dinner, good music and a great atmosphere try Semiramis (➤ 152).

Day Four

Morning/Lunch

See Chaniá's market, Archaeological Museum and Folklore Museum. Arrive promptly at 1 pm to get a table at Tamam (➤ 152).

Afternoon

Allow plenty of time to see the Byzantine Museum and the Naval Museum, and to enjoy the beautiful Venetian harbour.

Evening

Wander through the Turkish quarter to the superb Well of the Turk (➤ 152).

Day Five

Morning

Spend the day at the **Samariá Gorge** (left, ➤ 140–141). Take lunch and water with you.

Evening

Back in Chaniá, relax over a meal around the harbour, where the Amphora (➤ 151) is one of the best restaurants.

❶ Moní Arkadíou

(Arkadi Monastery)

Standing proudly at the end of a steep, twisting road on the edge of the Psiloreítis Mountains, Moní Arkadíou has one of the finest Venetian churches on Crete. But its striking façade is not the only reason to visit. The tragic events that took place here in 1866 have made it a national symbol of Crete's heroic struggle for independence.

Inside the church at Arkadíou

During the 1866 rebellion against the Turks (➤ 16), nearly 300 guerrilla fighters and some 700 women and children took refuge in the monastery. The Turks laid siege to it, and after three days broke through the gates on 9 November. As they rushed in, the abbot ordered the ignition of the gunpowder stores, killing hundreds of Cretans and Turks alike in the massive explosion: it was a heroic act of sacrifice that galvanised support for Cretan independence both at home and abroad.

Exploring the Monastery

Standing in the centre of the courtyard is the **church**, dating from 1587, with its lovely façade of golden stone and bell tower. Inside is a beautifully carved altar screen of cypress wood, executed in 1902. On the right-hand side is a large gilt-framed icon of Christ, part of a scene of the Resurrection from the church's original altar screen.

To the left of the church is the **refectory**, where 36 freedom fighters were massacred. You can still see sword marks on the long wooden table and benches. A room above the refectory is hung with portraits of Cretan patriots throughout history.

At the far left side of the courtyard you can step down into the roofless **gunpowder magazine** – formerly the monks' wine cellar – where the holocaust took place. A simple shrine commemorates the tragedy.

On the opposite side of the courtyard, the old **cloisters** with their arched stone arcade are very atmospheric. Above, a small **museum** houses historic items from the monastery, including a fragment of the Sacred Banner, so called because after being taken by a Turk during the Turkish onslaught the banner survived and was returned to the monastery in 1870. You can still see the battered old refectory door with bullet holes visible.

The **ossuary**, housed in a former windmill outside the gate near the parking area, contains the skulls and bones of the people who died in the great explosion.

The skulls of the martyrs in the ossuary

TAKING A BREAK

With nothing else in the area, it's as well that the monastery has its own **restaurant** – simple but fine for a meal or snack.

✚ 181 E3 ✉ 25km southeast of Réthymno ☎ 08310-83116 🕐 Daily 8–7
🍴 Restaurant (€€) 🚌 Direct buses from Réthymno 💰 Inexpensive
❓ Photography allowed, except in church and museum

MONÍ ARKADÍOU: INSIDE INFO

Top tip If driving towards **Eléftherna** (➤ 142) note that the road is the one that appears to go through the monastery grounds. The signpost is at the far end.

Hidden gems Take a close look at the **crucifixes** high on either side of the church's altar screen. Each has a ladder propped up against the cross, and a skull and crossbones at the foot.

• In the courtyard outside the refectory you'll find an ancient **cypress tree** with a shell from the Turkish siege still embedded in its trunk. An arrow marks the spot.

2 Réthymno

Réthymno's massive fortress – thought to be the biggest the Venetians ever built – dwarfs its tiny Venetian harbour. Nearby, the compact old quarter, punctuated with crumbling mosques and overhanging closed wooden balconies, bears traces of Turkish rule. This is Crete's third largest town, and many prefer it to its bigger neighbour, Chaniá. It has charm as well as modern bustle, not to mention good seafood and one of the best beaches on the northern coast.

While little remains from the ancient Minoan settlement here, you can see plenty from the town's Greco-Roman days, when Réthymno was a busy port and trading centre. With the arrival of the Venetians in the 13th century the town positively boomed, adding a reputation for art and literature to its name. It is still considered the intellectual capital of Crete.

Réthymno boasts perhaps the biggest Venetian fortress in the world

The fortress towers over the city from its western promontory. Below, the tiny Venetian harbour is big enough to accommodate only the smaller craft of local fishermen. Bigger ferries have to moor along the breakwater outside the narrow entrance, beside which stands a graceful 16th-century lighthouse. These days there are far more lights from the dozens of fish restaurants that ring the inner side of the harbour than from boats; waiters almost drag you inside to look at the glistening fresh fish on display.

The Town's Main Sights

From the harbour, a long palm-lined promenade – somewhat marred by the parked cars alongside – stretches east along the

The flame still burns in the church at Réthymno's fortress

wide, sandy beach that runs for several miles. South of the seafront, the warren of streets that make up the old quarter lies between the fortress and Plateía Iroon.

The formidable Venetian fortress, or **Fortezza**, was built in the 1570s to guard against pirates and the increasingly powerful Turks. However, it did not hold the latter out for long as they stormed the fortress in 1646 after a 23-day siege. The spacious grounds feel rather like a town park, with the remains of administrative buildings, a church and barracks. The highlight is the **mosque** with its enormous dome and tiled prayer niche. This and other buildings often house art exhibitions. You'll get spectacular views from the ramparts and parapets, but to fully appreciate the Fortezza's size walk around its base beside the rocky shoreline.

Opposite the entrance to the fortress is Réthymno's small but excellent **Archaeological Museum**. Among the highlights are neolithic finds, a collection of delicate and detailed bronze vessels from the tomb of an athlete dating from the 1st century BC, bronze figurines recovered from a shipwreck off Agía Galíni, and a fine clay model of a small Minoan temple

The mosque inside the fortress

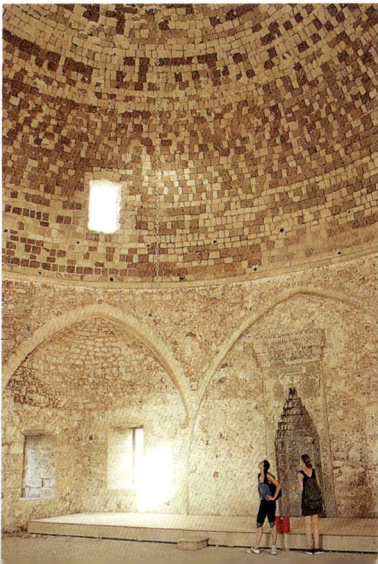

(2100–1600 BC). The artwork of bulls and other animals on the Minoan sarcophagi is also marvellous. Among the more unusual objects are a soldier's helmet made from boars' tusks, an ivory-handled bronze mirror of the Post-Palace period (1400–1150 BC), and a small collection of red-figure vases dating from the 4th to 1st century BC on which the keen-eyed observer might spot some erotic scenes.

Near by is the **Réthymno Centre for Contemporary Art**, also known as the Kanakakis Municipal Gallery. This wonderfully restored old building has wooden rafters and white-painted Venetian arches on the ground floor. Although small, the centre has a sense of light and space, and the two floors usually house two or three changing exhibitions featuring Cretan artists. In the streets of the old town a few smaller galleries exhibit one-person shows.

Réthymno's other major museum is the **Historical and Folk Art Museum**, housed in an elegant early 17th-century Venetian mansion. The ground floor displays are of little interest if you don't speak Greek, containing mainly documents, letters and photographs on social aspects of Réthymno life. The upstairs rooms, however, contain a fascinating collection of folk art, with detailed information panels in both Greek and English. In the large main room there are superb displays of embroidery and weaving, as well as figures wearing traditional costumes.

A smaller room is filled with ceramics and Cretan baskets, together with a potter's wheel and an interesting display on bee-keeping. The next room contains more examples of embroidery, delicate crochet and threadwork. The final room concentrates on agriculture, with scale models of a watermill, an olive press and a fulling mill – a device used for cleaning tough goatskins, traditionally made into cloaks. Picture panels on breadmaking show how the intricate decorated loaves are made for different celebrations.

Minaret of the Nerantzes Mosque

Hidden Charms

Some of Réthymno's greatest charms are found simply by wandering through the atmospheric streets of the old quarter, where you'll discover hidden fountains, decorative doorways gracing old Venetian mansions, and the overhanging wooden balconies added by the Turks.

Further along Vernardou Street from the folk museum is the **Nerantzes Mosque**, with its slender minaret soaring over the old town. It is now a music conservatory and concert hall.

Below: Flowers in the old town

The Venetian lighthouse guards the harbour

Near by, at Plateía Petiháki, the delightful **Rimondi Fountain** has waterspouts in the shape of the heads of the lions of St Mark. It dates from around 1626 when, it is claimed, the Venetian governor of Réthymno was envious of the Morosíni Fountain in Irakleío. This small square, packed with bars and cafés, buzzes day and night.

Just back from the inner harbour, the 16th-century **loggia** is one of the finest examples of Renaissance architecture on Crete, once used as a gathering place for the city worthies. Today it houses the **Museum Shop** (➤ 153).

Souliou and Ethnikis Andistasis streets lead up to the **Porta Guora**, the only remnant of the old city walls. Through this archway the busy Plateía Martíron, with the large modern **Church of the Four Martyrs** at one end, marks the end of the old town. Opposite are the lush **public gardens**.

TAKING A BREAK

The restaurants around the tiny harbour look appealing, but the persistent waiters can be a nuisance. **Walk further west** to a quieter row of restaurants which are just as good; the **Fanari** (➤ 151) is one of the best.

Réthymno
+ 181 D3

Venetian Fortress
🕐 Tue–Sun 8–7; last admission 6:15 pm
👣 Moderate ❓ Photography allowed

Archaeological Museum
✉ The Fortezza ☎ 08310-54668
🕐 Tue–Sun 8:30–3 👣 Inexpensive ❓ No flash photography

Réthymno Centre for Contemporary Art
✉ Himaras 5 ☎ 8310-55847; email: rca@ret.forthnet.gr; www.rca.gr 🕐 Tue–Fri 9–2, 7–10; Sat–Sun 11–3 👣 Inexpensive
❓ No photography allowed

Historical and Folk Art Museum
✉ M Vernardou 30 ☎ 08310-23398
🕐 Mon–Sat 9:30–2; Wed, Fri 9–2 only in winter 👣 Moderate ❓ No photography allowed

---

RÉTHYMNO: INSIDE INFO

Top tip Parking is a nightmare and the town a warren of narrow one-way streets. On arrival, use one of the large, inexpensive **public car parks** adjacent to the ferry dock or the public gardens, then seek advice from your hotel if you are staying.

Hidden gems The city's two other surviving mosques, both closed, are **Kara Musa Pasa**, at the end of Arkadiou Street near Plateía Iroon, and **Veli Pasa**, with a graceful minaret and three domes, set in an overgrown garden south of the town hall at the end of Dimoukratias.

One to miss The entire **ground floor** of the Historical and Folk Art Museum could be missed. Head straight into the garden and up to the first floor.

3 Chaniá

The island's second city has been called the Venice of Crete, not because of its canals (there aren't any) but because of its lovely Venetian architecture. One of the most beautiful spots on the whole island is Chaniá's Venetian harbour, especially at night when the lights come on and the crowds are out enjoying the many cafés and restaurants. Behind here the narrow streets of the old town are a delight to wander in, and with its wealth of museums, shopping, nightlife, town beach and good restaurants, Chaniá is a joy to visit.

Chaniá is thought to be one of the oldest continually inhabited cities in the world. There was a Minoan settlement here and modern Chaniá bears influences of a steady stream of invaders: Roman, Byzantine, Venetian, Genoese, Turkish and, during World War II, German.

The Venetian lighthouse at sunset

The Harbour

The greatest legacy is the Venetian harbour, actually two harbours joined together. They meet at Plateía Sindriváni, or Harbour Square. Here, the **Mosque of the Janissaries** was built in 1645, the same year that the Turks took Crete from the Venetians, making it the oldest Turkish building on the island. Now renovated, it is sporadically used for staging exhibitions.

Follow Aktí Tombázi east past the yachts and fishing boats moored in the inner harbour. On the right you'll pass the remains of the Venetian *arsenali*, or shipyards. You can walk all the way around the inner harbour and along the sea wall to the Venetian **lighthouse**, beautifully restored and a symbol of the city. There are lovely views back over the town and harbour.

To the west of Harbour Square the waterfront, lined with lively pavement cafés, bars and restaurants, leads to the Venetian **fortress**, or Firkas, where restoration is in progress. Inside the bastion is the **Naval Museum**, which is well worth

The Venetian shipyards still line the harbour

Bottom: Greek
flags mark the
Naval Museum

visiting even if you're not that interested in naval matters. The upper floor has an extensive exhibition on the Battle of Crete (➤ 17–19). This excellent display shows what life was like on the island at that time, particularly around Chaniá where much of the initial action took place. Part of the display is very harrowing, especially photographs of Cretan villagers being led to their execution, but it should not be missed.

The rest of the museum includes a beautifully detailed scale model of Venetian Chaniá, models of ships from ancient triremes (Greek warships powered by oarsmen) to modern battleships, a room full of sea shells ranging from a metre across to the size of a pin-head, and interesting models of famous sea battles.

On the western side of the fortress is the delightful **Byzantine Museum**, whose bright modern displays are housed in a small renovated church. Whereas many Byzantine museums concentrate almost solely on icons, this one covers all aspects of Byzantine culture including sculptures, mosaics, jewellery and frescoes. There are fragments of wonderful 11th-century wall frescoes that have survived marvellously, their colours shiny and bright.

In a side gallery, the **San Salvatore collection** of Byzantine coins includes finds from graves, with lovely necklaces of glass beads, crosses, rings, domestic pottery and a 6th- to 7th-century bronze lamp with a cross in its handle. At the far end, note the icon of St George slaying the dragon. This skilful work was done by Emmanuel Tzanes Bouniales (1610–90), one of the leading lights of the Cretan School of artists (➤ 32).

The Old Town

To reach the town beach continue along the waterfront for about ten minutes, though Chaniá's better beaches are found west of town. Otherwise, turn left along Odós Theotokopoulou outside the Byzantine Museum to enter the narrow and mostly traffic-free streets of the **old town**, which lies between the harbour and the old city wall. Just wandering around here is a delight. Gift shops alternate with Venetian palaces, many now turned into some of the city's most characterful hotels. Look for ornate doorways, balconies and other remnants of Venetian splendour as you head towards the picturesque Renieri Gate.

A Roman
mosaic in the
Archaeological
Museum

Odós Halidhon, the major thoroughfare running south
from Harbour Square, marks the edge of the old town. Tucked
back off a narrow passageway, beside the Catholic church, is
the **Cretan House Folklore Museum**, a tiny, charming place
with tableaux of weavers, basketmakers and other artisans.
The two founders of the museum have a workshop here
where their own weavings and embroideries are for sale.

Near by, Chaniá's splendid **Archaeological Museum** is
atmospherically housed beneath the arched roof of the
restored Venetian Church of San Francesco. You'll find plenty
of information in both Greek and English as you tour the
exhibits in clockwise fashion. Case 10 holds one of the most
interesting exhibits: rare seals with Minoan Linear A script,
accidentally preserved in a fire, are shown alongside examples
of Linear B. Kastélli Chania is the only place outside Knosós
where both Linear A and B have been found. Though Linear
A remains a mystery, here some symbols have been deciphered. Pictographs for such things as sheep, ox, wine, olive
oil, figs and numerals – a simple circle represents 100 – indicate an advanced system of accounting.

Carpets are
still handwoven
in Chaniá

The museum has many other
fine objects, including toys belonging to Minoan children, which
were used as burial offerings, and
magnificent Roman floor mosaics
from Chaniá houses. In a small
annexe, the Mitsotakis Collection
comprises Minoan and Mycenaean
items, vases, pots, figurines, early
Iron Age vases and bowls, Minoan
metalwork and many other fine
items. At the far end of the gallery
a central case contains the only
known bronze vessel to be
embossed with a Linear A inscrip-

tion, found at the peak sanctuary at Kofinas. It was originally made in Egypt around 1800–1425 BC, then brought to Crete and engraved on the island.

Beyond the Old Town

From the museum, Odós Halidhon leads south past the rather nondescript cathedral to modern Chaniá. Turn left on Odós Skridlof to reach the bustling **covered market**, with butchers, honey and cheese vendors, fruit and vegetable stalls and other shops lining the cross-shaped aisles.

Between the market and the inner harbour, the **Spiantza quarter** is one of the most atmospheric places in Chaniá. As you wander around the residential streets of this former Turkish area, you'll find cobbled streets, charming old houses with wooden balconies and archways, and minarets peeking out above the rooftops.

Below: A hint of old Venice in Chaniá's harbour

TAKING A BREAK

Anywhere on the **Venetian harbour** has a great setting and atmosphere, but if you care about your food try the **Amphora** (➤ 151).

Chaniá
🗺 179 E4
Naval Museum
✉ Akti Kountourioti ☎ 08210-26437
🕐 Daily 10–4 💶 Inexpensive ❓ No flash photography

Byzantine Museum
✉ The Fortress 🕐 Tue–Sun 8:30–3
💶 Free ❓ No photography

Cretan House Folklore Museum
✉ Odós Halidhon 46B ☎ 08210-90816
🕐 Mon–Sat 9–3, 6–9, Apr–Oct
💶 Inexpensive ❓ Photography allowed

Archaeological Museum
✉ Odós Halidhon 21 ☎ 08210-90334
🕐 Tue–Sun 8:30–3 💶 Inexpensive
❓ No flash photography

CHANIÁ: INSIDE INFO

Top tip If driving into Chaniá, there is **good parking** just to the west of the fortress, allowing easy access to the old town and most of the city's attractions.

Hidden gems The **Etz Hayyim Synagogue** off Odós Kondylaki is still in use but can be visited for its small historical displays and lovely peaceful garden.
• In the Kastélli quarter behind the inner harbour archaeological digs are uncovering the remains of **Minoan Kydonia**. Sites can be seen along or just off Odós Kanevaro.

4 Samariá Gorge

The awesome scenery of the Samariá Gorge (Farángi Samariás) makes it Crete's most spectacular natural wonder. This is the longest gorge in Europe, stretching 18km from the Omalós Plateau, 1,100m high in the Lefká Óri (White Mountains), to the Libyan Sea. The trek from top to bottom is long, hot and tiring, rather than difficult, but do it if you're reasonably fit – it's an experience you'll never forget.

The Samariá Gorge became a national park in 1962. It shelters a fascinating array of plants and wildlife, including ancient pine and cypress, wild orchids and dittany, and endangered species such as the golden eagle and the Cretan ibex, or *krí-krí* (► 27). This dramatic ravine was formed by a river, which slows to a trickle in summer but becomes a raging torrent after winter snow and rains. Thus the gorge is only open from May to October, weather permitting.

Thousands of people hike the gorge every year, and in high season it can seem an endless procession. Do use common sense before undertaking the trek and make sure you (and your young children) are up to the entire 16km walk, which takes 5 to 7 hours – there are no short-cuts out of the gorge once you start. It requires stamina, especially in the heat, and although it is downhill all the way knees and ankles will soon feel the strain.

Samariá the Lazy Way
Tour companies offer an easier option. A ferry takes you to Agía Rouméli, where you can walk up the gorge to the dramatic Sideróportes.

Take a hat, sunglasses and sun block, as there is no shade for the last few kilometres, and bring at least a litre of water per person – there are places to top up with spring water along the way. Above all, wear appropriate shoes with good support and strong soles to withstand sharp rocks. If you follow those simple guidelines, you'll enjoy the walk and feel a great sense of achievement at the end.

The easiest way to walk the Samariá Gorge is with an organised tour; transport details are sorted out for you, and a guide will accompany your group. But you can also take an early bus from Chaniá to the top of the gorge. From Agia Rouméli at the lower end you catch a ferry to Chóra Sfakia to connect with a return bus. Check all times locally.

Hiking the Gorge
The *xilóskalo* (wooden staircase), cut from the rock, makes a steep, winding descent into the gorge. The mountain views are breathtaking, with the sheer rock face of Mount Gíngilos (2,080m) towering magnificently above through the pines. The path becomes flatter after about 4km, when you reach the stone chapel of **Ágios Nikólaos**. Baby *krí-krí* sometimes venture down to graze at this shady spot beside the river.

Looking up to
Mount Gíngilos
at the entrance
to Samariá

Climb over the dry boulders and continue on to the aban-doned village of **Samariá**, whose residents were relocated when the park was formed. The Church of Óssia María (Mary's Bones) dates from the early 14th century. This is nearly the halfway point, and a good picnic spot. You will find a warden's station here.

Beyond, the gorge deepens beneath dramatic cliffs and you criss-cross the stream several times on the approach to the **Sideróportes** (Iron Gates). These sheer rock walls rise up over 300m high but are only 3.5m wide, the narrowest point in the gorge. Beyond, the path abruptly opens out to a flat, shadeless riverbed. At the end of the park it's a further gruelling 2km in the hot sun to **Agia Rouméli**, whose taver-nas are a welcome sight.

TAKING A BREAK

Bring a **picnic** as there are no refreshments until you reach the end of the gorge.

➕ 179 E2   🚌 Bus from Chaniá for Omalós/Samariá

SAMARIÁ GORGE: INSIDE INFO

Top tips Don't be fooled by the kilometre markers; they only mark distances with-in the park, not the full length of the walk.
• **Park wardens** patrol the gorge to make sure no one is left overnight, and mules stand by to rescue the injured.
• Get an **early start**. You'll have more time to linger without worrying about missing the boat.
• If your **footwear is inadequate** you may not be allowed to enter the gorge.

At Your Leisure

5 Melidóni Cave

Whereas other caves on Crete are filled with myths and legends, the Melidóni Cave is filled with the spirits of the people who died there, and it is one of the most chilling memorials on the island. In 1824, while the Cretans were fighting for their independence from the Turks, 300 villagers hid inside the cave from approaching Turkish forces. When asked to surrender the villagers refused, at which point the Turkish commander blocked the cave entrance to stop the air supply. The villagers created new air holes in the network of passages but the Turks were equally quick to seal these. They then opened the cave entrance slightly and lit fires at the mouth so smoked poured in and everyone inside choked to death. A memorial in the centre of the cave marks the spot where the bones of the people were gathered together years later and buried.

Without this background the cave would merely be an interesting natural phenomenon, comprising one large chamber at the foot of a staircase carved out of the rocks. This can be slippery and is also very poorly lit, so take a torch if you can. New areas of the cave are still being explored, and though shown on the map in the official booklet they will not be open until about the year 2005.

➕ 181 F4 ✉ Near Melidóni ⏰ Daily 9–6.30/7 pm, Apr–Nov 🚌 Bus to Pérama from Réthymno 🎫 Moderate 📷 Photography allowed

At work in the potters' village of Margarítes

6 Margarítes

There can be no better place on the island to buy ceramics than in the hill village of Margarítes, where pottery is a tradition and many artisans have their workshops. As the main road winds through the village, bright displays of pottery can be seen on every corner. Several of the craftsmen produce similar goods (bowls, jugs, plates, vases) distinguished only by their patterns and colours, but a few produce work of a very distinctive style and to a very high standard, so take the time to explore the different workshops. Even if you don't plan to buy, the pretty town is a delightful place to wander around.

➕ 181 F3 🚌 Bus from Réthymno

7 Eléftherna

The site of the city of Archéa Eléftherna (Ancient Eléftherna) is one of the most impressive on the island, set on a ridge in a valley high in the hills between two villages. Don't stop in the village of Eléftherna itself (you can

Spíli and its lion fountain (inset)

reach the site from there but it is a long walk) but go on to Archéa Eléftherna from where the remains are more easily reached. Like Lató (▶ 104), Eléftherna was a major Doric city and later a Roman settlement before falling into ruin. Not too many remains can be seen today, but the setting is superb.

🚹 181 F3 🖂 Archéa Eléftherna
🕐 Open access 🚌 Bus from Réthymno 💷 Free ❓ Photography allowed

🎱 North Coast Beaches

The beaches along the north coast in this part of the island include long stretches of golden sand, with several busy holiday spots among them. East of Irakleío the first two main resorts are **Bali** (▶ 182 A5) and **Pánormos** (▶ 181 F4), the latter being the smaller but with the better beach. It is only west of here, though, that the beaches come into their own.

East of Réthymno, and in the town itself, are some lovely stretches of sand, with more to be found if you carry on driving west towards Chaniá. Look for the sign for Petres Bridge, where there is access to a

beautiful long beach with a few cafés, sunbeds and parasols. Parking and more facilities can be found opposite the turning for Episkopí, with golden sand running for miles.

One of the most attractive resorts is **Georgioúpoli** (▶ 180 B3), with a wide sandy beach backed by dunes. The town itself has not lost its character despite being popular with visitors. **Kalýves** (▶ 180 A4), closer to Chaniá, also has a good sandy beach. **Plataniás** (▶ 179 D4) is a large, lively resort west of Chaniá with a booming nightlife scene in summer.

🟒 Spíli

One of the main towns between Réthymno and the south coast, Spíli is the ideal place to break a journey. Huddled beneath mountain slopes, its back streets are those of a busy hill town, a world away from the holiday resorts on the coast. In the centre of the town on a small square a delightful Venetian fountain comprises a row of 19 lions' heads spouting water into a stone trough.

🚹 181 E2 🚌 Bus from Réthymno

10 Moní Préveli

The monastery at Préveli is one of the loveliest in the whole of southern Crete and has a revered place in Greek history for its role in the Battle of Crete (► 17–19). During World War II the monks here risked the wrath (and worse) of the Nazis by providing shelter to Allied troops trapped on Crete after the evacuation, and subsequently aided the Cretan resistance movement.

Originally dating back to the 17th century, the monastery's isolated setting and grounds dotted with palm trees and pomegranate trees are irresitible to the photographer. Within the "lion-coloured" walled enclosure is a chapel, the cells where the monks still live and peaceful courtyards.

One of the monastery's cellars has been effectively turned into a small museum, a long and narrow vaulted room whose alcoves and cabinets contain icons, vestments, bibles and other religious items. The magnificently adorned chapel has an elabo-

The Monastery at Préveli

rate gold and red Bishop's Chair, an ornate pulpit, icon-covered walls and, in the centre, a cross said to contain a piece of the True Cross.

In the courtyard near by an old fountain exhorts visitors to wash their faces and wash their sins away. For those who want to bathe more fully, there are several good beaches close by, including **Préveli Beach** and **Palm Beach**, both accessible by following the main road eastward from the monastery.

🕂 181 D2 ☎ 08320-31246 🕐 Daily 8–7, 25 Mar–31 May; Mon–Sat 8–1:30, 3:30–7pm, Sun 8–7, 1 Jun–31 Oct 🚌 Buses from Réthymno and to/from Plakiás 💷 Inexpensive ❓ Photography allowed except inside church and museum

11 Plakiás

With its long, wide beach backed by tamarisk trees, Plakiás is a terrific south coast retreat for those who want to get away from it all without completely leaving civilisation behind. There are a few hotels, bars and restaurants, and although the resort bears little resemblance to what it was 20 years ago, it's still attractive, with

a long promenade, a more remote feel than many other resorts on Crete and plenty to do. A long curve of sand sweeps away at the eastern end of town, and you'll find more good beaches if you continue along the coast to the west. You can take hill walks to the north or walk to the monastery at Préveli (see above), while drivers can enjoy two of Crete's most dramatic gorges, **Kotsifoú** and **Kourtaliótiko**, to the north.

➕ 180 C2 🚌 Buses from Réthymno and Agía Galíni

12 Fragkokástelo

The Venetian fortress at Fragkokástelo is one of the largest on the island. Built in this remote setting in 1371 to help protect the

Dew in the Morning

In May 1828 the Greeks raised their flag at the fortress in defiance of the ruling Turks and in the subsequent battle 385 Cretans were killed. Locals claim that every year, on 28 May, these souls can be seen marching towards Fragkokástelo. The dead are called *droussoulites*, or dew shades, because they are said to appear with the morning dew.

south coast from pirates and other raiders, it was also used to keep unruly local Cretans in check. However, the fortress's imposing nature is somewhat undermined when you discover that today it is a mere shell, with nothing inside the sturdy walls. Still, it stands on a lovely spot with good beaches and marshland where wildlife flourishes close by.

➕ 180 B2 ⚙ Open access 🍴 Several beach tavernas, including Flisbos and Korali (€/€€) 🚌 Plakiás–Chóra Sfakia buses pass by

13 Ímpros Gorge

Samariá (▶ 140–141) may be more famous and more dramatic, but the Ímpros Gorge (Farángi Ímprou) offers a good half-day's walk through some of southern Crete's most spectacular scenery. It is also more accessible and not as crammed with other walkers. The entrance is just south of the village of Ímpros and the gorge runs for about 6km towards the sea, stopping just short of the coast. It can be tackled easily by anyone who is reasonably fit, and the rock formations, deep sides and abundant wild flowers in spring are superb. Tour companies in nearby towns offer organised trips, which are worth considering, as a one-way walk – even if you have your own car – needs a little organising.

➕ 180 A2 ⚙ Open access 🍴 Café serving light meals at start and end of walk (€) 🚌 Buses to Ímpros village from Chaniá and Chóra Sfakia

Looking down the Ímpros Gorge

14 Chóra Sfakia

The main town of southern Crete's Sfakia region has an atmosphere all its own. Its lazy charm and lovely coastal setting, together with the peace that descends when the day's visitors have left, will captivate anyone who spends a few days here. The focus of the town is its small harbour, lined on one side with cafés and restaurants. Beyond here the streets start to rise, some steeply, hemmed in as the town is by the lower slopes of the Levká Óri, or White Mountains. It was through these mountains that Allied troops were evacuated after the Battle of Crete (▶ 17–19), arriving exhausted at Chóra Sfakia to await the rescuing

Pleasant waterside restaurants overlook the harbour at Chóra Sfakia

ships. Today there is only a small pebble beach, but there are better beaches along the nearby coasts, good walks in the mountains and a get-away-from-it-all feeling.

🚹 179 F1 🍴 Numerous cafés and tavernas line the harbour (€/€€)
🚌 Bus from Chaniá

15 Gávdos Island

The largest of Crete's offshore islands, Gávdos is also the most southerly point in Europe. It takes a bit of a hike to get to the island's southern tip, but a visit here will show you a part of Crete that few people see. With a resident population of about 50, facilities are few, but you might find a room to rent and many people camp here in the summer. One or two small cafés serve simple food in summer and beaches are good, if you don't

mind a walk to get to them as there is no public transport. However, while Gávdos might seem like heaven to some people, it is not for everyone.

➕ 179 D1 🍴 Some cafés (€)
🚢 Summer ferries from Chóra Sfakia and Palaiochóra

🔟6 Loutró

Loutró, with its blue and white buildings set around a cove against a stunning mountain backdrop, is one of the most picturesque villages on the island. There is nothing to do here – the tiny village is little more than a waterfront strip with several tavernas and rooms to rent – but that is where the attraction lies for many visitors. You needn't waste time looking for the road to Loutró, as there isn't one: you either need to walk from the nearest road a few kilometres away, or do what most people do and take the boat in and out. If you tire of the small pebble

beach there are good coastal walks in both directions to better beaches, or you can head inland to the mountains. Despite the influx of visitors in summer, vastly outnumbering local people, in comparison to most places on Crete Loutró remains an idyllic retreat.

➕ 179 F1 🍴 Several simple cafés (€/€€) 🚢 Boats from Chóra Sfakia and other south coast towns

Allied graves at Soúda

🔟7 Soúda and the Akrotíri Peninsula

The Akrotíri Peninsula, to the immediate east of Chaniá, is often neglected by visitors but it offers lovely hill scenery, ancient monasteries and some of the most peaceful spots on the north coast – despite the fact that Chaniá's airport and

For Children

The **Fortezza** at Réthymno (➤ 133)

The **Little Trains** in Chaniá and Réthymno

Horse and buggy ride in Chaniá

Melidóni Cave (➤ 142)

The **beach** and **castle** at Fragkokástelo (➤ 145)

Beaches everywhere

No roads lead to Loutró

ferry port are both located here. The easiest way of getting to the peninsula from Chaniá is to drive east out of the town centre towards the airport and follow the occasional signs for the Venizélos Graves. These are on a hillside in a small garden, with terrific views over the city. Crete's premier politician and one-time Greek leader, Elefthérios Venizélos, lies buried here, and close by is the grave of his son, Sophocles.

Further out on the peninsula are three monasteries – **Agia Triáda, Gouvernétou** and **Korakies**. Agia Triáda, with its orange-coloured walls, is particularly beautiful and should not be missed. The others are a few kilometres beyond up a winding road.

Soúda, on the bay of the same name, is on the far side of the peninsula. On the outskirts of the town is the beautiful and peaceful **Allied War Cemetery**, where lie hundreds of soldiers who died during World War II. The headstones look out over the water, the young men buried in the soil of the island they tried to defend.

The growing resort of Palaiochóra

✚ 179 E4 Allied War Cemetery
✉ 1km northwest of Soúda 🕐 Open access 🍴 Plenty of cafés and restaurants in Soúda (€) 💶 Free
❓ Photography allowed

🔟 Palaiochóra

The major resort in southwest Crete is Palaiochóra, an appealing town with two beaches either side of a headland and a great deal of easy-going charm. Standing on the headland are the ruins of a Venetian fortress dating back to 1279, with a sandy beach to the west and a pebble beach to the east. The south coast can be quite windy, and they do say that if one beach is affected by the wind the other one will be sheltered, but that isn't always the case.

The town has developed rapidly as a tourist resort over the last ten years or so, and many hotels, rooms to rent, souvenir shops, travel agents and restaurants have sprung up. Despite that, its identity as a town has not been lost, especially on the main street at night when traffic is banned, chairs spill out from cafés and bars, the air is filled with the chatter of conversation and people enjoy wandering round in a very relaxed atmosphere.

✚ 178 B2
🍴 Numerous cafés and restaurants (€–€€€)
🚌 Bus from Chaniá

Where to... Stay

Prices

Prices are for a double room per night in high season including taxes

€ under €60   €€ €60–€100   €€€ over €100

Casa Delfino €€€

The best place in town is this 17th-century former palace, built around a fabulous Venetian-style courtyard. It has studio rooms, ordinary rooms and suites, all of which are bright and cheerful and superbly decorated with old photos on the walls. Air-conditioning, mini-bar, satellite TVs and marble Jacuzzi baths are standard. There's also a large bar, a breakfast room, a roof terrace and a lounge with internet access for guests, tucked away in the old quarter.

✚ 179 E4 ⊠ Theofanous 9, Chaniá ☎ 08210-87400/93098; fax: 08210-96500; email: casadel@cha.forthnet.gr; www.casadelfino.com

Doma €€

Though about 3km east of the town centre, this hotel is convenient if you are arriving at or departing from the airport. Either way, a stay in this converted century-old mansion is memorable. The historical feel is apparent in the general décor, although all rooms are en-suite with air-conditioning and TV. The third-floor dining room has great views towards the town, and front rooms have views out to sea. Luxurious it is not, but it is inexpensive and charming. Booking is advisable in high season.

✚ 179 E4 ⊠ Eleftherion Venizélou 124, Chaniá ☎ 08210-51772; fax: 08210-41578 ⓖ Apr–Oct

Hotel El Greco €€

Perfectly situated on an almost traffic-free street in the old town, just a minute's walk from the harbour, the El Greco is a family-run hotel with only 23 rooms. They are all a good size and well appointed, some being suites with extra living space. They all have air-conditioning, TVs, phones and the welcome bonus of a fridge. There's a relaxing bar downstairs and a terrific roof garden with wonderful views over the roofs of the old town to the sea.

✚ 179 E4 ⊠ Theotokopoúlos 49, Chaniá ☎ 08210-94030/9432/91818; fax: 08210-91829; email: hotel@elgreco.gr ⓖ Mar–Nov

Hotel Fortezza €€

This fairly new hotel has been built in traditional style, echoing the Venetian feel of the old town around. It is in one of the quieter areas of Réthymno, mostly pedestrianised and close to the Venetian fort that gives the hotel its name. The best rooms have balconies and

overlook the small swimming pool, so try to get one of these. Booking is recommended, even in low season.

✚ 181 D3 ⊠ Melisinou 16, Réthymno ☎ 08310-23828/55551; fax: 08310-54073; email: mliodak@ret.forthnet.gr

Galaxy Rooms €

Galaxy is one of the most pleasant of the many "rooms to rent" options in Palaiochóra. Front rooms, above the Galaxy Fish Restaurant, have large balconies overlooking the town's pebble beach and the sea. The en-suite rooms are a good size and surprisingly well equipped with TV, fridge, phone and washing line. They are also clean and well maintained. Though no breakfast is served, there are several choices near by. The owner also has more rooms across town near the sandy beach.

✚ 178 B2 ⊠ Palaiochóra ☎ 08230-41059/41514; fax: 08230-41518/41279 ⓖ Apr–Oct

Grecotel Creta Palace €€

Although a de luxe standard hotel, prices are reasonable given its quality and location; it's about 4km east of Réthymno centre, beyond the wonderful town beach. The rooms are simple but bright and clean, and the hotel has all the facilities you might expect including three swimming pools (one indoors), restaurants, bars, gym, tennis courts and watersports.

🕂 181 D3 ⊠ Misiria Beach, Réthymno ☎ 08310-55181; fax: 08310-54085; email: sales_cp@cp_grecotel.gr; www.grecotel.gr ⏰ Apr–Oct

Hotel Ideon €€

In a wonderful location overlooking the harbour, the Ideon is set back from the main road and has a public car park (vital in Réthymno) directly opposite. The hotel has 100 rooms, all with balconies overlooking either the sea or the private swimming pool. The rooms are modern, with phone, radio, safe, air-conditioning and bath. The slightly pricier suites also have a fridge and TV.

🕂 181 D3 ⊠ Plateía Plastíra 10, Réthymno ☎ 08310-28667; fax: 08310-28670; www.helsun.gr ⏰ Mar–Oct

Ifigenia Rooms and Studios €€

Not one hotel but several places close together near the Venetian harbour, all are owned by the same enterprising young man and all have the same flair when it comes to the decoration. Some of the rooms are stunningly designed with stone arches, four-poster beds, galleried areas and open-plan baths adding to the striking look. As well as the Ifigenia I, II and III there are the Ifigenia Studios, Pension Orio and Hotel Captain Vassilis.

🕂 179 E4 ⊠ Angelou 18 and others, Chaniá ☎ 08210-99184 or 0944-501319 (mobile); fax: 08210-94357; email: nin1955@otenet.gr; www.ifigenia.com

Palazzo Hotel €€

You'll find this delightful small hotel on a quiet street in the old town. It was once a mansion and the 11 rooms, named after Greek gods and heroes, are full of wood-panelling and old-fashioned touches, though with modern bathrooms, TVs, fridges and phones. The generous breakfast is one reason to stay here, others being the friendly service and ideal location: use the public car park west of the harbour if you are driving.

🕂 179 E4 ⊠ Theotokopoulou 54, Chaniá ☎ 08210-93227; fax: 08210-93229 ⏰ Mar–Nov

Palazzo Rimondi €€€

Tucked away in the back streets of the old town, the Rimondi is a small, stylish hotel that spreads over several 15th-century Venetian houses. The conversion has been very tastefully done, retaining such features as the decorated ceilings, while giving the rooms every modern convenience. The 21 rooms are more like mini-suites, with separate living and kitchen areas, and there's a small swimming pool in the inner courtyard.

🕂 179 E4 ⊠ Xanthoudídou 21, Réthymno ☎ 08310-51289; email: rimondi@otenet.gr

Vritomartis Hotel and Bungalows €€

One of the best and best-run hotels on Crete, the Vritomartis has its own pool and restaurant, and grounds lush with vegetation. It is also Greece's only naturist hotel, though non-naturists are also welcome and nudity is not allowed inside the hotel buildings. The rooms are big, bright and white, and all have balconies though some only overlook the car park. There is also a large bar and a restaurant, and plenty of organised activities and tours.

🕂 179 F1 ⊠ Chóra Sfakía ☎ 08250-91112; fax: 08250-91222; email: vritna@otenet.gr; www.naturism-crete.com ⏰ Apr–Oct

Where to...
Eat and Drink

Prices
Prices are for a two-course meal for one person, excluding drinks and tips

€ under €9   €€ €9–€14.5   €€€ over €14.5

Amphora €€
The only thing that distinguishes this unassuming restaurant from the others at the western end of the harbour is the fact that there is no waiter outside trying to coax you in. The food, however, is excellent. Fresh fish naturally features but *meze* are a speciality here, and the mixed Greek plate can certainly be recommended. The fact that they use only virgin olive oil to prepare their dishes certainly shows in the results.

🚹 179 E4 ⊠ Akti Koundouriotou 49, Chaniá ☎ 08210-93224 🕒 Daily 10 am–midnight, Apr–Oct

Avli €€€
The best spot to choose here is the lovely open-roofed garden court-yard planted with large palms, though there are also tables on the street outside and in another indoor area. The menu advertises "Gastronomic experiments with Cretan produce and an open mind", and to find out if they succeed try one of the house specialities such as wild kid goat cooked with honey and thyme.

🚹 181 D3 ⊠ Xanthoudidou 22/Radamanthyos, Réthymno ☎ 08310-26213 🕒 Daily noon–2.30, 6–midnight

Cavo d'Oro €€€
There are numerous fish restaurants cheek-by-jowl around the little Venetian harbour in Réthymno, and with every waiter trying to persuade you to eat in their estab-lishment it can be very hard to choose between them. It is worth making the effort to find the Cavo d'Oro, which looks like all the rest with its displays of fresh fish and seafood, but is rated the best by the local people.

🚹 181 D3 ⊠ Nearchou 42–43, Réthymno ☎ 08310-24446 🕒 Daily lunch and dinner

Fanari €
Walk west of the inner harbour – where the waiters almost drag you physically inside – to this quieter stretch where locals tend to go. Here you will find a much more laid-back atmosphere, with the restaurant on one side of the road and the outdoor seating area, with bright yellow and white tablecloths, on the other overlooking the sea.

Check the *meze* for some interest-ing options, perhaps followed by grilled meat and a glass or two of the tasty house wine.

🚹 181 D3 ⊠ Kefalogiani 16, Réthymno ☎ 08310-54849 🕒 Daily 11 am–late

Galaxy Fish Restaurant €€
This excellent fish restaurant has roadside seating directly opposite the pebble beach, an upper open patio beneath a red-tiled roof and a further raised indoor seating area. Stretched across the back wall of the latter is a large fisherman's net hung with crab shells, lobsters, starfish and other sea creatures. Although there are meat options on the menu, and old Greek favourites, the speciality is quite simple, as the menu states: "fresh fish from Palaiochóra". Enjoy the wine from the barrel, too.

🚹 178 B2 ⊠ Palaiochóra ☎ 08230-41059/41514; fax: 08230-4518/41279 🕒 Daily lunch and dinner, Apr–Oct

O Gounas €€

There are only a few tables on the narrow street outside O Gounas as all the action takes place inside, where live music is staged nightly – but don't show up too early as the restaurant doesn't open until 8 pm and it takes a while to get going, though early birds are more likely to get the best tables. The stage is at the far end of the cellar-like interior, beyond an archway. The menu makes no concessions to fashion and is resolutely Greek, plain and tasty, but the place really buzzes.

➕ 181 D3 ✉ Koroneou 6, Réthymno
☎ 08310-28816 ⏰ Daily 8 pm–1 am

Kyria Maria €€

You'll find Maria's original little restaurant in a narrow alley tucked away behind the Rimondi Fountain. Tables covered with dark red and black striped woven table-cloths of traditional designs line both sides of the street, and cages of twittering birds hang from the buildings. So successful has Maria's home-cooking become (her lamb *kleftiko* is a deliciously tender speciality) that she now has two other restaurants, at Fotaki 22 and Himarras 8.

➕ 181 D3 ✉ Moshovitou 20, Réthymno ☎ 08310-29078
⏰ Daily 8 am–1 am

Semiramis €€

The outdoor seating of this large taverna runs alongside one whole block of a narrow street, and there is also a charming garden area with a fountain; this is much in demand, so expect to wait for a table. In season, Cretan musicians play here and in the main taverna building over the street nightly. The food is nothing out of the ordinary, consisting of the usual Greek fare of grills, fish and meat dishes, but there is chatty atmosphere and the whole operation is run briskly and in a friendly fashion.

➕ 179 E4 ✉ Skoulon 8, Chaniá
☎ 08210-98650 ⏰ Daily 10 am–
late, Apr–Nov

Sultana's €€

A 15th-century Venetian palace in the heart of the old town is the setting for this characterful place, built around a courtyard now set out with tables. For a time it was home to a Turkish official who walled off the courtyard to shield his harem from public view, hence the name. The food is traditional Greek fare but there is live music nightly in season and the setting makes for a great night out.

➕ 179 E4 ✉ Moshon 2, Chaniá
☎ 08210-97128 ⏰ Daily 7 pm–late

Tamam €€

Some of the best food in town can be sampled at the former Turkish bathhouse, hence the nightly queues for a table by both locals and visitors alike. Despite the passing crowds, most people prefer to sit outside in the narrow street to enjoy the imaginative dishes combining the best of the Mediterranean, from Italian risotto via Greek baked red peppers to

Middle Eastern lamb with rice and yoghurt. There's a good range for vegetarians, too. The wine list runs to almost four pages and includes many wines from the mainland as well as from Crete.

➕ 179 E4 ✉ Zambeliou 49, Chaniá
☎ 08210-96080 ⏰ Daily 1 pm–
12.30 am

Well of the Turk €€

Allow plenty of time to find this back-alley place, near Plateía 1821. The search will be rewarded, though, as British owner Jenny Payavla, who lived in Tangier, combines the best of Cretan and North African cuisine. Dishes range from simple shish kebabs and couscous to specialities including calamari (squid) stuffed with seafood, herbs and rice and served with turmeric rice. There's also a bar inside. Don't forget to ask to see the actual Well of the Turk.

➕ 179 E4 ✉ Kalinikou Sarpaki 1–3,
Chaniá ☎ 08210-54547
⏰ Wed–Mon 7 pm–late

Where to...
Shop

The best shopping in western Crete is in Réthymno and Chaniá. For ceramics, visit the pottery village of **Margarites** (➤ 142). Two potters worth seeking out for quality wares are Manólis Kallérgis (tel: 08340-92262) and Nikos Kavgalákis at the southern end of the village.

RÉTHYMNO

You could think of Réthymno's warren of streets as one giant bazaar. Souvenir shops abound and there is a good selection of clothing since this is the main shopping area for locals too, particularly along Odós Arkadíou. There are also many jewellery shops around town. The loggia now houses the **Museum Shop for the Ministry of Culture** (open 8–3:30), where you can buy reproductions of ancient art from major museums. For genuine antiques, try **Palaiopoleíou**, Soulíou 40. Artistic woodturner **Nikos Síragas**, at Petaliotí 2, creates beautiful bowls, vases and sculptures from olive and carob wood. Also try **Olive Tree Wood**, Arambatzoglou 35, for wooden crafts.

Manólis Stagakis and his son Michalis are two of the last lyra makers who carve instruments by hand. Their workshop is at **Dimakopoulou 6** where you can order your own custom-made lyra.

Ethnikís Andístasis is the market street near the Porta Guora, with delicious foodstuffs. There is also a Thursday **market** on Dhimitrakaki, by the public gardens. Among those bookshops carrying English titles are **International Press**, at Venizélou, and **I Petihaki**, near the waterfront. English books are expensive, but you may find a bargain at one of the second-hand bookshops around town.

CHANIÁ

Most of the old town south of the fortress is given over to tourist shops. On **Theotokopoulou**, the main street, two gift shops stand out: **Paraoro** (No 16), selling beautiful handmade glass, ceramics and metal sculpture; and **1885** (opposite at No 11), selling handmade silver and clothes.

Roka Carpets, 61 Zambelíou, is stacked with colourful rugs, blankets and wall hangings, all handwoven on a traditional loom here in the shop. At **Top Hanas**, 3 Angelou, by the Naval Museum, old Cretan blankets and rugs are displayed in an old house. For beautiful embroidery and tablecloths made on a loom, try **Pili**, 40 Kriari Street, below the tourist office.

Meli, 45 Odos Kondilaki, is one of the best shops on the island for Cretan natural products. You can buy vinegar, olive oil, raki and wine in beautiful decorative glass bottles, honey and organic olives. At the **covered market** (➤ 139), shop for Cretan cheeses, herbs, spices and other foodie gifts.

Nearby **Odós Skrídlof** is the place for leatherware, and though the old workshops are mostly gone you'll find some of the best prices for belts, bags, sandals and other goods, even Cretan high boots. **Odós Sifaka** is the street of the knife-makers if you want an authentic Cretan dagger – try the **O Arménis** workshop.

The **Local Artistic Handicrafts' Association**, at the old harbour behind the mosque, carries a range, in both price and quality, of ceramics, sculpture, glass and jewellery, including some very artistic pieces. **Verekinthos Craft Village**, just outside town at Chania Industrial Park, on the south side of the National Highway, is another good place for traditional handicrafts.

Where to...
Be Entertained

RÉTHYMNO NIGHTLIFE

Most of the big discos can be found east of town among the large hotels. In the centre try the **Opera Club** on Salaminos, **Rock Café Fortezza** by the inner harbour and, around the corner, **NYC-Metropolis**. A number of rock bars are clustered around Plateia Petihaki and the streets behind the inner harbour. **Odysseas**, on Venizélou, has nightly live Cretan music and dancing geared for tourists.

CHANIÁ NIGHTLIFE

Chaniá's largest discos are also out of town, mainly west along the coast at Plataniás. **Splendid, Privilege** and **Mylos Club** are always packed. In town, the main clubs are along the inner harbour, behind the mosque. These include **Club Xania** and **Klik Dancing Bar**, with **Platiá** upstairs offering live Greek music. Further along the inner harbour are **Four Seasons** and **Prime Vision Ariadne**, the latter a popular venue for live modern Greek music. Chaniá's largest discos are **Energy**, at Halidhon, and **Skalidhi**, near the Schiavo Bastion.

MUSIC AND FESTIVALS

For traditional and contemporary Greek music in **Chaniá**, look for handbills advertising Cretan musicians. They often play at **Lyrakia**, a bar by the waterfront, and **Café Kriti**, behind the *arsendi* at 22 Kalergon. Chaniá's cultural calendar of performances runs from mid-July to September; enquire at the tourist office (▶ 37).

The main cultural event in **Rethymno** is the **Renaissance Festival**, with international theatre and music performances held in August and September in the Venetian fortress. The programme is announced in mid-July; contact the town hall (tel: 08310-53383) for information and tickets. There is also a **Wine Festival** held in the Municipal Park in July.

BOAT TRIPS AND WATERSPORTS

Dolphin Cruises in Réthymno (tel: 08310-57666) run boat trips to pirate caves and beaches on the north coast; or cruise to Bali on a pirate ship with **Captain Hook** (tel: 08310-57666).

Boat trips are offered all along Chaniá's old harbour. These include a half-day cruise on **Aphrodite** (tel: 0930-2977292). Alternatively, take a trip on a glass-bottom boat with

Evagelos (tel: 0945 874283) or the **Posidon Sea Discoverer** (tel: 08210-55838).

Limnoupolis Waterpark (tel: 08210-33246, open May–Oct 10–6:30), is 7km from Chaniá on the Omalós road.

Two dive centres in Réthymno are **Paradise Dive Centre**, 73 and 75 El Venizélou (tel: 08310-26317) and **Dolphin Diving Centre**, Hotel Rethymno mare-Scaleta (tel: 08310-71703). In Chaniá, try **Blue Adventurers Diving**, 69 Daskalogianni Street (tel: 08210-40608).

OTHER ACTIVITIES

In Réthymno, **Olympic Bike Travel** (tel: 08310-72383) offers organised bike rides in the countryside and mountain biking. **The Happy Walker**, 56 Tompazi Street (tel: 08310-52920), organises guided walks in the countryside.

Englishman **Tony Fennymore** (tel: 08210-87139) leads walking tours around Chaniá.

Walks & Tours

1 ZARÓS & THE ROÚVAS GORGE

Walk

This exhilarating walk takes you to a mountain monastery and up a rocky gorge, rich in flora and fauna, with beautiful views of central Crete's Psiloreitis range. Start early to avoid the worst of the midday heat.

1–2

Zarós, nestling at the southern foot of Mount Ída (Psiloreítis), is famous throughout Crete for its spring water, bottled on the edge of town. Drive west through town and park on the main road near the post office. (To shorten the walk, drive to the lake.)

2–3

Continue along the main road until you see signs for the Ídi Hotel and Lake Votomos just past a modern fountain. Turn right and follow the narrow road up the hill to the **Ídi Hotel** (▶ 92), about 1km from town.

Checking out the Roúvas Gorge trail

DISTANCE 8km
TIME 3–4 hours
START/END POINT Zarós ✚ 182 B2

3–4

The road makes a sharp bend to the left. Continue uphill past the trout farm – its fish is a Zarós speciality. After 15 minutes you reach small **Lake Votomos**, formed by the Zarós springs, with a good taverna on the south side.

4–5

Both the right- and left-hand paths lead round the shore of the lake and up stone steps. Go through the gate and proceed along the dirt path that ascends above the olive groves. As you round a bend you will see **Moní Ágios Nikólaos** ahead on your left. Although the complex appears modern, the church has frescoes dating from the 14th century.

5–6

Opposite a little wooden bridge beside the monastery a set of rock steps on your right leads up to the tiny chapel of **Ágios Efthímios**, filled with icons. Cross the bridge and follow the path as it turns sharply to the right and zigzags up and away from the monastery. Follow the yellow arrows and markings painted on the rocks to guide you through the boulders. You are now entering the **Roúvas Gorge**, which the locals also call Ágios Nikólaos Gorge, after the monastery.

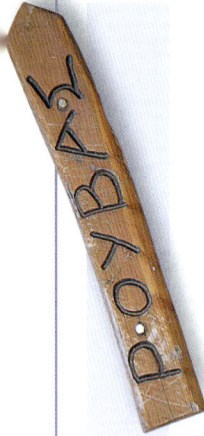

6–7

After a short, steep climb you come to a fence. Go right, following the arrow as the path curves around the next hill. Take the stone steps up and through a gate. The 1.6km path through the gorge alternates easy stretches along the herb-covered hillsides with steeper climbs up stone steps. The route is well marked with yellow arrows.

7–8

The path follows the steep side of the gorge, then drops down through the ravine and doubles back on the far side. Here it becomes a wide track leading uphill to a signpost. To extend the walk to a full day, follow the trail up through the peaks for 2.7km to the mountain **Church of Ágios Ioánnis.**

8–9

To return, follow the sign for Votomos and Ágios Nikólaos. This dirt track is narrow and steep at first, so go slow. There are beautiful views down the gorge to Zarós. After passing some beehives turn left on to a wide dirt

road that leads downhill to the monastery. Follow the sign for Votomos round behind it to the wooden bridge, and return to Zarós the way you came.

The church at Ágios Nikólaos

Taking a Break

Taverna Oasis, opposite the post office in Zarós, is a cheerful spot. The Idi Hotel's pretty courtyard bar, the **Votomos Taverna** (▶ 94), and the **taverna** at Lake Votomos are other options.

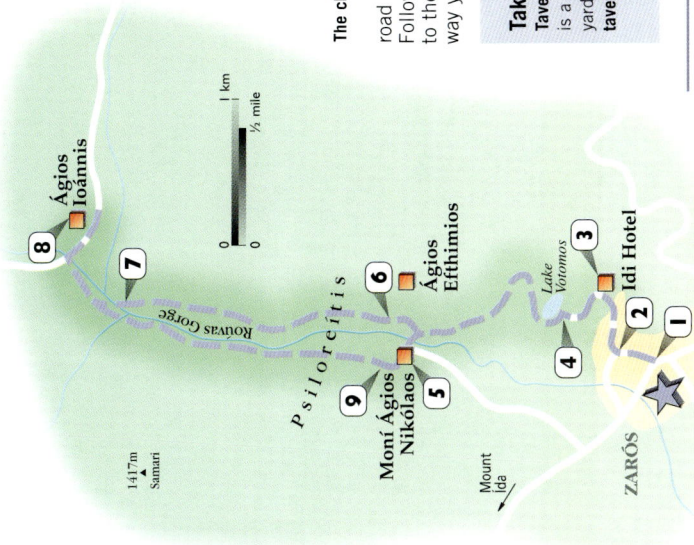

Map labels

- 8 Ágios Ioánnis
- 7
- Roúvas Gorge
- Psiloreítis
- 1417m Samari
- 9 Moní Ágios Nikólaos
- 5
- 6 Ágios Efthimios
- Lake Votomos
- 4
- 2
- 3 Idi Hotel
- 1
- ZARÓS
- Mount Ida

0 ½ mile
0 1 km

2 ORCHARDS & OLIVE GROVES

Walk

You will often see windmills from a distance while driving through Crete, but this walk enables you to view them right up close. Following tracks and quiet roads, it links three of eastern Crete's unspoilt villages while meandering through olive groves and orchards of lemon trees, apple trees and bright red pomegranates.

DISTANCE 5km
TIME 2 hours
START/END POINT Límnes ⊞ 184 C4

1–2

Driving west to east on the old road between Neápoli and Ágios Nikólaos, pass the first few buildings as you arrive in Límnes and park just after a bridge on the right of the road at a sharp bend. Cross the bridge and walk along the path between white stone walls, past windmills and vines. After 50m you reach a large taverna, where you turn left and immediately right. Pomegranate trees line one side of the path, olives and figs the other. Further on are patches of sweetcorn and cabbages, and lime and lemon trees.

2–3

At the next junction, turn left and immediately right again. The path is flanked with olive groves and passes, on the right, a red-roofed church surrounded by flowers and shrubs. The path goes slightly uphill as it brings you into the village of Houmeriákos,

Olive trees (left) and pomegranates (right)

where you turn right, passing a shrine and a memorial on your right. In the village's small square there are a few cafés and shops. Take the road that goes uphill on the left side of the square, passing the church and an old fountain in a wall on your left.

3–4

Turn right at the first T-junction you reach, then follow the path as it swings left and climbs uphill. Pause on the corner for a view

The chapel above Houmeriákos

back to Limnes to the right, with the rest of the village of Houmeriákos to the left. From here carry on uphill, ignoring the track to the right. The main track then swings right and carries on uphill, leaving the village behind. On reaching a tarmac road, turn right.

4–5

The road swings right past more olive trees and heads towards a white chapel on a small hill. The chapel is locked but climb up to it for lovely views of the land around. Far to the left is Neápoli, to the right in the distance the village of Nikithianós, and to the

right of that is Límnes, where the walk started. Up the hill to the immediate left is Vrýses, your destination.

5–6

Continue on this quiet road until you reach a rough T-junction. The left fork leads up the long way round to the main Lasíthiou–Neápoli road, and you can turn right into upper Vrýses. If you turn right, however, it is an easy walk into lower Vrýses, with its narrow streets and whitewashed houses with vine-covered terraces. To find a café or a shop you will need to pick your way up one of the sets of steps that leads up to the main part of the village. Afterwards, simply retrace your steps to Limnes where there are several tavernas.

Taking a Break

There are simple tavernas and cafés in **Limnes, Houmeriákos** and **Vrýses.**

LÍMNES

NIKITHIANÓS

Neápoli

E75/90

HOUMERIÁKOS

Ágios Nikólaos

Chapel

Neápoli

VRÝSES

Lasithiou

750 metres

750 yards

3 THE LASÍTHIOU PLATEAU

Drive

The Lasíthiou Plateau stands 850m high in the Dikti Mountains, and is one of the most picturesque areas of the island. Orchards and olive groves cover the floors and slopes of the plateau.

DISTANCE 80km **TIME** 2–3 hours
START POINT Neápoli 🕂 184 C4
END POINT Mália Archaeological Site 🕂 184 B4

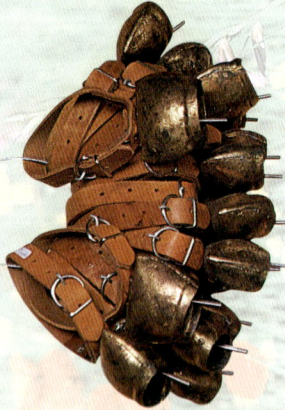

1–2

From the main square in Neápoli, follow the signs to the south for the "Plateau of Lasíthiou" (sometimes spelt "Lasíthi"). The route is well signed almost all the way. The good tarmac road quickly winds up through olive groves and the upper part of the village of Vryses. After turning right, again signed, you'll see lovely views of the Seléna Mountains ahead.

2–3

The road now descends to irrigated olive groves then climbs up the other side of the little valley into a stark and rocky landscape. About 12km from Neápoli you pass through

Traditional goat and sheep bells made in Neápoli

the hamlet of Káto Amygdáloi, and soon afterwards its big brother, Áno Amygdáloi.

3–4

After Áno Amygdáloi you reach the delightful village of Zenía, a cluster of vine-covered houses. At the far end of the village look for the spoon carver sitting outside his little house on the left.

4–5

The road winds higher now. Soon, on your right as you round a bend, you will see your first stone-based windmill. Next follows a series of small villages with women in traditional dress, donkeys with pack saddles, and villagers by the side of the road keen to sell you their honey, apples and *rakí*.

Poppies on the plateau

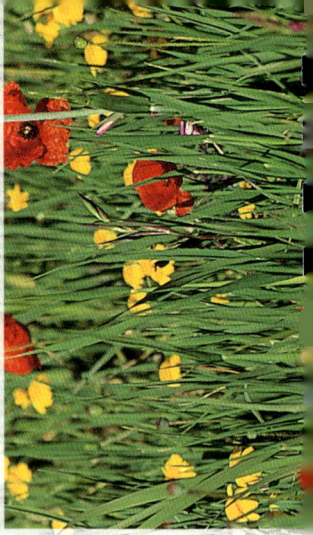

Konstandínos, where several shops sell weaving and textiles. From here, windmills start to appear more regularly in the fields.

7–8

In Ágios Geórgios, drive up past the church and go to the left following the signs for the **Diktaean Cave** (► 114) and the Venizélos Museum. Look for a bend to the right where a sign points left to the **Cretan Folklore Museum** and the **Venizélos Museum**. Park on the main road and walk up, as there is not much space to park above. Both little museums are worth seeing. The guidebook for the Folklore Museum has an old photo showing hundreds of white-sailed windmills ranged across the plain.

Map labels:

- Vrachási
- Voulisméni
- Neápoli E75/90
- Límnes
- Vrýses
- Ágios Nikólaos
- Káto Amygdáloi
- Áno Amygdáloi
- Zénia
- Roussapídia
- Argiró Neró
- Éxo Potamoí
- Mésa Lasíthi
- Ágios Konstandínos
- Mésa Potamoí
- Seléna
- 1599m
- Seléna
- Tavérna Skaranís
- Tzermiádo
- Cretan Folklore Museum
- Venizélos Museum
- Ágios Geórgios
- Psychró
- Avrakóntes
- Lasíthiou Plateau
- Pinakianó
- Diktaean Cave
- Kerá
- Krási
- Moní Kardiótissa
- Seli Ambélou Pass
- Káto Metóchi
- Pláti
- Mochós
- Stalída
- Mália
- Mália Palace
- E75/90
- Óros Díkti
- Óros Seléna

Map scale: 0 – 5 km / 0 – 3 miles

Looking for Zeus in the Diktaean Cave

5–6

The road gets increasingly steep as it crosses over the mountains, beyond which is the Lasíthiou Plateau itself. A good panoramic view can be had from the Tavérna Skaranís. As you descend there is a good view of the plots and fields on the flat central plain, and more villages to pass through where you'll find tavernas, shops and petrol stations.

6–7

After passing through Mésa Lasíthi you reach a T-junction. Turn left towards Ágios Geórgios. The first village after the T-junction is Ágios

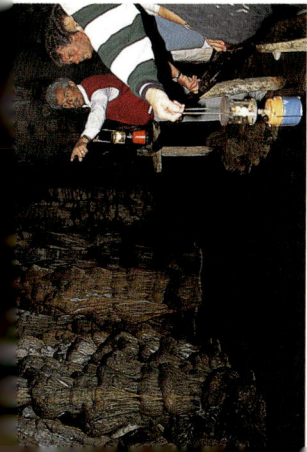

Taking a Break

Almost all the villages you pass through have tavernas and cafés. In Tzermiádo, the **Restaurant Kri-Kri** (tel: 08440-22170) has good local food, and the **Kali Mera** (tel: 08440-31913), just west of Psychro, has simple food and great views. The **Platanos taverna**, beneath the plane tree at Krasi, is an atmospheric spot.

8–9

Drive on out of the village and turn left at the sign for the Diktaean (Dhiktaean) Cave. The narrow road passes through more villages but take care when driving. Numerous tour buses use this route and the drivers are notoriously aggressive. Just beyond the town of Psychro, a sign points left up the hill 2km to the Diktaean Cave. There are more good views of the Lasithiou Plateau from the official car park.

9–10

Drive back down to Psychro and turn left, continuing the drive around the plateau. Orchards and farms are still plentiful, with olive groves and cows grazing on the plain.

A few kilometres beyond the village of Káto Metóhi, the road splits. Ignore the left turn to Irakleío for the moment but carry straight on to Tzermiádo, the largest old provincial town in the region. It's a pleasant old provincial town with handicrafts for sale and several restaurants. After a break you should return the way you came in, this time taking the road towards Irakleío.

10–11

Next follows one of the best parts of the drive, through the Selí Ambelou Pass.

Windmills can be seen along the ridge, to which you can walk if you want close-up views. As you descend from the pass, watch for the convent of Moní Kardiótissa (Our Lady of the Heart), on the outskirts of Kerá on your left. The little stone church contains lovely 14th-century frescoes.

11–12

The road curves down the mountain – an exhilarating drive through trees and olive groves, but watch for the sharp right turn to Krasí. Look for the enormous gnarled old plane tree in the village, and the nearby spring where locals fill their water bottles. Carry on through the village and rejoin the main road, simply following signs now for

Málía. The road curves back up over rocky hills, then switchbacks steeply back down again, a pretty and majestic drive through a dry rocky landscape.

12–13

This road brings you into Málía a back way. Turn right at the stop sign towards Ágios Nikólaos to reach the entrance to **Málía Palace** (▶ 102–103), a lovely place to end an impressive drive.

The way of life is slow to change in Lasithiou

4 THE AMÁRI VALLEY

Drive

The Amári Valley is one of the most beautiful and fertile regions of Crete. Here you will enjoy breathtaking views, orchards, vineyards and olive groves, and experience genuine Cretan hospitality in the lovely villages encountered en route. You can start from Réthymno and join the route at Agía Foteiní (31km from Réthymno), thus missing the winding roads with spectacular views out of Agía Galíni.

1–2

Take the only road out of Agía Galíni. Ignore the first two roads going off to the left. After 5km take the left turn for Amári and Réthymno. As you now head north you see the southern slopes of the Psiloreítis range ahead of you to the right. After 2km a sign in Greek indicates the left turn to **Agía Paraskeví**, which you take. The road is asphalt but watch out for the potholes. Olive groves lie on either side, and high in the hills

DISTANCE 100km
TIME 4–5 hours
START/END POINT Agía Galíni ✚ 181 F1

to your left is the mountain village of **Mélampes**.

2–3

In Agía Paraskeví the Church of the Panagía has fine 16th-century frescoes, though you will have to park and ask for directions as it is hidden away, off the main road. This road winds up through Agía Paraskeví and becomes more gravelly with sharp uphill bends. The high peak on the left on the far side of the valley is **Kédros** (1,776m).

Looking out over Amári town from the church tower

Detail from the 14th-century Panagía Church, Méronas

3–4

At the next junction take the left fork towards Réthymno. This is a wonderful road that snakes down into the valley and up the other side, with many a sharp bend. Look out for eagles and vultures circling overhead. Some 9km after the junction you reach an unmarked junction. Turn right and in 2km is the sleepy hamlet of Hordáki, and a few kilometres beyond that the hill town of **Áno Méros**, where white houses cover the hillside and there are a few cafés and shops.

4–5

About 4km beyond Áno Méros is **Vrýses**, with more shops and cafés and, on the right of the main road, a large white war memorial. These Amári Valley villages may look peaceful now, but after the kidnapping of the German

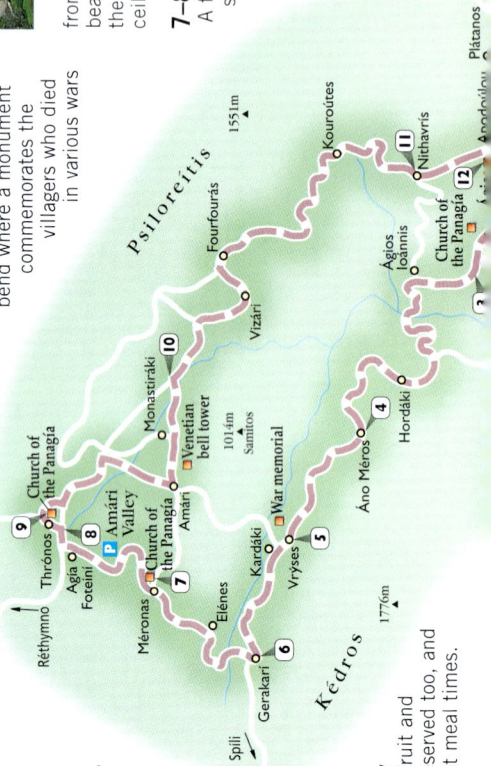

General Kreipe during World War II (▶19), German troops destroyed them by way of reprisal, slaughtering the village men, looting and burning the houses, and even dynamiting schools and cemeteries. The villages you pass through today were rebuilt after the war, although a few old churches survived the destruction.

5–6

About 5km after Vryses is **Gerakarí**, the centre of the cherry-growing area of the valley. If you pull over at the Taverna Yerákari on the right of the main street you can sample cherry brandy or cherry preserve, made by the owner. Other fruit and vegetables are preserved too, and food is available at meal times.

The glorious Amári Valley spreads out below

6–7

Continue through Gerakarí, ignoring the left turn to Spíli and various minor turns and staying on the main road towards **Méronas**. In Méronas look for the old church on the right. Park around the next bend where a monument commemorates the villagers who died in various wars from 1717 to 1949. Walk back to look at the beautiful 14th-century Byzantine Church of the Panagía with its fresco-covered walls and ceilings.

7–8

A few kilometres beyond Méronas is a picnic stop on the right, with fabulous views of the valley. Soon after this is the village of Agía Foteiní, where you meet a main road: turn right, signposted for the Asomáti School. After 1km turn left for **Thrónos**.

8–9

In Thrónos is the wonderful 11th-century Church of the Panagía, on the right. Though it is usually

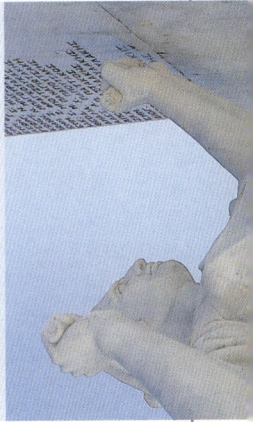

Byzantine church in the valley

locked, part of a lovely mosaic can be seen on the floor outside the church, and beyond it good views of the valley.

9–10

Beyond Thrónos the road forks. Turn right to loop back down and meet the main road again, where you turn left. When you reach the next few houses take the sharp right turn to the village of **Amári** itself. In Amári, park in the small square outside the taverna and walk

up the nearby narrow street that heads up towards the Venetian bell tower. You can climb the tower to enjoy the views but there is no guardrail, so take care. Drive out of the village square the way you came in, keeping straight on past the police station and on through Monastiráki to rejoin the main road.

10–11

At the main road turn right, signposted Vizári. Drive on through Vizári to Fourfourás. Continue through Fourfourás and Kouroútes and, as you leave the next village, Níthavris, take the road to Tympáki, ignoring the right turn to Ágios Ioánnis.

War memorials stand in every village

11–12

At **Apodoúlou**, if time allows, park in the village and look for the signs to the Minoan site, which is still being excavated, and to the 14th-century Church of Ágios Geórgios.

12–13

Beyond Apodoúlou, ignore the left fork marked Plátanos and keep on the main road to the right (not signed). Rejoin the main road and turn left towards Tympáki, then at the next junction turn right back to Agía Galíni.

Taking a Break

There are numerous options, the best for a meal being the **Taverna Yerakári** and the **Noukákis** in Amári.

5 WEST COAST OF CRETE

Drive

In the Agía Sofía cave

Some of Crete's best sandy beaches lie on the island's far western coast, and their remote location has so far brought only minimal development, leaving them largely unspoiled. The dramatic mountain and coastal scenery is well worth the long day's drive. Drive with care on the narrow mountain roads.

DISTANCE 110km
TIME 3–4 hours driving, 1 day with stops
START/END POINT Kastélli Kissámou (43km west of Chaniá) ✚ 178 B4

1–2

From Kastélli Kissámou on the north coast, take the Old Road east towards Chaniá for about 2km to Kaloudianá. Turn south to **Topólia**, a pretty whitewashed village clinging to steep slopes. The Church of Agía Paraskevi, with its striking Italianate bell tower, has late Byzantine frescoes.

2–3

Just beyond town a tunnel marks the start of the **Koutsomatádos ravine**. Only 1.5km long, it is highly dramatic, the narrow road clinging to the western slope with sheer cliffs rising 300m above a river bed. Near the end of the gorge, steep steps on the right lead up to **Agía Sofía** cave, one of the biggest on Crete. The huge cavern is filled with stalagmites and stalactites, and there is a small chapel. It was occupied in neolithic times. Just beyond is **Koutsomatádos** village with a couple of tavernas.

3–4

About 3km further on, you can detour along a twisting mountain track to **Míli** (signposted), a beautifully restored traditional farming village. Or continue straight ahead on the main road through the Tyflós Valley, lush with olive groves and tall plane and chestnut trees.

Kólpos Kissámou

Chaniá
Kaloudianá
Kastélli Kissámou
Agios Geórgios
Lardás
Kalyviani
Ancient Falásarna
Falásarna
Órmos Livádi
Plátanos

4–5

At **Élos**, the road winds up the hillside to the centre of this pretty village, the largest of the nine *kastanohória*, or chestnut villages, which harvest the crop for export. A chestnut festival is held here each year in late October.

5–6

As you climb higher out of Élos, look back at the spectacular views over the valley and its terraced hillsides. Pass Perivólia, and at the T-junction turn left for Elafonísi. The road curves down a pretty, peaceful valley, passing through **Váthi**, another chestnut village, and **Plokamianá**.

6–7

A good asphalt road enables a fast descent to the sea, 10km away with a

the 13th century. This one dates from the 19th century and contains an ancient icon of the Virgin.

7–8

It's a further 6km to the white sands of **Elafonísi**, at the southwestern tip of the island. The paved road ends after 4km, and a gravel track leads down to the beach. The turquoise waters are warm and shallow, seldom reaching above waist height, and you can wade across the sandbar to **Elafonísi Island**. Despite its remoteness, this idyllic spot is always busy in high season; there are a few snack bars and plenty of sunbeds for hire.

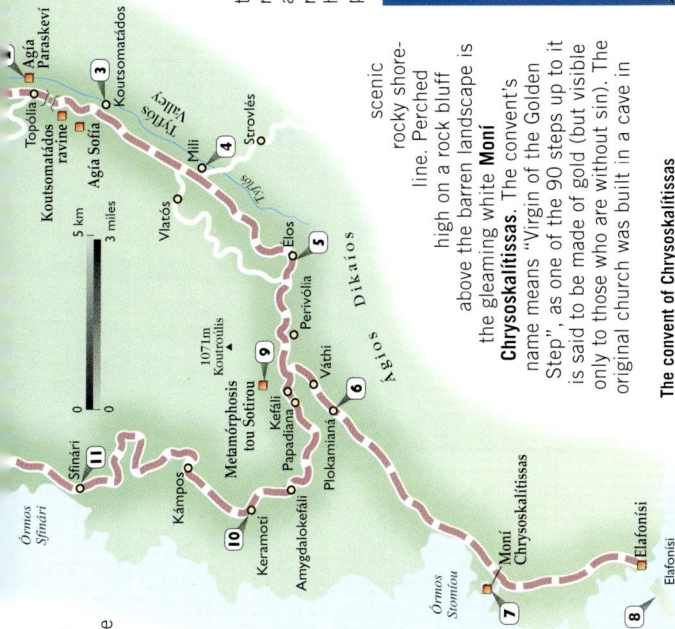

scenic rocky shoreline. Perched high on a rock bluff above the barren landscape is the gleaming white **Moní Chrysoskalitissas**. The convent's name means "Virgin of the Golden Step," as one of the 90 steps up to it is said to be made of gold (but visible only to those who are without sin). The original church was built in a cave in

The convent of Chrysoskalitissas

Sand and dunes at Falásarna

8–9

Return on the same road, and after Váthi take the left fork through **Kefáli**. Its 14th-century church, Metamórphosis tou Sotírou (Transfiguration of the Saviour), contains fine Byzantine frescoes as well as graffiti from early travellers. A path beside the *kafeníon* leads to the church.

9–10

Beyond the next village, tiny Papadiana, the road becomes a series of tight, narrow switchbacks climbing up the mountainside. Look back across the valley for stunning views to the glistening sea. After Amygdalokefáli, wide vistas of the western coast open out as the long, slow descent begins through old mountain villages such as Keramotí. You only realise how high you are when you glimpse the sea and the coastal fields far below.

10–11

Kámpos, 14km from Kefáli, is a larger, pleasant village with pretty stone houses clinging to the slopes around a ravine. After winding through it you make a magnificent descent into the canyon lined with rock walls of red and gold covered in greenery, and on to **Sfinári**.

11–12

The road climbs again, affording a stupendous view over the bay and beach below. The big peak of Mount Manna looms ahead. After 9km turn left for **Plátanos**, a large whitewashed town perched on a high plateau. Drive through town. Most signs are in Greek only, making the ill-marked turn for Falásarna more difficult to see (it's better signposted from the other direction). As you leave town look for an EKO petrol station on the left, and just beyond a blue BANK sign. Turn left on to the small road here. Shortly after the turn follow the brown and yellow sign for Ancient Falásarna. As you descend to the coastal plain, turn right at the signposted junction for Falásarna.

12–13

Falásarna has lovely stretches of golden sand set between rocky inlets that are great for beachcombing. Facilities are basic, with a handful of small hotels and tavernas scattered along the road. North of the beach a dirt track leads to the ruins of ancient Falásarna, a port city dating back to the 6th century BC. Return to Plátanos and continue north to Kastélli, 11km away.

Taking a Break

The **Kastanofolia taverna** in Élos serves good food. There are snack bars with drinks and sandwiches at Elafonísi. On the coast road the larger villages of Kámpos and Sfinári have tavernas. The **Sun Set taverna** at Falásarna is a simple but pleasant spot.

ΟΔΟΣ
25ΗΣ ΑΥΓΟΥΣΤΟΥ

Practicalities

44

IONIAN
BANK

GETTING ADVANCE INFORMATION

Websites
- www.explorecrete.com
- www.infocrete.com
- www.interkriti.org
- www.cretetravel.com
- www.ktel.org

In the UK
Greek National Tourism
Organisation (GNTO)
4 Conduit Street
London W1R 0DJ
☎ 020 7734 5997

In the USA
Greek National Tourism
Organisation (GNTO)
645 Fifth Avenue
New York, NY 10022
☎ (212) 421-5777

BEFORE YOU GO

WHAT YOU NEED

		UK	Germany	USA	Canada	Australia	Ireland	Netherlands	Spain
●	Required								
○	Suggested								
▲	Not required								
△	Not applicable								
Passport/National Identity Card		●	●	●	●	●	●	●	●
Visa		▲	▲	▲	▲	▲	▲	▲	▲
Onward or Return Ticket		▲	▲	▲	▲	▲	▲	▲	▲
Health Inoculations (tetanus and polio)		▲	▲	▲	▲	▲	▲	▲	▲
Health Documentation (► 174, Health)		▲	▲	▲	▲	▲	▲	▲	▲
Travel Insurance		○	○	○	○	○	○	○	○
Driver's Licence (national)		●	●	●	●	●	●	●	●
Car Insurance Certificate		●	●	●	●	●	●	●	●
Car Registration Document		●	●	●	●	●	●	●	●

WHEN TO GO

▭ High season   ▭ Low season

JAN	FEB	MAR	APR	MAY	JUN	JUL	AUG	SEP	OCT	NOV	DEC
12°C	12°C	14°C	17°C	21°C	23°C	25°C	26°C	25°C	21°C	18°C	14°C

Very wet	Wet	Cloud	Sun	Sun/ Showers

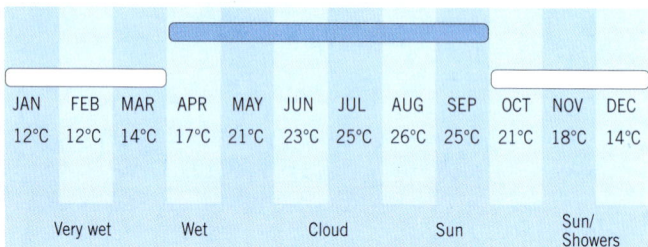

April and May are probably the best two months to visit, when temperatures are pleasant without being too hot, there is very little rain, the island is not yet too busy and there is a profusion of wild flowers to see. **September and October** can also be pleasant, but more suited to swimmers than botanists. The landscape will be looking burnt out, but the sea temperatures will still be in the mid-70s. In **July and August** there is no rain at all. Temperatures remain mild all through the year, but in winter it does get wet. The holiday season usually runs from **Easter to late October**, and outside this period many hotels and restaurants will be closed. There are still plenty which open all year round, but your choice will be more limited.

GETTING THERE

By Air Crete has two international airports, at **Irakleío** and **Chaniá**, although the one at Irakleío is the major airport and much more frequently used. They are about two hours apart by road, with Irakleío best for eastern Crete and Chaniá for western Crete. There is also a small domestic airport at **Siteía** in eastern Crete. A new airport is being built at Siteía, and will be capable of taking international flights (► 36). There are no direct scheduled flights to Crete, though there are **numerous charter flights** from various European airports from April to October. Scheduled flights involve flying to Athens and changing there to an internal flight. There are 20 to 30 flights a day from Athens to Crete in season, with the national carrier Olympic Airways, or its privately operated competitors Aegean Cronus Airlines and Air Greece. There are also air links with Rhodes and Thessaloníki.

By Sea From **Piraeus** in Athens there are daily ferry services to **Irakleío**, **Chaniá** and **Réthymno**, and several a week to **Ágios Nikólaos** and **Siteía**. Journey time is about 12 hours, or less in good weather. There is also a new fast ferry in operation from Minoan Lines, which cuts the journey time to between 6 and 7 hours. There are also numerous other connections to Crete: from Gíthio on the Peloponnese, from Thíra (Santorini) and other Cycladic islands, from Rhodes, Karpathos and other Dodecanesian islands, and from Israel and Cyprus.
Bear in mind that **ferry schedules can often be affected** by stormy or windy weather, not only off the coast of Crete itself but throughout the Aegean. This applies as much in high summer, when winds can be strong, as at any other time of year. Always leave at least a day's grace if you need to connect to onward flights or ferries.

TIME

Like the rest of Greece, Crete is two hours ahead of Greenwich Mean Time (GMT+2), and adjusts to summer time at 4 am on the last Sunday in March until 4 am on the last Sunday in October.

CURRENCY AND FOREIGN EXCHANGE

Currency The monetary unit of Crete is the Euro (€). Euro notes are in denominations of €5, €10, €20, €50, €100, €200 and €500, and coins in denominations of €1 and €2, and 1, 2, 5, 10, 20 and 50 cents. Other currencies such as the US dollar and the pound sterling can still be widely exchanged.

Credit cards Credit cards are widely accepted in the resorts and ATMs are common in large towns and cities.

Exchange Cash and travellers' cheques can be exchanged in banks, at exchange bureaux and often in travel agencies and tourist information centres. Post offices in Greece no longer offer currency exchange facilities. Banks generally give the best exchange rates, although commission charges can vary quite a bit from bank to bank, so shop around.

GMT 12 noon	Crete 2 pm	USA (NY) 7 am	Germany 1 pm	Spain 1 pm	Sydney 10 pm

WHEN YOU ARE THERE

CLOTHING SIZES

UK	Greece	USA	
36	46	36	Suits
38	48	38	
40	50	40	
42	52	42	
44	54	44	
46	56	46	
7	41	8	Shoes
7.5	42	8.5	
8.5	43	9.5	
9.5	44	10.5	
10.5	45	11.5	
11	46	12	
14.5	37	14.5	Shirts
15	38	15	
15.5	39/40	15.5	
16	41	16	
16.5	42	16.5	
17	43	17	
8	34	6	Dresses
10	36	8	
12	38	10	
14	40	12	
16	42	14	
18	44	16	
4.5	38	6	Shoes
5	38	6.5	
5.5	39	7	
6	39	7.5	
6.5	40	8	
7	41	8.5	

NATIONAL HOLIDAYS

1 Jan	New Year's Day
6 Jan	Epiphany
Feb/Mar	Shrove Monday (41 days pre-Easter)
25 Mar	Independence Day
Mar/Apr	Good Friday, Easter Monday
May/Jun	Whit Monday (50 days after Easter)
1 May	Labour Day
15 Aug	Feast of the Assumption
28 Oct	Ochi Day
25/26 Dec	Christmas

Restaurants and tourist shops may well stay open on these days, but museums will be closed.

OPENING HOURS

○ Stores
● Offices
● Banks
● Post Offices
● Museums/Monuments
● Pharmacies

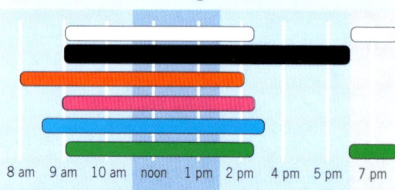

□ Day   ▨ Midday   □ Evening

Many shops in tourist areas stay open late. In larger towns, some banks and post offices may open on Saturday mornings.

Pharmacies These are normally open weekdays only, but some open on Saturdays and each one displays details of the nearest 24-hour pharmacy.

Churches Churches are often open all day, though some may open early morning and evenings only.

Museums Museum hours vary from place to place. It is advisable to check, especially if travelling out of season or making a special journey.

	POLICE 100
	FIRE 199
	AMBULANCE 166
	ELPA (CAR BREAKDOWN) 104

PERSONAL SAFETY

Crete is one of the safest places in Europe. Crime is rare, although petty theft can occur so don't be too careless with your valuables. Report any crime to the police immediately.

- Leave valuables in your hotel or apartment safe, never on the beach or visible in a car.
- Women may be pestered by local lotharios, but these are usually a nuisance rather than a serious threat. Persistent refusal usually works.

Police assistance:
 100 from any phone

TELEPHONES

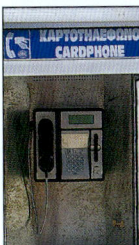

To make a call from a street phone you must have a phone card, available at numeous outlets.

Otherwise use the street kiosks. Simply dial and pay the attendant at the end according to the meter.
For the domestic operator dial 151. For the international operator dial 161, or 162 from Athens. The cheapest way to call internationally is at one of the OTE offices.

International Dialling Codes
Dial 00 followed by

UK:	44
USA/Canada:	1
Ireland:	353
Australia:	61
Germany:	49

POST OFFICES

All towns and many large villages have a post office, either in the form of a large yellow caravan or a building on the main square or street. Normal hours are Mon–Fri 7:30–2:30, but in main towns and busy tourist resorts they may stay open until 8 pm, and also open Saturday mornings.

ELECTRICITY

The power supply in Greece is 220. Sockets accept two-round-pin plugs. Visitors from
 continental Europe should bring an adaptor.
Visitors from the US will require a voltage transformer. Power cuts happen from time to time.

TIPS/GRATUITIES

Tipping is expected for all services. As a general guide:

Restaurant waiters (service not included)	leave change
Cafés/bars	leave change
Taxis	change from bill
Porters	€3 per bag
Chambermaids	€2 per day
Hairdressers	change from bill
Tour guides	€3

CONSULTATES

UK
0810-224012

USA and CANADA
(010) 721 2951
(Athens)

Germany
0810-226288

Australia
(010) 645 0404
(Athens)

Netherlands
0810-283820

HEALTH

Insurance EU nationals carrying an E111 form are entitled to free medical treatment. More often you will be asked to pay and claim a refund when you return home. Medical insurance is recommended, especially if hiking in Crete's rugged gorges and mountains.

Dental Services There are many good dentists in Crete, mostly in the major towns of Irakleío, Chaniá and Réthymno. Services are much cheaper than elsewhere in Europe.

Weather The summer sun can be fierce, and even in spring and autumn you must take precautions against sunburn. Even if there is some cloud cover, still use protection as the rays and reflections will burn.

Drugs Prescription and non-prescription drugs are widely available at pharmacies. Look for the Green Cross. Pharmacies work a rota system out of hours and will have a notice indicating the nearest open one. Bring sufficient supplies of any medication with you, plus a prescription indicating generic and not brand names in case you need more. Be aware that codeine is banned in Greece, so check the contents of any medical supplies in case you fall foul of the law.

Safe Water Tap water is safe to drink throughout Crete. Bottled water is available everywhere. Drink plenty to avoid dehydration in the hot summer months.

CONCESSIONS

Students/Youths Students Holders of an International Student Identity Card (ISIC) are entitled to reduced-price admission at most public museums and monuments. Privately run museums may not give a concession. No travel concessions available.

Senior Citizens Senior citizens receive few if any concessions. Some sites and museums will offer reduced admission if you can prove you are over 60. Sometimes this is limited to EU citizens. No travel concessions are available.

TRAVELLING WITH A DISABILITY

Crete is not ideal, so check first if your accommodation is going to be suitable. Few special facilities exist, and archaeological sites are difficult to get around. That said, Cretans are always willing to help anyone in need so the personal touch may see you through where public facilities let you down.

CHILDREN

Cretans love children and they are welcome everywhere. You will often see a group of Greek children eating at one table while the adults dine together at another. Children under 8 travel free on buses, but over-8s pay full fare.

TOILETS

There are free public toilets in most main towns, but not always well signposted. Standards vary. Most people prefer to use a bar or café toilet, and proprietors don't usually mind. Remember not to put the paper into the toilet, but into the basket provided.

CUSTOMS

The import of wildlife souvenirs sourced from rare or endangered species may be either illegal or require a special permit. Before buying, check your home country's customs regulations.

THE GREEK ALPHABET

Alpha A α
Beta B β
Gamma Γ γ
Delta Δ δ
Epsilon E ε
Zita Z ζ
Eta H η
Theta Θ θ
Iota I ι
Kappa K κ
Lambda Λ λ
Mu M μ
Nu N ν
Xi Ξ ξ
Omicron O o
Pi Π π
Rho P ρ
Sigma Σ σ
Tau T τ
Upsilon Y υ
Phi Φ φ
Chi X χ
Psi Ψ ψ
Omega Ω ω

TRAVEL

Airport **Aerodhrómio**
Harbour **Limáni**
Bus station
Stathmós leoforíon
Bus stop **Stási**
Bus **Leoforío**
Car **Aftokínito**
Taxi **Taxí**

DAYS OF THE WEEK

Monday **Deftéra**
Tuesday **Trití**
Wednesday **Tetárti**
Thursday **Pémpti**
Friday **Paraskeví**
Saturday **Sávato**
Sunday **Kiriakí**

OTHER USEFUL WORDS & PHRASES

Good morning **Kaliméra**
Good afternoon/evening **Kalispéra**
Good night **Kaliníkhta**
Okay, all right **Endáksi**
Very well **Polí kalá**
I'm fine **Kalá iméh**
I think so **Nomízo**
I'm not too bad **Étsi kyétsi**
Enjoy your meal **Kalí órexi**
Cheers! **(Stín)** yía más
What can I do for you? **Oríste?**
What's your name? **Pos sas léne**
Be careful **Ópa**
Take your time **Sigá sigá**
Who **Pyós**
What **Ti**
When **Póte**
Why **Yiatí**
How **Pos**
How much? **Póso**
How many? **Póses?**
A little **Lígho**
Open **Aníkto**
Closed **Klistó**

SURVIVAL PHRASES

Yes (formal) **Ne (málista)**
No **Óchi**
Hello (formal) **Yiásu (hérete)**
Goodbye (formal) **Yiásu (adío)**
How are you? **Ti kanís (tí káneteh)?**
Please **Parakaló**
Thank you (very much) **Efharistó (párapolí)**
Excuse me **Signómi**
I'm sorry **Signómi**
You're welcome **Parakaló**
Do you have…? **Boríte na moú dósete…?**
How much? **Póso íne?**
I'd like **Tha íthela**

DIRECTIONS

Where is…? **Poú íne…?**
- the beach **i paralía**
- the bank **i trápeza**
- the bus stop **to stási**
- the church **i eklissía**
- the post office **to tachidromío**
- the hospital **to nosokomío**
- the hotel **to xenodohío**
- the sea **i thálassa**
- the telephone **to tiléfono**
- the toilet **i toualéta**
Left **Aristerá**   Right **Deksiá**
Straight on **Ísia**
How far is it? **Póso makriá íne?**
Near **Kondá**   Far **Makriá**

NUMBERS

0	midhén	12	dhódheka	30	tríanda	120 ekatón íkosi
1	éna	13	dhekatría	31	tríanda éna	200 dhiakósia
2	dhío	14	dhekatéssera	32	tríanda dhío	300 triakósia
3	tría	15	dhekapénde			400 tetrakósia
4	téssera	16	dhekaéxi	40	saránda	
5	pénde	17	dhekaeftá	50	penínda	500 pendakósia
6	éxi	18	dhekaochtó	60	exínda	600 exakósia
7	eftá	19	dhekaenyá	70	evdhomínda	700 eftakósia
8	ochtó	20	íkosi	80	oghdhónda	800 ochtakósia
9	enyá			90	enenínda	900 enyakósia
10	dhéka	21	íkosi éna	100	ekató	
11	éndheka	22	íkosi dhío	110	ekató dhéka	1,000 hílya

IF YOU NEED HELP

Help! **Voíthya!**
Could you help me, please? **Boríte na me voithísete, parakaló?**
Do you speak English? **Miláte angliká?**
I don't understand **Den katalavéno**
Could you call/fetch a doctor quickly, please? **Parakaló, kaléste/idhopíste ghríghora éna yatró?**
Could I use your telephone? **Boró na chrisimopiíso to tiléfono sas?**
Police **Astinomía**
Ambulance **Asthenofóro**

TIME

What time is it?
  Ti óra íne?
Today **Símera**
Tomorrow **Ávrio**
Yesterday **Kthés**
In the morning
  To proí
In the afternoon
  To mesiméri
In the evening
  To vrádhi
At night **To níchta**

DRIVING

Petrol **Venzíni**
- leaded
  aplí venzíni
- unleaded
  amólivdhi
fill **yemízo**
Petrol station
  Pratírio venzínis
Diesel **Dízel**
Oil **Ládhi**
Tyre **Lásticho**
Garage **Garáz**

RESTAURANT (ESTIATÓRIO)

I'd like to book a table **Boró na klíso éna trapézi**
A table for two **Éna trapézi yía dhío átoma**
Can we eat outside? **Boróome na fáme kyéxo?**
Could we see the menu/wine list?
  Boróome na dhóome ton gatálogho/ton gatálogho krasyón?
Could I have the bill please?
  To loghariazmó, parakaló?

MENU READER

bíra beer
chortofághos
  vegetarian
dhípno dinner
gála milk
hórta vegetables
kafés coffee
- **nescafé** instant
karáfa carafe
krasí wine
  - **áspro** white
  - **mávro** red

- **kokkinélli** rosé
kréas meat
khímos fruit juice
neró water
orektikó -hors
  d'oeuvre
proinó breakfast
psitós grilled
tighanitós fried
tsai tea
voútiro butter
vrazménos boiled

MENU A–Z

afélia pork cubes
  cooked in red-
  wine-and-
  coriander sauce
aláti salt
anginári
  artichoke
angoúri
  cucumber
antsóoya anchovy
avgó egg
avgolemóno egg-
  and-lemon
  soup
bakláva pastry
  filled with nuts
  and honey
banána banana
brandy brandy
domátes
  tomatoes
eliés olives
eleóladho
  olive oil
fakés lentils
fasólia beans
fétta goat's
  cheese
glyká fruit in
  sweet syrup
hálloumi ewe's
  cheese
hirómeri
  cured ham
húmmos
  chickpea dip
kalambhóki
  sweetcorn
karóto carrot
keftédhes
  meatballs
kerásya cherries
kétsap tomato
  sauce
kléftiko oven-
  baked lamb
kolokitháki
  courgette
kounoupídhi
  cauliflower
kotópoulo
  chicken
kounélli rabbit
koupépia minced
  meat and rice
  wrapped in vine
  leaves

krém karamél
  crème caramel
kremídhi onion
láchano cabbage
ládhi salad oil
lemóni lemon
loukániko sausage
loúntza smoked
  pork loin
makarónya
  spaghetti
mandaríni mandarin
manitária
  mushrooms
maroúli lettuce
melitzána aubergine
mídhya mussels
milópita apple pie
moussaká minced
  meat, aubergine,
  potatoes, etc, in a
  bechamel sauce
paidháki lamb chop
pagotó ice-cream
patátes potatoes
pepoúni melon
pikándikos spicy
pipéri pepper
pipérya pepper
  (vegetable)
pítta flat bread
portokáli orange
pourgoúri
  cracked wheat
psári fish
psiménos roasted
psomí bread
saláta salad
sáltza sauce
sardhéles sardines
skórdho garlic
soujoúkos almonds
  in grape juice
soupá soup
souvláki grilled
  meat on skewer
spanáki spinach
stafília grapes
stifádho beef
  stewed in onion-
  and-tomato sauce
sheftália lamb
  sausage
táhini sesame
  seed dip
taramás fish-roe dip
vodhinó kréas beef
yaoúrti yoghurt
zambón ham

Atlas

Chaniá
178/179
Palaiochóra

Réthymno
180/181

IRAKLEÍO
182/183
Moíres

Agios
Nikólaos
184/185
Ierápetra

Sitía
186

Gávdos

To identify the regions, see the map
on the inside of the front cover

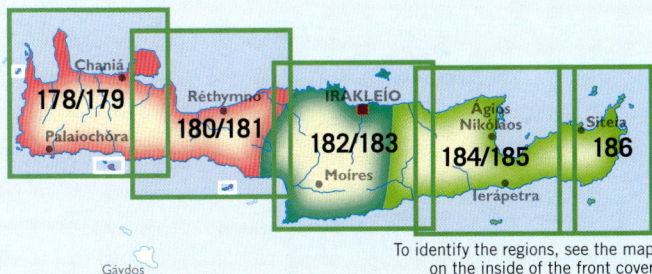

Regional Maps

—·—·—	Regional boundary	▢	City
═══	Motorway	▫	Major town
━━━	Major route	○	Other town
───	Main road	○	Village
───	Other road	▧	Featured place of interest
⊢══⊣	Tunnel	■	Place of interest
·········	Long distance trail	✈	Airport
─ ─ ─	Ferry route	▲	Mountain peak

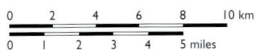

0 2 4 6 8 10 km
0 1 2 3 4 5 miles

Akrotíri Spánta

Akrotíri Skála

Pýreás, Kýthira,
Gíthio, Andikíthira

Rodópou

748m
▲ Ónychas

Ágria
Gramvoúsa

Akrotiri Voúxa

Ímeri
Gramvoúsa

Akrotíri Tigáni

Afráta

Rodópos

Kolymvári

E65/90

Máleme

Kólpos
Kissámou

Ravdoúcha

Tavronítis

Germaniko
Nekrotafeío
Polémou

Spilía

E65/90

Nóchia

Polemárchi

762m
Geroskinós

Archéa
Falásarna

Kalyvianí

Kastélli
Kissámou

Nopígeia

Vasilopoulo
Episkopí

Zounáki

Neriáná

Pondikonísio

Akrotíri Koutrí

Falásarna

90

Ágios
Geórgios

Lardás

Káto
Palaiókastro

Kaloudianá

Voukoliés

Karés

Órmos
Livádi

Plátanos

Polirínia

Rókka

Sfakopigádi

Deliana

Nterés

Lousakiés

Voulgáro

899m
Platanianí

890m
▲ Manna

Kalathénes

Koukounará

Maláthyros

Áno Kefála

Órmos
Sfinári

Sinenianá

Topólia

Agía
Paraskeví

Kakópetros

Akrotíri Kórakas

Sfinári

Koutsomatádos

928m
▲ Agrixokefala

Michaliana

Kostogiánnides

Koutsomatádos

Sasálos

Vlatós

Tyflós

Mili

Flória

Kámpos

1071m
Koutroúlis

Strovlés

1331m
▲ Apopigádi

Keramotí

Kefáli

Agía Eiríni

Amygdalokefáli

Perivólia

Élos

Aligoí

Psarianá

Epanochóri

Papadiána

Váthi

Drýs

Kántanos

Anisaráki

Akrotíri
Máyros

Plokamianá

Ágios Dikaios

Plemenianá

Kampanós

Órmos
Stomíou

Moústakos

Chondrás

Moní
Chrysoskalítissas

Kalámios

Kefáli

Kakodíki

Rodováni

Moní
Koustogérako

Voutás

Kádros

Papadiana

Sklavopoúla

Kálamos

Prodromi

Elafonísi

Kontokynígi

Ágioi
Theodoroi

Ánydroi

Soúgia

Órmos
Soúgias

Elafonísi

Kaladikiános

Palaiochóra

Koundoúra

Akrotíri
Kríos

Akrotíri
Trachíli

Akrotíri
Floriés

Gávdos

K R I T I K Ó   *P É L A G O S*

5

Akrotíri
Trypití

Moní Agíou Ioánnou
tr Gouvernétou

Stavrós

Akrotíri
Mavromoúri

Koumarés

Moní Agías
Triádas

*Órmos
Kalávas*

Chorafákia

Kalórrouma

Risoskloton

Kampáni

Pervolitsa

K ó l p o s   *C h a n i ó n*

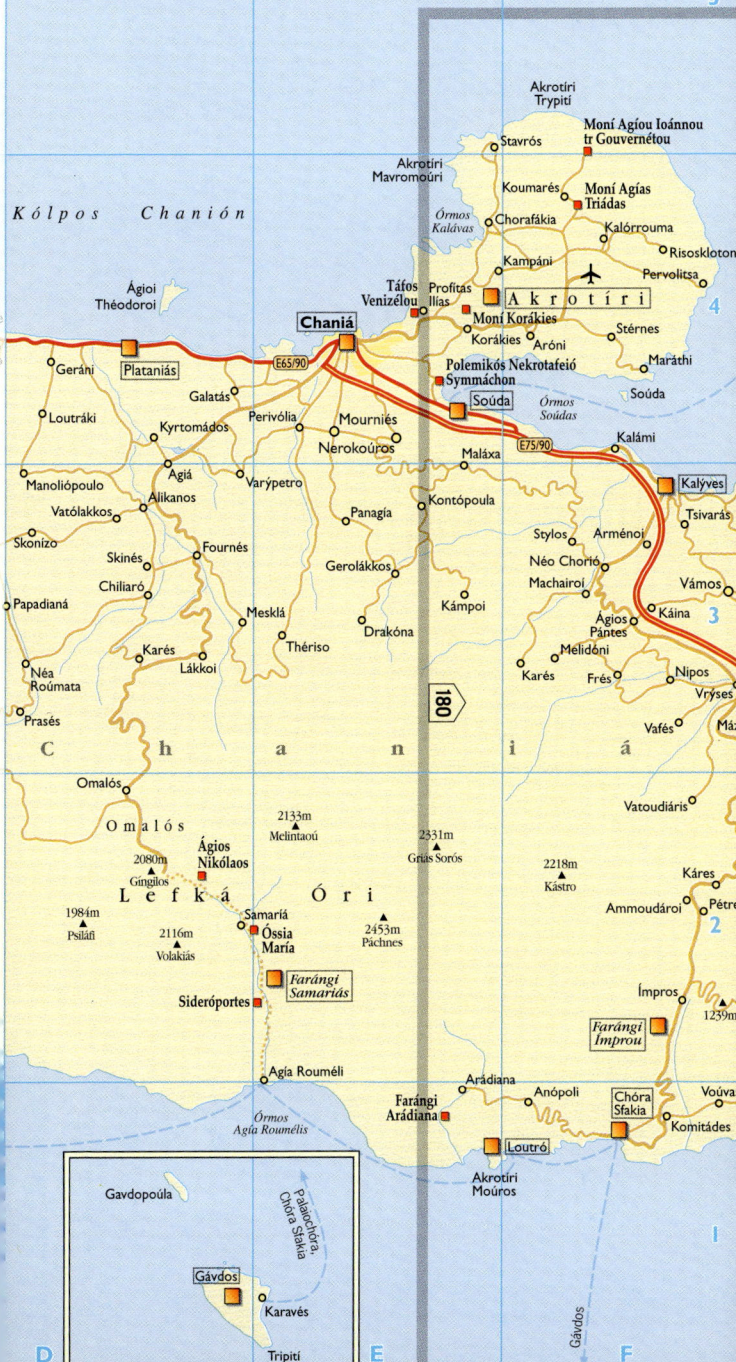

Ágioi
Théodoroi

Tráfos
Venizélou

Profítas
Ilías

A k r o t í r i

4

Moní Korákies

Korákies

Aróni

Stérnes

Maráthi

Soúda

Geráni

Plataniás

Chaniá

Galatás

E65/90

Polemikós Nekrotafeió
Symmáchon

Soúda

*Órmos
Soúdas*

Loutráki

Kyrtomádos

Perivólia

Mourniés

Nerokoúros

Maláxa

E75/90

Kalámi

Manolíopoulo

Agiá

Alikanos

Varýpetro

Panagía

Kontópoula

Stylos

Arménoi

Kalýves

Tsivarás

Vatólakkos

Néo Chorió

Skonizo

Skinés

Fournés

Gerolákkos

Kámpoi

Machairoí

Vámos

Káina

3

Papadianá

Chiliaró

Mesklá

Drakóna

Ágios
Pántes

Melidóni

Karés

Frés

Nipos

Vrýses

Karés

Lákkoi

Thériso

Néa
Roúmata

Prasés

Vafés

Máza

C   h   a   n   i   á

Omalós

Vatoudiáris

O m a l ó s

2133m
Melintaoú

2331m
Griás Sorós

2218m
Kástro

Káres

2080m
Gíngilos

Ágios
Nikólaos

L e f k á   **Ó r i**

Ammoudároi

Pétres

2

1984m
Psiláfi

2116m
Volakiás

Samariá

**Óssia
María**

2453m
Páchnes

Ímpros

1239m

*Farángi
Samariás*

*Farángi
Ímprou*

Sideróportes

Agía Rouméli

Aráthiana

Anópoli

**Chóra
Sfakiá**

Voúvas

*Órmos
Agía Roumélis*

*Farángi
Arádiana*

Loutró

Komitádes

Akrotíri
Moúros

1

Gávdos

Gavdopoúla

*Palaiochóra,
Chóra Sfakía*

Gávdos

Karavés

Tripití

180

Akrotíri
Trypití

Stavrós

Moní Agíou Ioánnou
tr Gouvernétou

Koumarés

Moní Agías
Triádas

Órmos
Kalávas

Chorafákia

Kalórrouma

Kampáni

Risoskloton

Pervolitsa

Profitás
Ilías

A k r o t í r i

Moní Korákies

Korákies

Aróni

Stérnes

Polemikós Nekrotafeió
Symmáchon

Maráthi

Soúda

Akrotíri
Drápano

Soúda

Órmos
Soúdas

Maláxa

Kalámi

E75/90

Kontópoula

Kalýves

Kókkino
Chorió

Pláka

Stylos

Arménoi

Tsivarás

Drápanos

Néo Chorió

Gavalochóri

Machairoí

Vámos

Kefalás

Kámpoi

Káina

Ágios
Pántes

Mélidóni

Sellía

Likotinariá

Órmos   Almyroú

Karés

Frés

Nipos

Kal Alexándrou

Vrýses

Georgioúpoli

E75/90

Geráni

Vafés

Máza

Asprouliáni

Drámia

Káto
Valsamónero

331m
is Sorós

Alíkampos

Límni
Kourná

Episkopí

179

Vatoudiáris

Kávallos

Koúfi

2218m
Kástro

Kournás

Ágios
Geórgios

Kalonyktis

Káres

1493m
Trýpali

Argyroúpoli

Roústika

Ammoudároi

Pétres

A s k í f o u

Asigonía

Moúntros

1511m
Agkathés

Ímpros

Myriokéfala

Vilandrédo

1239m

Asfendos

1312m
Kryoneritis

Alónes

Kánevos

Farángi
Kotsifoú

Arádiana

Anópoli

Chóra
Sfakia

Voúvas

Patsianós

Áno
Rodákino

Káto
Rodákino

Selliá

gi
na

Loutró

Komitádes

Skalotí

Myrthios

Plakiás

Akrotíri
Moúros

Fragkokástelo

Akrotíri
Kalógeros

Órmos
Pláka

Akrotíri
Kakomouri

Gávdos

L I V Y K Ó

P É L A G O S

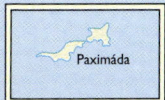

K R I T I K Ó   P É L A G O S

5

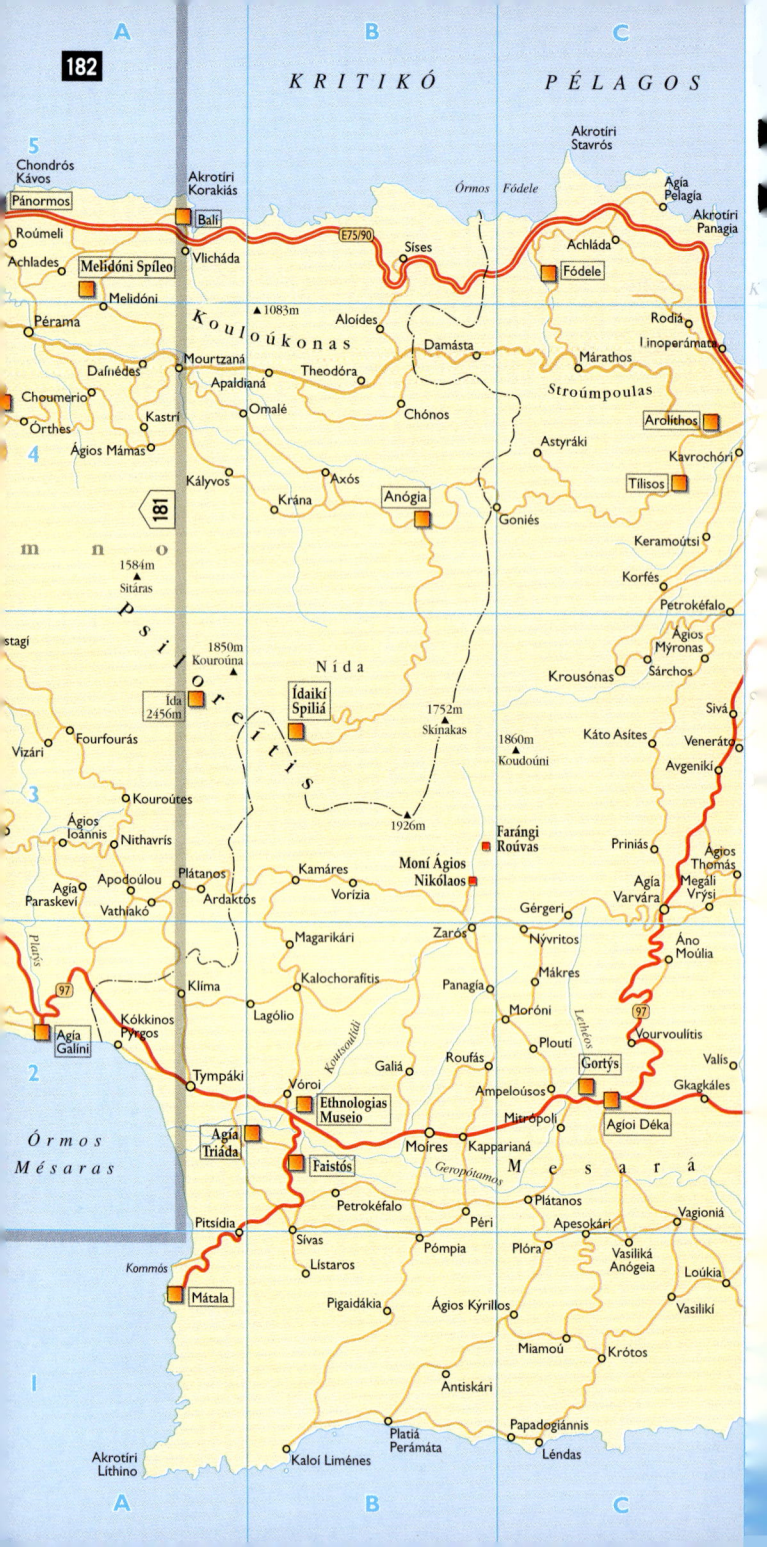

Chondrós Kávos
Pánormos
Roúmeli
Achladés
Melidóni Spíleo
Melidóni
Akrotíri Korakiás
Bali
Vlicháda
E75/90
Síses
Akrotíri Stavrós
Órmos Fódele
Agía Pelagía
Akrotíri Panagía
Achláda
Fódele

4

Pérama
Dafnédes
Choumerío
Órthes
Kastrí
Ágios Mámas
Mourtzaná
Apaldianá
Omalé
Theodóra
▲1083m
Aloídes
Damásta
Márathos
Rodiá
Linoperámata
Stroúmpoulas
Arolíthos
Kavrochóri
K o u l o ú k o n a s
Astyráki
Goniés
Keramoútsi
Korfés
Petrokéfalo
Kályvos
Krána
Axós
Anógia
Tilisos

m   n   o

1584m
▲ Sitáras

1850m
Kouroúna ▲
Ída 2456m

N í d a
Ídaikí Spiliá
1752m
▲ Skinakas
1926m
Farángi Roúvas

Ágios Mýronas
Sárchos
Krousónas
Káto Asítes
1860m
▲ Koudoúni
Sivá
Veneráto
Avgenikí

P s i l o r e í t i s

3

stagí
Vizári
Fourfourás
Kouroútes
Ágios Ioánnis
Nithavrís
Agía Paraskeví
Apodoúlou
Vathiakó
Plátanos
Ardaktós
Kamáres
Vorízia
Moní Ágios Nikólaos
Magarikári
Zarós
Gérgeri
Nývritos
Mákres
Priniás
Ágios Thomás
Megáli Vrýsi
Agía Varvára
Áno Moúlia

2

Platýs
Agía Galíni
Kókkinos Pýrgos
Klíma
Lagólio
Kalochorafítis
Panagía
Moróni
Ploutí
Roufás
Galiá
Ampeloúsos
Mitrópoli
Kapparianá
Moíres
Gortýs
Vourvoulítis
Valís
Gkagkáles
Agioi Déka
Letheós
Tympáki
Vóroi
Ethnologías Museío
Agía Triáda
Faistós
Kommós
Mátala
Pitsídia
Petrokéfalo
Sívas
Lístaros
Pigaidákia
Pómpia
Plóra
Ágios Kýrillos
Péri
Apesokári
Plátanos
Vasiliká Anógeia
Miamoú
Krótos
Loúkia
Vasilikí
Vagioniá
M e s a r á
Geropótamos

Ó r m o s   M é s a r a s

I

Akrotíri Líthino
Kaloí Liménes
Antiskári
Platiá Perámata
Papadogiánnis
Léndas

181
97

D E F

Patra, Ancona, Kefalónio
Thessaloníki, Pireás, Kykládes, Sporádes
Thíra
Thíra, Ródos
Kúsadasi, Kárpathos, Lemesós

Día
Paximadi
Akrotíri Stavros

Kólpos Irakleíou

Akrotíri Chersónisos

IRAKLEÍO
Néa Alikarnassós
Ammoudára
Amnisos
Vathianós Kámpos
Kokkini Hani
Káto Goúves
Svoúrou Metóchi
Limín Chersónisou

E75/90
Réma
Gournes
Goúves
Goúrnes

99
Knosós
Knosós
Spília
Elaía
Anópoli
Kainoúrio Chorió
Kóxari
Chersónisos

Gioufyrákia
Kalésa
97
Foinikiá
Vasileíes
Epáno Vátheia
Galifá
Smári
Kaló Chorió
Potamiés

Voutes
Ágios Sýllas
Episkopí
Káto Karouzaná

Stavrákia
Kounávoi
Sgourokefáli

Archánes
Myrtiá
Apóstoloi
Askoí

811m
Gioúchtas
Pezá
Sampás
Kastélli
Xidás
Amarianó

Dafnés
Ágios Vasíleios
Ag Paraskiés
Sklaverochóri
Lilianó
Máthia

Profítis Ilías
Meléses
Vóni
Thrapsanó

Kypárissos
Choudétsi
184

Roukáni
Parthéni
777m
Alágni
Chouméri
Geráki

Doúli
802m
Stíronas
Arkalochóri
Nipíditos
1414m
Virgioméno

Metaxochóri
Panórama
Zínda
Mousoúta
Avlí
Panagía

Amourgélles
Pártira
Áno Pouliá

Charáki
Kasános
Thomadianó

Melidochóri
Pyráthi
Badiá
Ínio
Karavádos

Laráni
Teféli
Vakiótes
Martha

Kastélli
Drapéti
Garípa
97

Atsipádes
Ligortýnos
Skiniás
Káto Vriánnos

Sokarás
Kalývia
Demáti
Chóndros

Stóloi
97
Protória
Káto Kastelliená
Favrianá

Loúres
Asími
Mesochorió
Keratókampos

Dionýsio
Chárakas
Pýrgos
Rotási
Órmos Keratokámpou

Stávies
Stérnes
979m
Asfentiliá
Tsoútsouros
Órmos Tsoútsourou

Ethiá
Achentriás

A s t e r o ú s i a
1231m
Kófinas
Paránymfoi
Treís Ekklísies

Kapetanianá
Akrotíri Martélos

I r a k l e í o
Gioúfyros
Kartterós
Aposelémis
Parastiá
Anapodáris

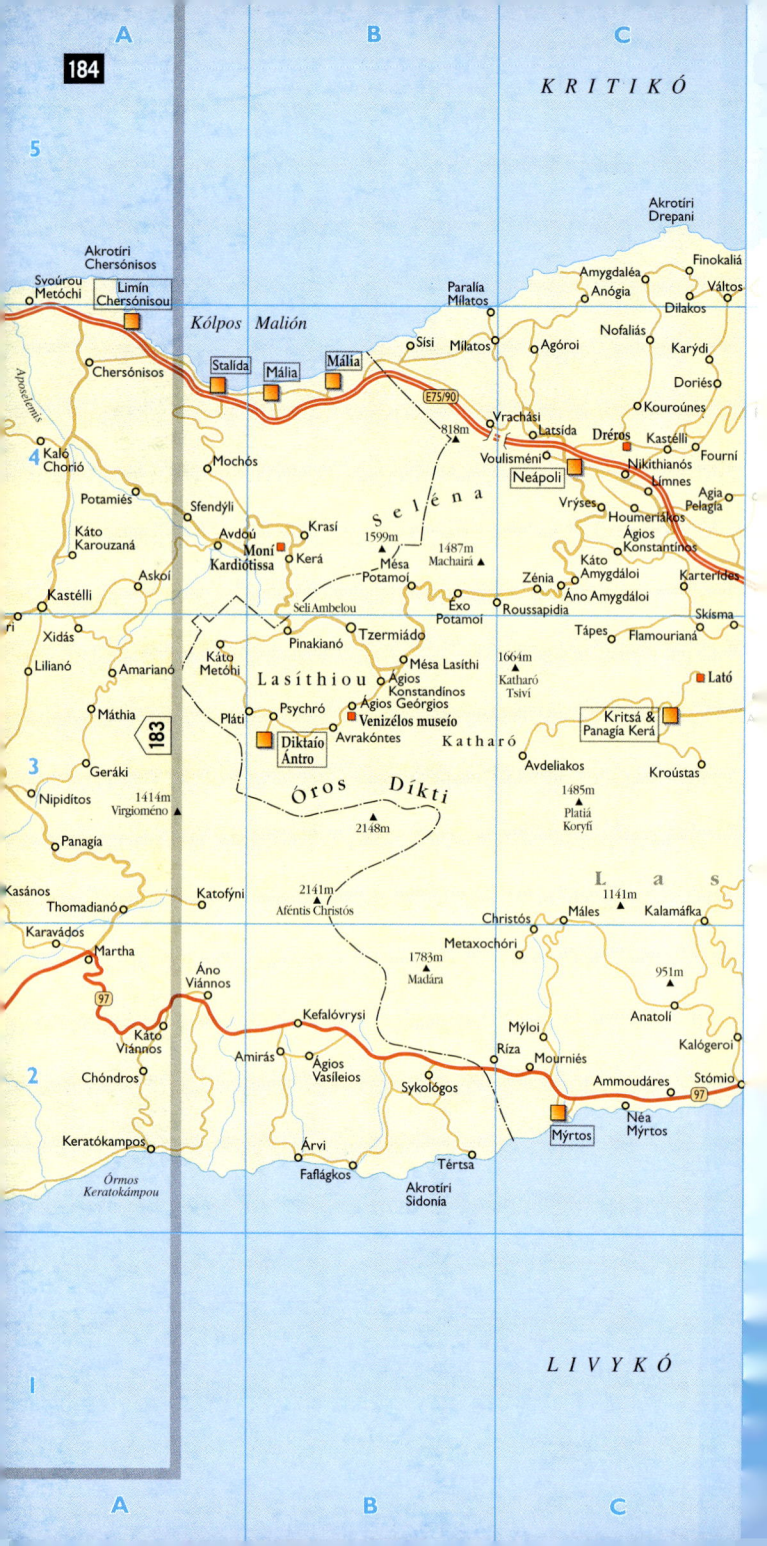

K R I T I K Ó

5

Akrotíri
Drepani

Svoúrou
Metóchi
Limín
Chersónisou

Akrotíri
Chersónisos

Amygdaléa
Anógia
Finokaliá
Váltos
Dílakos

Chersónisos

Kólpos Malión

Paralía
Mílatos
Nofaliás

Stalída Mália Mália
Sísi Mílatos Agóroi
Karýdi

Doriéso

E75/90
Kouroúnes
Vrachási
818m Latsída Dréros Kastélli
Fourni

4

Kaló
Chorió
Mochós
Voulisméni Neápoli Nikithianós
Límnes

Potamiés
Sfendýli Vrýses
Houmeriákos
Agia
Pelagía

Káto
Karouzaná
Avdoú Krasí
Seléna
1599m Ágios
Konstantínos

Askói
Moní
Kardiótissa Kerá
1487m
Machaíra Káto
Amygdáloi
Karterídes

Kastélli
Mésa
Potamoí Zénia Áno Amygdáloi

Xidás
Selí Ambélou Exo
Potamoí Roussapídia Skísma

Lilianó Amarianó
Pinakianó Tzermiádo Tápes Flamouriana

Máthia
Káto
Metóhi Lasíthiou Mésa Lasíthi 1664m
Katharó
Tsíví Lató

Pláti Psychró Ágios
Konstandínos
Ágios Geórgios
Venizélos museó Kritsá &
Panagía Kerá

3

Geráki
Diktaío
Ántro Avrakóntes Katharó

Nipídtos 1414m
Virgiómeno Óros Díkti Avdeliakos Kroústas

Panagía 2148m 1485m
Platiá
Koryfí

Kasános
Katofýni 2141m
Aféntis Christós L a s
1141m Máles Kalamáfka

Karavádos
Thomadianó
Martha Christós
Metaxochóri

97 Áno
Viánnos 1783m
Madára 951m Anatolí

Káto
Viánnos Kefalóvrysi Mýloi Kalógeroi

2

Chóndros
Amirás Ágios
Vasíleios Ríza Mourniés Ammoudáres Stómio
97

Keratókampos Árvi Sykológos Néa
Mýrtos

Órmos
Keratokámpou Faflágkos Tértsa
Akrotíri
Sidónia Mýrtos

1

L I V Y K Ó

A B C

D E F

5

P É L A G O S

Akrotíri
Ágios Ioánnis
Vlychádia
Sélles Myronikítas
Vrouchás
Epáno
Loúmas Spinalógka
Pláka
Spinalógka
Pines Mavrimianón
Kolokythía
Eloúnta
Ólous

4

Kalós
Lammos
Lénika
Katsíkia
Xirókampos
Ág Pántes Pseíra
Kalavrós Skopí
Chamézi
Ágios
Nikólaos Móchlos Myrsíni Paraspóri
E75/90 Tourlotí Éxo
Mardáti *Kólpos* Thólos Mésa Mouliana
Ammoudára *Mirampéllou* Sfáka Mouliana Skordilo
Lástros
O r n ó

3
E75/90 Kavoúsi 1238m Ge
Ístro ▲Askordaliá Dáfni 186
Pýrgos Pachiá 937m ▲
Kalo Choriό Ammos Chrysopigí
T h r y p t í s Lápithos
Prína Gourniá Thryptí Oreinó Stavrochóri
▲1476m Péfkoi
í t h i Vasilikí Aféntis Ágios Stéfanos
Meseléroi Monastiráki Stavroménos
Makryliá Stavrós Papadianá Schinokápsala Tsikkalariá
Episkopí Kalyvítis Análipsi
Kentrí Káto Choriό Ágios Koutsourás Pilalímata
Ioánnis Makrýgialos Kaló
Vainiá Agía Neró
Bramianá Koutsounári Fotiá Mávros
Agiasménos Kólympos 2
Gra 97
Lygiá Ierápetra

I

P É L A G O S

Mikronissi

Chrýsi

D E F

A   B   C

5

Paximáda

Dionisádes   Dragonáda

Giannisáda

Kassos,
Karpathos, Ródos

Akrotíri
Síderos

Órmos
Ténda

Akrotíri
Mavro   Elása

Ítanos ■ Erimoúpolis

Vái ■ Vái Finikodasos

Vái

Órmos
Grántes

Metoxi

Akrotíri
Faneroméni

4

Akrotíri Vamvakia

Órmos Siteías

Moní
Tóplou

Grántes

Akrotíri
Plaka

✈

Siteía

Palaíkastro

Angathía

■ Triptos

Petrás   ● Agía Fotiá

E75/90   Roússa
Ekklisía

97

Cháméxi   Skopí   Kimouriótis   Piskokéfalo

Kryonéri

Lagkáda

Órmos
Karoúmpes

Parapóri   Achládia   Stavroménos

Chochlakiés

Éxo
Moulianá   Maroniá   Zoú   803m
Priniás

Kellária

Azokéramos

Akrotíri Avláki

Skordilo

Sfákia

Karýdi

Adravástoi

Áno
Zákros

Zákros

Ágios
Geórgios   Epáno
Episkopi   Katsidóni   Sítanos

Náa Praísos

Káto Zákros

Dáfni   185
937m ▲

Vorí   Ágios
Spyrídonas   Kateliónas   810m ▲

Akrotíri
Zákros

Lamnóni

óri   Péfkoi   Etiá   Chandrás
Arménoi   Ziros

Ágios Stéfanos   Lithines

Chamaítoulo

Análipsi   Pezoúlas   Kaló Chorió   Xerókampos

rýgialos   Pilalímata   Kaló
Neró   Agía Triáda

Órmos
Makrýgialos   Goúdouras

Akrotíri
Goudoúra

Stenon Konfonisou

Strongilo

Koufonísi

Koufonísi

Trahilos

L I V Y K Ó   P É L A G O S

I

A   B   C

Index

Index 189

Picture credits

Abbreviations for terms appearing below (t) top; (b) bottom; (l) left; (r) right; (c) centre.

The Automobile Association wishes to thank the following photographers and libraries for their assistance in the preparation of this book.

Front and Back Cover (t) AA Photo Library/Philip Enticknap; (ct) AA Photo Library/Ken Paterson; (cb) AA Photo Library/Ken Paterson; (b) AA Photo Library/ Philip Enticknap; Spine AA Photo Library/Ken Paterson

THE ART ARCHIVE 33; BRUCE COLEMAN COLLECTION 27, 28b; DONNA DAILEY 25t, 30t, 30c, 30r, 31t, 31b, 86, 89, 91t, 110t, 156t, 156b, 158, 158l, 158r, 159, 160c, 163r, 167; KOBAL COLLECTION 34t; MARY EVANS PICTURE LIBRARY 6/7, 7t, 13c

The remaining pictures are held in the Association's own library (AA PHOTO LIBRARY) and were taken by NIGEL HICKS with the exception of 173t, 173r STEVE DAY; 2i, 2ii, 2iii, 2iv, 3ii, 5t, 11b, 12/13, 12b, 15b, 17/19, 18t, 18b, 19, 24, 25c, 34b, 35, 45, 46b, 50, 53, 54c, 55, 58, 59t, 71, 73, 74b, 77b, 81, 88c, 91c, 105, 110b, 125, 164, 168 PHILIP ENTICKNAP; 3iii, 3iv, 8, 9t, 9b, 10l, 10r, 11tc, 11tr, 13t, 14, 14/15, 15t, 16t, 20t, 20/21, 22c, 23t, 28t, 46c, 48c, 49t, 50/51, 52/53 (background); 52, 52/53, 54b, 62, 63t, 64b, 72b, 75b, 78/79, 79t, 82/83, 82, 90c, 90b, 100t, 100b, 101b, 102/103, 108/109, 111, 112, 114, 115t, 116c, 117, 118, 127, 133t, 144l, 145c, 145b, 147b, 148, 155, 157, 160, 161, 162, 163c, 165l, 165r, 166, 173l 169 KEN PATERSON

The authors would like to thank Sunvil Holidays in England for arranging their flights and car hire, and also the Istron Bay Hotel for help with accommodation.

SPIRAL GUIDES

Questionnaire

Dear Traveler

Your comments, opinions and recommendations are very important to us. So please help us to improve our travel guides by taking a few minutes to complete this simple questionnaire.

Send to: Spiral Guides, MailStop 66, 1000 AAA Drive, Heathrow, FL 32746–5063

Your recommendations...

We always encourage readers' recommendations for restaurants, nightlife or shopping – if your recommendation is added to the next edition of the guide, we will send you a FREE AAA Spiral Guide of your choice. Please state below the establishment name, location and your reasons for recommending it.

Please send me AAA Spiral_____
(see list of titles inside the back cover)

About this guide...

Which title did you buy?

_____ AAA Spiral

Where did you buy it? _____

When? m m / y y

Why did you choose a AAA Spiral Guide? _____

Did this guide meet your expectations?

Exceeded ☐   Met all ☐   Met most ☐   Fell below ☐

Please give your reasons _____

continued on next page...

Were there any aspects of this guide that you particularly liked?

_____

_____

_____

_____

_____

Is there anything we could have done better?

_____

_____

_____

_____

_____

About you...

Name (Mr/Mrs/Ms) _____

Address _____

_____

_____ Zip _____

Daytime tel nos. _____

Which age group are you in?

Under 25 ☐   25–34 ☐   35–44 ☐   45–54 ☐   55–64 ☐   65+ ☐

How many trips do you make a year?

Less than one ☐   One ☐   Two ☐   Three or more ☐

Are you a AAA member? Yes ☐   No ☐

Name of AAA club _____

About your trip...

When did you book? _ _ / _ _   When did you travel? _ _ / _ _

How long did you stay? _____

Was it for business or leisure? _____

Did you buy any other travel guides for your trip?   ☐ Yes   ☐ No

If yes, which ones? _____

_____

Thank you for taking the time to complete this questionnaire.